Emilius A. de Cosson

The Cradle of the Blue Nile

A visit to the court of King John of Ethiopia

Emilius A. de Cosson

The Cradle of the Blue Nile
A visit to the court of King John of Ethiopia

ISBN/EAN: 9783743407206

Manufactured in Europe, USA, Canada, Australia, Japa

Cover: Foto ©ninafisch / pixelio.de

Manufactured and distributed by brebook publishing software (www.brebook.com)

Emilius A. de Cosson

The Cradle of the Blue Nile

THE CRADLE

OF

THE BLUE NILE.

A VISIT TO THE COURT OF KING JOHN
OF ETHIOPIA.

BY E. A. DE COSSON, F.R.G.S.

IN TWO VOLUMES.
VOL. II.

WITH MAP AND ILLUSTRATIONS.

LONDON:
JOHN MURRAY, ALBEMARLE STREET.
1877.

[All rights reserved.]

LONDON
BRADBURY, AGNEW, & CO., PRINTERS, WHITEFRIARS.

CONTENTS.

CHAPTER XVIII.
	PAGE
THE ROYAL CAMP AT AMBACHARA	1

CHAPTER XIX.
| LIFE AT THE ETHIOPIAN COURT | 23 |

CHAPTER XX.
| WE PREPARE TO VISIT LAKE TZANA | 49 |

CHAPTER XXI.
| THE GREAT LAKE | 66 |

CHAPTER XXII.
| SPORT ON THE LAKE CONTINUED—OUR RETURN TO AMBACHARA | 91 |

CHAPTER XXIII.
| I BID ADIEU TO THE KING—ARRIVAL AT THE CITY OF GONDAR | 109 |

CHAPTER XXIV.
| THE RIDE TO THE FRONTIER | 138 |

CHAPTER XXV.
| GALABAT AND ITS SLAVE MARKET | 156 |

CHAPTER XXVI.

FROM GALABAT TO KATARIF 173

CHAPTER XXVII.

A CAMEL RIDE ACROSS THE PLAINS 192

CHAPTER XXVIII.

JOURNEY DOWN THE BLUE NILE, AND ARRIVAL AT KHARTUM 213

CHAPTER XXIX.

KHARTUM CONTINUED—DEPARTURE FOR BERBER . . . 235

CHAPTER XXX.

BERBER—DEPARTURE FOR SUAKIN 261

CHAPTER XXXI.

DESERT JOURNEY CONTINUED—THE STORY OF LEILA . . 281

APPENDIX 303

ILLUSTRATIONS TO VOL. II.

THE SLAVE MARKET AT GALABAT . . . (*Frontispiece*)

                                                                      PAGE

A WICKED HIPPO 88

A NIGHT ENCOUNTER 162

THE LAST DROP OF WATER 198

THE CRADLE

OF

THE BLUE NILE.

CHAPTER XVIII.

THE ROYAL CAMP AT AMBACHARA.

WHEN day dawned I returned to my tent, where I found Bo-Galla had been spending his leisure moments in trying to empty the gumbos of *tedge*, and having in consequence got frightfully drunk, had amused himself by smashing my pith helmet, English saddle, and one or two other things that could not possibly be replaced. I was so angry with him that I paid him and dismissed him on the spot, retaining only my gun-bearer Sinké, to whom I was forced to convey most of my orders by signs, as he could speak nothing but Tigre. It was embarrassing to have nobody by whom I could make myself understood, but having once forbidden Bo-Galla the tent, I was resolved not to recall him, as the surest way for a European to gain an ascendance over the Abyssinians, is to convince them that he is entirely independent of their assistance.

I had not been long alone before one of the king's principal officers, Likamanguas Warki, called to enquire after my health in his majesty's name. He was splendidly dressed in a robe of flowered silk, with an embroidered *kuarie* of Indian muslin draped round him, and a silver-mounted pistol in his sash. As all my knowledge of Abyssinian was confined to a few nouns, a few simple words of command, and one or two vigorous adjectives more useful among the wild tribes of the mountains than the denizens of a court, we unfortunately could not communicate our ideas very freely; however, the courtly manner of the Likamanguas quite made up for all deficiencies of speech, and we were soon good friends. He was one of four officers who bear the title of "Likamanguas," and are as inseparable from the king as his shadow. Each Likamanguas has the privilege of wearing the same dress as his sovereign, and when the King of Abyssinia goes into battle they wear the same arms, so that the king's person may not be distinguished from them. Formerly, I believe, the kings of Ethiopia were seldom killed in battle, the royal insignia being always respected by their foes, but alas! radical ideas have crept even into Ethiopia, and her kings are no longer treated with such reverence.

The Likamanguases rank among the principal officers of the state; they serve the king with food, transmit his orders, and, in short, are his private chamberlains. I have read * that time was when all those who served

* "Dictionnaire des Faits et Dits mémorables de l'Histoire." Paris: 1768.

the kings of Ethiopia had to share their sufferings, even to the breaking of their own legs and arms should the royal legs or arms happen to get broken. Thus, says the chronicler, the kings were served with great zeal, and their servants attended to their interests as to their own. But this appears to have been another good old custom that has fallen into disuse in Ethiopia. *O tempora! O mores!*

After many expressions of amity the Likamanguas left me, as he said, to tell his Majesty of my welfare; while I set to work to mend my saddle and repair as much as possible the damage done by Bo-Galla the Franzoui. At 3 P.M. the king's interpreter Maderakal came to summon me to the royal banquet, an invitation I was much pleased to receive, for the king does not as a rule like strangers to be present at his banquets, lest they should draw invidious comparisons between his court and the courts of other kings, less powerful, but more civilized.

Seeing me plainly dressed in grey cloth, Maderakal asked if I was not going to wear a uniform. I told him that being on a simple sporting expedition I had not brought one with me, and that with us a gorgeous dress was not the necessary symbol of social position that it is in the East, and that indeed we often showed our pride by dressing our servants far more splendidly than ourselves. At this moment the king's *gasha-zagry*, or esquire, bearing his sword and shield, came for us, and Maderakal, daring to delay no longer, led me to the front of the royal enclosure.

As I entered, a salute was fired from a battery of brass howitzers, and the air reverberated with the sound of drums and trumpets. In the centre of the enclosure stood a large oblong building made of boughs, interlaced with the stems of young trees let into the ground, and covered with a flat roof of rushes. A sort of double colonnade of tree-trunks ran up the centre of this hall to where stood the king's throne, or divan, raised high above the earth, and draped with rich purple velvet. A short way in front of the throne a bright wood fire was blazing merrily, and immediately at the foot of it, and on either side, were spread several rich carpets, presents from her Majesty to the king when he was Prince Kassa of Tigre. The king himself,

"In rough magnificence arrayed,"

sat cross-legged on his divan, with a pair of English rifles, loaded and cocked, resting on the cushions to the right and left of him, and his slippers, of solid silver filigree, lying on the carpet before him. By his side was a beautiful sword, with a sheath of velvet and enamel; while on his head the great triple crown of Ethiopia flashed with gold and jewels. The royal robe was of cloth of silver, and over the king's brows hung a long cloth of crimson silk, worn under the crown, and falling in heavy folds round the face, so as to conceal the features. Bruce says that formerly the kings of Abyssinia, like the kings of the Medes and Persians, never permitted the profane gaze of their subjects to rest on the royal countenance, but the necessity of con-

The Royal Camp at Ambachara.

stantly leading their armies in person has forced the Abyssinian sovereigns to abandon this custom, and it is now only on very solemn occasions that the king thus veils "the terrors of his brow," and places the great triple crown on his head.

On either side of the throne stood two gigantic eunuchs, over six feet high, clad in shirts of purple and green silk, and holding drawn sabres in their hands. A swarthy guard of honour, dressed with almost equal magnificence, stood, also with drawn sabres, behind; while all around crowded the great officers of state, and noted warriors, sumptuously arrayed in long robes of silk and velvet of every colour, the scarlet scabbards of their swords gleaming with gold and silver filigree, and their necks adorned with the skins of the lion and black panther. The Likamanguases, nearly as richly dressed as their lord, stood grouped round the throne, two on each side of it, and the air shook with the wild notes of the trumpets and drums of the royal band. Thrice— as we pushed our way through the crowd of courtiers and attendants that thronged the lower end of the hall, towards the foot of the throne where the veiled king sat, like the veiled prophet of Korassan, surrounded by the barbaric splendour of his warlike court—Maderakal prostrated himself till his forehead rested on the ground, and his lips kissed the dust. I, as an Englishman, of course confined myself to the plain bow of our European receptions, and the king, when I reached him, stretched his hand from the folds of his robe and shook mine, saying at the same time a few courteous words of welcome in Tigre. He then motioned me to sit down on a carpet at his right hand, and immediately all the rest of the assembly sat down on the ground, taking their places nearer or farther from the king according to their rank. Soon afterwards, a tall, stout man, with a very handsome, though somewhat sensual, face, walked up the centre of the hall, carrying a rifle in one hand, and a round shield, beautifully ornamented with plates of silver and filigree work, in the other. This was the redoubtable Ras Warenia, the newly subdued chief, who, before, had ruled over all Amhara as an absolute prince, but now was forced to prostrate himself in the dust before his master, and take his place on my right as a guest, in the same spot where others had so often bowed to him as lord—*Sic transit gloria mundi!*

Round his neck he wore a splendid tippet of black panther skin, enriched with clasps and bosses of gold filigree, which had belonged to the king, and been presented to him that morning as a mark of honour. For King Yohannes was politic, and sought to gild the chains of this proud chief, and reconcile him to his fall. At the side of the Ras hung a long straight sword, also handsomely ornamented with gold filigree, and his carefully platted hair was covered with a thin piece of white muslin, fixed with a golden pin; but his feet—like those of all the rest of the courtiers—were bare. His robe, however, was of the richest silk, and round his right wrist was clasped a silver-gilt gauntlet, studded with gems, an ornament which was also worn by several

CH. XVIII. *The Royal Camp at Ambachara.* 7

of the officers of the king's household, and is conferred by the Abyssinian sovereigns as a mark of especial favour.

To the left of the throne sat the principal minister of state, a man advanced in years, with a remarkably intelligent countenance, but it would tax the ingenuity of a court newsman to describe the appearance of the many striking figures that were grouped around. One, however, I cannot pass without a mention. He was a veteran warrior, the oldest of all the king's personal attendants. The grey hairs of his beard mingled with the tawny mane of the lion's skin thrown over his shoulders, and his thin locks were bound with a sort of silver crown; his tall, gaunt figure was almost as straight as the long silver-mounted matchlock he held in his hand, and the fire in his dark eyes was unquenched, though nearly ninety years had passed over his head, and marked their course by many a deep furrow on his broad and handsome brow. Indeed, the Ethiopic monarch's court, thronged as it was on this day with all his greatest chiefs, was a grand and striking sight, well worth my hard ride through the mountains. And now a long line of slaves made their way up the hall, bearing on their heads round baskets covered with crimson cloth. One of these baskets was placed on the ground before each of the principal guests, and contained the usual flat cakes of *tef*, or bread, which serve the triple purpose of food, napkin, and table-cloth, to the Abyssinian epicure. Meanwhile, several cows had been slaughtered on the threshold of the hall, according to the proper traditions of native hospitality, and large hunks of the raw and smoking meat were placed on the baskets before us, I, as the stranger guest, being first served. Two attendants then went round, one, distributing knives from a case he carried at his side, and the other offering an antelope's horn full of mixed salt and red pepper, for us to season the meat with. All the company then set to, and began to devour the raw cow's flesh with the greatest avidity, cutting off huge pieces, which they swallowed with much smacking of lips and gesticulation.

I fear my pen is not powerful enough to describe in sufficiently picturesque colours this barbaric banquet. The gorgeous robes of every dye, the glittering shields and swords, the dark faces of more than two hundred guests, with gleaming eyes and teeth, clutching the red pieces of raw beef of which their feast was composed, formed a picture I must leave to the imagination of the reader.

I need hardly say I did not touch the raw meat before me, and when the king noticed this he whispered to his master of the ceremonies, an active personage, robed in purple velvet, and armed with a white wand, which he did not scruple to apply to the shoulders of those who disobeyed him. The *Agafâree*, as this official is called,* thereupon took a piece of meat, which he placed on the fire, and, after leaving it there for

* In Abyssinian, *Agafâree* signifies door-keeper. Two of them always stand by the king's throne.

about a minute, brought to me. Though the meat was of course still quite raw, I felt constrained to eat a few mouthfuls of it, in acknowledgment of the courteous attention, and then, at Maderakal's suggestion, passed the remainder to the attendants and courtiers of humble degree standing behind, who divided it amongst them with great gusto. Most of the chiefs did the same with what remained of their portions, and thus the whole company was fed.

After the raw meat had been all consumed, pieces of meat slightly braised in the fire were handed round, and I was given a dish of curry prepared by the king's own reverend cook. This ended the dinner. Each guest was then allowed a small portion of arrakee; and after that,· *tedge, ad libitum*, was served to the whole company. I was presented with the king's glass to drink my tedge out of; it was one of the presents that had been sent him in her Majesty's name after the Magdala campaign, and had a beautifully painted head of Cupid on the front. This glass was afterwards sent to my tent for me to use during the rest of my stay at the camp, and I was often asked whether the head painted on it was not a portrait of her Majesty's eldest son! Great quantities of *tedge* were consumed, but the revelry of the guests was much hushed and awed by the presence of royalty, and nobody drank excessively, though it was just perceptible that one or two of them had been *looking* at somebody drinking, as they say in Connemara.

We presently heard a great deal of shouting and

singing at the lower end of the hall, and a party of natives came dancing up to the foot of the throne, led by a man wearing a lion-skin over his shoulders, who every now and then fired his gun in the air, and danced to the wild chanting of his companions. Maderakal explained to me that this man had slain a lion, and had now come to boast of it before the king, for, in Abyssinia, to kill a lion single-handed is considered a greater feat than to slay a dozen men in battle. After the lion-slayer had been dismissed, two slaves entered leading an enormous lioness, who walked majestically up the hall, uttering every now and then a low growl. At a sign from the king, the slaves occasionally loosened the cord attached to her neck, and allowed her to make in the direction of some of the groups of guests, who rushed away in the greatest consternation, upsetting one another, and causing great laughter to those who were at a safe distance. Seeing that the beast was really entirely under the control of her keepers, I allowed her to come quite close, and I do not think I ever saw a finer specimen. Of a rich tawny yellow, with firm lean flanks, enormously powerful forearms and claws, a broad forehead, and square cut jaws armed with a splendid array of glittering white teeth, she looked truly a worthy consort for the king of beasts, and a noble plaything for an African sovereign. After the guests had been sufficiently frightened by the lioness, a monkey was brought in and made to confront her; much fresh laughter being excited by the grimaces of the poor beast, who did not feel at all comfortable in such noble company. These rude sports brought the entertainment to a close, and I rose to go, repeating to the king a few words of thanks in his own language, which appeared to please him much. I then returned to my tent, and slept till late the next day.

April 22nd.—Murcher, the head interpreter, and a Swiss, called Louis, who was in the service of the king, came to breakfast with me. I also had a visit from Maderakal, with whom I had a long conversation about the slave trade in this part of Africa, which I shall have occasion to speak of in another chapter. Likamanguas Warki, too, paid me an official visit, and informed me that his Majesty had ordered a hundred *naphteñas* to escort me to his banquet on the previous day, but that, owing to a mistake of the king's page, they had not appeared at the right time, and that I should be happy to hear that the boy had been soundly flogged for his error. I was not at all happy to hear it, but, as in duty bound, thanked the courtly Likamanguas for this polite attention.

April 23rd.—A very wet day, and, as my tent was just like a shower-bath, I was again forced to take refuge in Murcher's hut for shelter. I had a long talk with him about Bruce's story, that the Abyssinians feasted off live cow. He assured me that the oldest men in the country had no recollection of such a custom ever having prevailed, though it was quite true that the Abyssinians were very fond of raw meat, as I had been able to see for myself at the king's banquet, and that they liked the flesh fresh and smoking from the carcase.

April 24th.—A messenger brought me a letter from my brother to say that he and K. would not be able to reach Ambachara for two days. A couple of regiments of *naphteñas* were therefore dispatched to meet them and help them on with the baggage. In the afternoon the king again invited me to dine with him. This time the royal dinner was quite *sans cérémonie*, and the king and all his court were simply clad in the white blanket with a crimson stripe down it, called a *kuarie*, which forms the ordinary costume of all the people of Tigre and Amhara, from the king to the humblest peasant.*

King Yohannes sat on an *alga* at the upper end of the hall, with his two English rifles beside him. He wore no covering on his head or feet, but each of his ankles was adorned with a small string of silver beads, and these, with a diamond pin stuck in his carefully platted hair, were the only ornaments about him. I had now a good opportunity of studying his face, and rarely have I seen a more intelligent countenance, or one that a physiognomist like Lavater would have examined with greater interest.

The brow was beautifully moulded, though small and slightly retreating; the nose aquiline, with very delicately-formed nostrils; the eyes deep-set, and not very large, but singularly courageous and penetrating; the cheek bones high for an Ethiopian; the mouth and

* See Appendix, note E.

chin sharply chiselled; and the ears almost as tiny and shell-like as a woman's. His Majesty's age was about thirty-five, and his stature somewhat under the middle height, but his figure was perfectly proportioned, and he seemed possessed of great strength and endurance, though his hands and feet were exceedingly small and delicately shaped. That King Yohannes is an astute diplomatist has been proved by the masterly manner in which he has placed himself at the head of the large and turbulent empire, which, at the death of Theodorus, was left to be disputed for by several great and warlike chiefs, some of whom were not less powerful than Kassa himself,* and yet Prince Kassa obtained his present supremacy with comparatively little bloodshed. He had the sagacity to cultivate the friendship of the English, and obtain a supply of muskets for his followers, who, though few in numbers, were soon twice as well armed and disciplined as those of any other chief. Having once obtained this moral lever, he worked it so firmly and judiciously that it was not long before he was able to have himself crowned the successor of Theodorus. But, though the king has always preferred policy to warfare, I was assured by K. that he is a hardy and fearless soldier, prompt in action, and ever to the forefront in battle. Indeed, his personal attendants said that they often had hard work to keep up with their royal master when once he was on his war-horse, so recklessly and furiously would he ride through the ranks of the

---

* I have before mentioned that King Yohannes was formerly known as Prince Kassa of Tigre.

foe, nor is it a pleasant thing for his enemies to be within range of his English rifle, as he is a splendid shot. But he possesses other qualities besides those of a soldier and statesman, for he is of a studious disposition and well read in the laws and history of Ethiopia. Nor is his outward sobriety and piety of life less remarkable.

At little after 3 A.M. he is wont to rise every morning, and read the Psalms of David by candle-light for a couple of hours; then he goes to church, after which he frequently sits fasting in open court to judge all cases that may be brought before him. The rest of the day is divided between the necessary hospitalities of the camp, riding out to indulge in the martial game of *goaks*, and attending to state affairs. Two or three hours being always reserved by his Majesty for study, while by nine o'clock he is generally in bed, as becomes one who rises so early.

I think Markham's opinion that Kassa is a "poor weak creature," is an erroneous conclusion, probably arising from the peculiarly quiet and unobtrusive demeanour of the king, and the great secretiveness of his character, which renders him loath to talk, or to appear to notice what is passing around him, though—in after conversation—I often found that there are few things that escape his observation, and that he does not carefully revolve in his mind. Crabbe's words would not inaptly describe him :—

> ' Yet might observers in his sparkling eye
> Some observation, some acuteness spy ;
> The friendly thought it keen, the treacherous deemed it sly.

> Yet not a crime could foe or friend detect,
> His actions all, were, like his speech, correct.
> Chaste, sober, solemn, and devout, they named
> Him who was this, and not of this ashamed."

But it must not be supposed for a moment that I am judging the king by a European standard. I merely wish to point him out as a remarkable man in a country like Ethiopia, and among a people like the Abyssinians.*

The dinner consisted of raw beef followed by braised beef as before; but this day *tedge* was the only drink. I made the acquaintance of the king's confessor, who was sitting near me. He was an amiable old man with a grey beard, and, when he saw me looking at him, he touched my boots with his hand and then kissed it in token of homage, saying at the same time that he was saluting St. Michael, for the Abyssinians think that white men are like St. Michael, and, in Wooma, the province governed by King Aba-Jubar, the people really believe that a white man is an angel come to visit them. Foreigners generally have a knack of paying ingenious compliments, but in the whole of my experience I had never before been taken for a saint, and I really felt quite at a loss how to look the part and not bring discredit on my new character. Alas! the good old times are passed, when, as Thomas Ingoldsby says:—

> "Saints were many, and sins were few,"

and I could not call to mind a single male saint of my

* See Appendix, note F.

acquaintance who would serve as a model, and had therefore to be content with looking as pre-Raphaelite and Fra-Angelic as I could, which, though I dare say it was very effective, was decidedly not comfortable. I also saw three ambassadors from the Galla country who had arrived at the camp. The Galla women are said to be wonderfully beautiful, but, if these three men might be taken as specimens, the sterner sex most assuredly do not share their good looks. They were short powerfully-built fellows, with a profusion of coarse black hair, which was unplatted and fell in heavy masses over their naturally low and retreating brows, making them look as if they had no foreheads at all, and the expression of their dark sensual faces was ferocious in the extreme; while at their girdles hung the horrible curved knives with which they emasculate their prisoners. Altogether, I do not think I ever saw a more truculent-looking trio, or one I should be less desirous to meet on a dark night if my rifle were empty; but though, even in Abyssinia, the savage ferocity of the Gallas is proverbial, I was told that if, which is rare, a Galla once becomes your friend, he will remain staunch to you and sacrifice his own life in your defence.

Several times during dinner I felt some of the courtiers near me, furtively feeling the texture of my coat, or examining my boots, cap, &c.; but what most struck their attention was my hunting-knife which was the only ornament I wore. It had once belonged to General Ortith de Rodas, the brother of the bloody president of Buenos Ayres, and the handle and sheath were of silver enriched with gold. When it was given to me, I was told that it had been the amiable general's custom to descend at night to the *oubliettes* where his brother's prisoners were confined, and cut their throats with this identical knife, so that there was a sort of gloomy interest attached to it, and the rude gorgeousness of its South American workmanship was greatly admired by the Abyssinians. I may here remark that it is very useful in Africa to have a knife with a blade of soft steel like a butcher's knife, as it is more easily sharpened, cuts meat better, and is less liable to chip or break than a knife of hard steel.

After the king's banquet I rode out to see a glorious blood-red sunset. At night the innumerable lights in the huts and tents made the camp look like some great city built round the base of Mount Ambachara. The weather being cold the king sent me a *kuarie* from his treasury as a cover for my bed.

April 25th.—I had now been five days at Ambachara, yet K. and C. had not arrived, and it was nine days in all since I had parted from them. Some of the king's soldiers were building me a house near the royal enclosure by his majesty's order, for now that the wet season had commenced my tent was uninhabitable. The Abyssinian mode of constructing a house is very simple. A long stake is driven into the ground, and six rather shorter stakes placed round it, forming a circle the diameter of which is about eight feet; the tops of these shorter stakes are then connected together by branches laid from one to the other, after which several long sticks are attached to the centre pole and placed sloping over the outer circle of uprights like the ribs of an umbrella. The ends of these sticks reach to within about three feet of the ground, and are attached to short uprights between which boughs are interlaced to form the wall of the house, the roof is then covered with branches and thatched with grass, and when all is firm, the centre stake is removed, the inner circle of uprights being now sufficient to support it. A hole is next scooped in the ground for the fire, and a bed of stones is built between two of the uprights and the wall for the owner of the mansion to repose on; this stony bed is generally placed opposite the door, which, like the wall of the hut, is only three feet high. Windows and chimney there are none, the smoke of the fire being considered rather good for the eyes, and generally strengthening.

I have omitted to mention that the king had kindly ordered a cow to be slaughtered daily for my private consumption, besides which he had sent me dishes of curry from his own table and an unlimited supply of *tedje*. Though my appetite in Abyssinia was remarkably robust, a cow a day was rather an *embarras de richesses*, and the pile of raw meat in my tent waxed higher and higher till I was nearly overwhelmed by it, and quite sickened by the sight and smell. At last I was forced to tell Maderakal to have it all cleared away and given to the soldiers, who accordingly held a grand feast.

CH. XVIII. *The Royal Camp at Ambachara.* 19

About 10 A.M. a native came into the camp with the news that K. and C. were in sight. I therefore mounted my horse and rode to meet them, accompanied by 200 of the king's *naphteñas* in charge of a Basha,* Madcrakal, and a little prince, a nephew of the king, who, though quite a child, rode his horse with much pluck and dexterity. Halting the escort on the top of a hill, I went forward alone to meet my brother and K., whom I found reposing by the side of a stream. They told me they had been suffering from all sorts of miseries, and had been forced to come forward without much of the baggage. The cold in the mountains had been extreme, and out of the two regiments of *naphteñas* sent to meet them the day before, only five men remained, the rest having all gone off plundering on their own account. Most of the villages they had passed through were swarming with vermin, and they had ghastly stories to tell of how they had been forced to sit up all night dismally feeding the lamp with fleas, while, to put a climax to their misfortunes, one of their porters had been accidentally shot by Tedla, the general's servant. We had always been careful to make our servants carry the breech-loaders empty and the muzzle-loaders uncapped, but it seems that Tedla thought this beneath his dignity, and had purloined a couple of caps which he placed on the gun he was carrying. As might be expected, one day when the men were all clubbed in a narrow pass the gun went off in the midst of them, and

* *Basha* is the title given to an officer of *naphteñas*, or fusileers.

one of the porters at once went down with two charges of buckshot in his knees. Tedla tried to look as innocent as the rest, but an inspection of the muskets' soon pointed him out as the culprit. K. grimly asked my brother to lend him his stick, and Tedla, seeing there was no escape, began calmly to strip off his *kuarie* for the coming castigation, while my brother busied himself cutting the shot out of the wounded man's legs with a razor. The poor fellow behaved very well, never murmuring or complaining, and even interceded in Tedla's behalf. He was, however, too badly hit to be taken forward, and was therefore carried to a village and placed under the care of a *shoum*, who promised to give him every attention.

After a brief halt we mounted our horses and proceeded to join the escort. K. narrowly escaped being crushed in jumping a stream, as the bank gave way, and his horse rolled back on him. When the escort saw us they fired an irregular volley, and two fresh horses, with silver-mounted head-stalls and scarlet saddle-cloths, were led up for K. and C. We all then set off at a sharp trot, surrounded by a crowd of *naphteñas* and attendants running beside us. As we neared the camp two slaves came up to K., leading the king's own mule for him to ride, reminding one of the old days when he whom the king most esteemed was mounted on the royal mule, and led through the streets of the city, with loud shouts of "this is the man the king delighteth to honour." The mule was a magnificent beast, as fat as a prize ox, and beautifully caparisoned, with a bridle of solid silver. According to the old Abyssinian law it is high treason for a subject to sit on the king's seat, and the king never mounts again on a horse that he has once given to another to ride, therefore, when he sent K. his mule to ride into the camp, it was equivalent to making him a present of it.

All the troops crowded out to see us as we approached, and when we reached the royal enclosure a salute was fired, and Murcher came forward and led us before the king, "who sat upon his royal throne, and was clothed with all his robes of majesty, all glittering with gold and precious stones; and he was very dreadful."* Around the throne stood many of the potent, grave, and reverend signiors whom I had seen on the day of the feast. K. knelt and presented the great Abyssinian book of laws which Her Majesty's government had entrusted him with to give to the king, and which had been brought to England after the fall of Theodorus. King Yohannes bowed low as he received this valuable present, and also the letters from Her Majesty and Lord Granville. My brother was then presented, and we repaired to my tent, where we were visited by Murcher, Maderakal, and Likamanguas Warki. In the course of the afternoon two more tents were erected for my brother and K., while the construction of a couple of new houses was commenced for their future accommodation. The king's treasurer also supplied us with some carpets, and five cows, ten sheep, and several

* Esther, c. xv. v. 6.

gallons of *tedge* and *tella* were sent us to appease our appetites. Of course we had to hold a sort of levee and receive an endless string of dark visitors, who one and all desired to examine our guns and other appointments, but at length we cleared the tent and retired to court what slumber we could.

CHAPTER XIX.
LIFE AT THE ETHIOPIAN COURT.

April 26th.—K. was engaged with the king all the morning assisting in the translation of the dispatches he had brought from England. The king was so pleased with Her Majesty's letter to him that he ordered a copy of it, in Abyssinian, to be placed in all the churches, that his people might know, as he said, the graciousness of "his Mother of England."

I spent the morning, file in hand, attemping further improvements in the locks of my 16-bore gun. By placing wedges of wood between the springs I shortened the arms, and rendered them somewhat stiffer. Like yesterday, we had an endless influx of dusky visitors, who came and squatted in and around the tent, saying little, drinking much, and staring more. A guard of royal *naphteñas* was stationed outside the tent, commanded by the pretty little lieutenant who had met me on my arrival at the camp. Seeing that our rack of guns attracted his admiration, I asked him if he would like to discharge my big elephant rifle, as it wanted cleaning. He put three fingers down the muzzle, and then looking up in my face, said, "If you wish to kill me, master, do so, but not by making me fire off this." Several of our visitors were very curious to know how old we were, as they could not reconcile it to their ideas that the chin of thoughtless youth, should be clothed with the beard of age and wisdom, and supposed, from our beards, that we ought to be already far gone in the sere and yellow leaf. One chief even took hold of my hand to try if there was any strength remaining in my aged muscles, but did not try a second time. According to our usual custom, we rode in the afternoon, and I endeavoured to teach my horse to stand fire from the saddle. I was much pleased with the success of the first lesson. When we returned we found one of our new houses finished, and determined all to remove there. Accordingly, three beds of stones were built round the wall—beautiful dry beds composed entirely of large angular lumps of hard serviceable granite that would not wear out however much we might toss about on them; and we *did* toss about a good deal at first, for it took a long time before we fitted our bodies comfortably into the angles of the stones, or rather the angles of the stones fitted themselves comfortably into our bodies. Getting seasoned to the fire was also rather a trying process, as the wood was damp, and the smoke preponderated, and, in the absence of a chimney, caused us all to weep copiously. However, when we did get to sleep we slept soundly, and I am convinced there is nothing like a hard bed for dreamless slumber, even though the hard bed be of hardest stone.

At 3 A.M. a low buzzing noise commenced which sounded very like the distant hum of a carouse, but it proved to be only the priests droning the Psalms of David, which they continued chanting in a monotonous way till sunrise. This-day, April 27th, was the old Abyssinian Easter, for the Ethiopians have two styles just as we have at home, though their styles do not quite correspond to ours, and, if I understood them right, the Abyssinian year is composed of twelve months of thirty days, and they do not count the remaining five days necessary to complete the year, considering them as having no existence, and whatever occurs on them as not having taken place. Would that we could do the same with some days of our lives!

It rained hard all the morning, and the king, who was holding a council in his great hall, had to run to his tent for shelter, as the water came through in bucketsfull. We had plenty of visits from distinguished natives, but there was as yet no sign of our baggage appearing, and indeed it was now so scattered over the country at Guldofellassie, Adowa, Axum, and along the highways and byways of the mountains, that my hopes of ever seeing it again were daily becoming smaller and beautifully less.

At 2 P.M. the weather cleared, and C. and I rode out. We saw large quantities of Francolin partridges in the bush that grew on the mountain sides, and there were also numbers of beautiful little green love parrots, with rose-coloured beaks, flitting among the trees.

The grey rocky cone of Mount Ambachara is surrounded on all sides by hills of lower height covered with grass and bush; and from the top of one of these which lies to the S.W. of the mountain, we obtained a magnificent view of the province of Dembea, a fine alluvial plain, stretching away at our feet to the shores of the great lake Tzana, which bounded the horizon like a vast sea. We could perceive the sharp outline of two headlands jutting into the lake, and some little green islands dotting its surface, but the opposite shore was quite out of sight. On the flat beach of the near shore long white lines of breakers were clearly visible as they rolled foaming in like the surf of the Atlantic, for it had blown almost a hurricane overnight. Thirty miles to our right was the plateau of Gondar, where stands the capital of Ethiopia beneath the shadow of the Mountain of the Sun; and over head squadrons of dark ragged clouds swept across the stormy sky like some shadowy host going to battle, but every now and then they were broken by the powerful rays of the sun, which, for a moment, glittered on the waters of the mighty lake, turned to gold the graceful clusters of trees that grew on the spurs of the hills bounding the fertile valley below, and lent a smiling aspect to Tzana's shores, which, the next instant, as the heavy thunder-clouds massed themselves together again, appeared dark and gloomy as the borders of Avernus.

We heard on returning that the king was likely soon to move his camp. A young man called McKelvie was talking to K. He had been brought out from England some years before by an English captain who had started an ivory hunting venture on the N.W. frontier of Abyssinia. The party of hunters consisted of the captain, McKelvie, and four others, their object being to shoot as many elephants as they could and sell the ivory. Each of the party had some special duty assigned to him—the captain's, if I remember right, being to cut wood for the camp-fire. Though Captain —— was a good sportsman the venture was not very successful, and when the party was broken up McKelvie remained behind in Abyssinia, and subsequently entered the service of the king, for, being an orphan, he had few ties to draw him back to England. One of the adventures that befell him while on the elephant-hunting expedition was so tragic that I must endeavour to describe it as well as I can from memory.

The little party of Europeans had been shooting for some time with varying success, when one day the captain wounded a large bull elephant which carried a fine pair of tusks. The elephant got away, but its track was followed by the hunters, who, after much weary marching, at last came upon it lying dead in the bush, in the country of one of the warlike tribes that dwell on the frontiers of Abyssinia, near the border of the Egyptian Soudan. McKelvie and his companions were preparing to secure the tusks of the elephant, when they perceived a strong party of natives approaching evidently with the same object. The natives had seen the dead elephant before, but were not aware of the presence of the Europeans, and these, fearing a collision with so strong a party, hid themselves and their camels in the bush, quite willing, as the captain said, that the natives should do their work for them, and cut out the tusks, though they were fully determined not to abandon their quarry if they could help it. The party of natives, meanwhile, never dreaming of snare or danger, began hacking out the ivory with much jubilation, but just as their work was completed, and they were preparing to march in triumph with their prize to the village, the white hunters, of whom each had marked his man, at a given signal fired a volley and shot six of the natives dead, while the remainder naturally took to flight at this sudden and unexpected attack. The hunters then without delay packed the ivory on their own camels, and directed the Arab drivers to follow a circuitous route through the bush and meet them again in the Egyptian territory, whither they decided to make their way as swiftly as possible, for they knew that it would not be long before the Abyssinians would be up in arms, and come down in numbers to exact blood vengeance for the death of their comrades. Their fears were destined only too soon to be realised. About sunset they descried a large force of armed natives winding down the side of one of the mountains so as to intercept them, and they knew that now the critical moment had indeed arrived. But the little party of Europeans was equal to the occasion. Deciding that resistance would be useless, they resolved again to have recourse to stratagem, and concealed their rifles and ammunition in the dry bed of a river, retained only their long hunting knives, which they secreted in the legs of their trowsers so as not to be visible. When the villagers surrounded them they made no resistance, and, being apparently unarmed, were led off without injury to the village, where the chief was to decide their fate on the following day. It never entered the heads of the simple Africans to search for hidden weapons, and, as their prisoners appeared quite submissive, they contented themselves with placing an armed sentinel over each, who at night lay down beside his captive with his hand firmly twisted in the folds of his dress so that he should not get away without waking him.

Gradually the fires waned low and darkness closed around. One by one the Abyssinians enveloped their heads in their *kuaries* and stretched themselves out to sleep, that sleep from which some would never wake again in this world. Soon all was hushed and quiet, the white prisoners appearing to slumber as calmly as the rest, notwithstanding the fate that awaited them on the morrow, but a terrible scene was yet to be enacted. At the dead of night, each of the prisoners drew forth his long hunting knife from its hiding-place, and with one sharp straight stroke drove it home to the heart of the man who held him. Not a hand seems to have trembled or failed in dealing the death-blow, each man successfully achieved his horrible task, and a horrible task it must have been to stab a man sleeping, even to men who knew, as they did, that their own lives would be forfeited if they faltered for a moment. However, the hunters had little time for such thoughts; having thus effectually released themselves from their gaolers they sprang up and escaped in the darkness, the subsequent panic and confusion which occurred among the natives only tending to help their flight. They succeeded in finding the place where their rifles were buried, and, having recovered them, made their way safely across the Egyptian frontier, where of course all pursuit was at an end.

I do not wish to make myself responsible for this story, but merely relate it as it was told to me by one who said he was an actor in it, and whom I have no cause to disbelieve.

It is rare that such tragic episodes do not lead to unhappy results. Some years later Powell went shooting in almost the same country, and unfortunately took with him as guide and general factotum an Alsatian who had been one of the above-mentioned party of hunters. The Alsatian was murdered by the natives, and it is believed in Abyssinia that his murder was partly, though not entirely, brought about by the feeling of hatred which existed against him on account of the affair of the elephant. The Alsatian's death led to the murder of poor Powell, his wife, and child, for the people said, as we have murdered the white man's servant we must murder the white man too, or he will assuredly come back and take vengeance upon us. Thus four more lives were perhaps indirectly sacrificed ; add to these about twenty lives taken when Prince Kassa punished the people of Bogos for the murder of Powell, and we have a total of thirty-six lives, twelve of which were directly, and the remainder, it is possible, indirectly, lost for a pair of elephant's tusks—*Tel jeu vaut-il la chandelle?* I think since the fatal day when Earl Percy rode a hunting in his neighbour's woods, the answer has been NO.

April 28*th.*—The weather was very wet, and we had been disagreeably awakened in the night by feeling large drops of rain falling on our noses. At 3 A.M. the priests as usual had begun chanting the Psalms of David close by, in tones as excruciating as a dozen Scotch bagpipes, so we had enjoyed little sleep. The morning was spent in repairing the thatch of our hut, and draping the inside with red and white *kuaries* and pieces of native cloth, which soon made it look quite bright and cheerful, our beds between the uprights having very much the appearance of boxes in a theatre. The fire still smoked horribly, but one of the servants converted himself into a human bellows, and squatted beside it, blowing all day, till his naturally dark complexion became almost black. The king dispatched another messenger after our baggage, which had not yet appeared, though, seven days before, K. and C. had left it only *one* day's march behind them. In the afternoon we were visited by a French missionary, a very unctuous young man, dressed in a long cassock of black velvet, with a sort of black velvet smoking-cap on his head, which gave him a picturesque though rather unclerical aspect. He had accompanied Powell to Massowah, then gone to Bogos, and lastly come to Amhara from Metemma. Some dissensions he had got into with the native priests and chiefs had led to his being placed in captivity, and he had now just been released by the king, with an intimation that he had better leave the country. While he was talking to us Maderakal came in, and the missionary at once accused him of having advocated his imprisonment; both parties became personal, and the quarrel was waxing hot, when my brother interposed, and reminded them that, as they were both his guests, he could not allow them to discuss their differences under his roof; the missionary apologised and peace was restored.

I confess I do not think it does much good to send isolated missionaries to preach in Africa, as they are not unfrequently induced to espouse the side of some one chief, for the sake of his support, and consequently get at issue with the rest; feuds then run high, and the alleged messenger of peace and goodwill becomes really an instrument for the exciting of party feeling and dissension among the people to whom he has professedly come to preach Christian love and charity.

Livingstone's great theory is, I honestly believe, the only true one. Open up the commerce of the country, establish colonies as centres of European civilisation, with missions attached, to educate the children, and teach the natives by *practical* example the advantages of industry and peaceful occupations. Religion will not be long in following on the steps of civilisation. Theoretically it may appear that civilisation ought to follow on the steps of religion. But religion takes a more lasting hold on a mind already developed by a little practical civilisation, and my opinion is that the other system will work by far the most rapidly and well.

Towards evening our baggage at last arrived. The

king's messenger said he had made prisoner the chiefs to whom it had been entrusted, and would keep them tied up until we had counted the packages. We told him to keep a guard on the chiefs, but *not* to tie them up. The weather was still very cold and tempestuous. Our guard of honour drank, caroused, burnt our wood, consumed our supplies, and generally enjoyed themselves, but would not assist in watching the cattle or make themselves useful in any way. In fact, if it had not been for the honour and glory of their presence, we began to feel we should be much better without them.

K. was occupied during the afternoon with the king, finishing the translation of the letters from Her Majesty and Lord Granville. The king, having no means of sending the answers to these letters safely through the Egyptian territory, wished to know if I would oblige him by taking charge of them on my way home. I said I should be glad to do so, but must first request that he would allow me to speak to him about the slave trade in Ethiopia, as I hoped that I might prevail on him to put an end to it.

M. Berlioux, in his pamphlet on the Slave-trade in Africa, laments that the difficulties encountered by travellers attempting to penetrate into Africa from the East coast have rendered our knowledge very limited as to the extent to which "man-hunting" is carried on the frontiers of Abyssinia and the country of the Gallas. He says—the tribes who live on the elevated terraces whence the Blue Nile descends, have retained some generous ideas with their disfigured Christianity, while the Arabs, who occupy the deserts at the foot of those mountains, keep them at war and in a state of siege, and have done so for ages. These wars are profitable to the slave-trade; robberies of children are constantly taking place, the details of which are not well known.

We had overcome the obstacles which the natives on the shores of the Red Sea, and even the Egyptian officials, throw in the way of a traveller attempting to visit these districts, and I was ambitious to obtain a thorough insight into the real state of this traffic in Abyssinian slaves; a traffic which appeared to me all the more horrible, because these slaves are not, like some of the negro races, creatures of a low type of humanity, without religion, and capable of little improvement, but Christians, who, though rude and primitive in their faith and customs, are yet naturally endowed with moral and physical qualities capable of high development. Moreover, having been fortunate enough to obtain the friendship of the king, I felt that I was bound in common humanity to employ what little influence I might have with him for the suppression of this infamous and unnatural trade. There is a Gaelic proverb which says: *Ge beag an t-ubh thig eun os*—Be the egg ever so small, a bird may come from it—and I did not altogether despair of success, though I could not but feel painfully how small my knowledge of the country was, and how difficult it might be to make a powerful and despotic prince move in such an important matter. However, I determined to do my best when the king should grant me an interview, and K. promised to second my endeavours, a promise he amply fulfilled.

April 29th.—At a little before six A.M. the king sent to say he was ready to grant us an audience. In this latitude the days are of pretty even length, and the sun does not rise before six. So we were all asleep in bed when the royal summons arrived. K. however got up, and explained to his Majesty that royalty in Europe was not usually so matutinal, whereupon His Majesty goodnaturedly postponed the audience till ten o'clock, at which hour we duly repaired to his presence. Besides my brother, General K., and myself, there were only three chiefs admitted to the audience, one of whom, Dedjatch Area, was the king's uncle. Maderakal acted as interpreter, and a Likamanguas sat in front of the king nursing the royal feet in his lap. His Majesty was dressed, in a plain *kuarie*, with his head and feet bare. He sat on an *alga* before a bright fire burning in an iron brasier, and, as soon as we had saluted him, motioned us to be seated on a carpet spread on his right hand. Both my brother and myself were much struck with the grace of his figure and the intelligence and refinement of his face. He spoke in a clear frank manly voice; and, after a few compliments, the conversation, as I had desired, turned on the slave trade.

In reply to my representations, his Majesty said it was true that slavery existed in his dominions. All his Christian subjects were in the habit of buying slaves; these slaves came chiefly from Wooma, Prince Aba-Jubar's country; they belonged to a sect of Christians who particularly reverence St. Michael, and were generally sold young by their parents to be slaves in Abyssinian families, where they were employed as servants and well treated. His Majesty went on to say that though his Christian subjects might buy slaves, they were not allowed to sell them, death being the punishment decreed for such an offence by an old, though rarely enforced, Abyssinian law. I now questioned him regarding his Mahometan subjects. These, he said, laboured under *no* restriction to prevent them from selling slaves, indeed, they were the great slave-merchants of the country, and procured all the slaves that were bought by his Christian subjects; they also drove large parties of slaves, whom they had collected in Wooma and the Galla countries, through Abyssinia to Galabat, and other towns on the frontiers of the Soudan, where there were regular markets at which the slaves were sold to merchants, who took them across the desert to the shores of the Red Sea, whence they were shipped to Arabia, in which country Abyssinian slaves were in great demand.

I need hardly pause here to remark that the Mahometan merchants do not confine themselves to legitimate buying of children from their parents, though that is bad enough. Great numbers of the young slaves carried into the Soudan are kidnapped, and the sufferings the poor little things have to undergo in the long marches across mountain and desert are too awful to be described. Girls of seven and eight are violated by their brutal conductors, and the weakly left to die on the road. Another way the Mahometan dealers have of obtaining slaves is by exciting feuds between neighbouring tribes and carrying off the prisoners, or making razzias on some peaceful mountain village when opportunity offers. But I shall have occasion to speak of these things again.

In Abyssinia all arguments are adduced in the form of questions, and I now spoke to the king accordingly, Maderakal, probably interpreting my speech somewhat in the following form: "Oh king! Is not slavery opposed to the tenets of the Christian faith? Is it right, then, that you should countenance it in your dominions? Should not a king be the Father of his people? Is it just, then, that you should allow your children to be carried off and sold into bondage? You claim to be the head and defender of the Christian faith in Africa; is it well that you should stand by and let your Christian subjects be transported to a Mahometan country, where they are forced to abandon the faith which you profess to uphold? Do not those who perish, and the souls of those who are forced to abandon the faith of their fathers, cry to you that this is wrong?" &c. I also represented to his Majesty that if, as he had declared, he wished to cultivate the friendship of the civilized nations of Europe, the first and best step towards proving the sincerity of his desire for the advancement of his country would be to put an end to an abuse which was fatal to the progress of civilization, and show that *he*, the king of Ethiopia, could set an example to Egypt and Turkey with all their boasted advancement; an act which could not but be appreciated in a country like England, which had ever been the first to advocate the abolition of slavery; and more to the same effect.

His Majesty, who had listened attentively while Maderakal translated my discourse, replied that he had thought gravely over these matters, and that it was true that slavery was distasteful to him as a Christian sovereign, but that no European power had ever before requested him, as I had, to abolish the slave trade, and that while he was only Prince of Tigre it would have been out of his power to do so, as the measure would have been opposed by many of his chiefs, whom he could not have controlled. He said that *now* he certainly had the power in his hands, and spoke with great modesty of the way in which he had attained it; he declared that he had never hoped to reach so high a position, but that God had helped him, and he trusted would favour his efforts to deliver his country from the attacks of the Mussulmans, and advance it in the friendship and esteem of England and the other civilized nations of Europe.

I hinted to his Majesty that he could take no step more conducive to this than setting himself earnestly to abolish slavery, which in itself would be a measure calculated to give great pleasure to my countrymen.

The king said he wished above all things to preserve the friendship of England, which had been a good friend to him from the time when he was fighting against

Theodorus, and in short, to my great joy, at last granted my request, telling me that the king could not lie, and that I had his promise that he would take immediate measures to enforce the punishment of death against all traders, Mahometan or Christian, who should in future attempt to buy, sell, or kidnap slaves in his country, or attempt to pass them through it.

I begged his Majesty, while he was doing so much, to complete the work by declaring free the slaves then existing in Abyssinia, as those who were contented with their lot would be no worse, while those who pined for liberty would be able to enjoy it like their fellow creatures. This also he said he would do, and, at my request, promised to pledge himself to the fulfilment of these things, in letters written under his great seal, which he would ask me to convey for him to our Government, to whom he hoped they would prove the sincerity of his friendship.

His Majesty then spoke to my brother of the ancient history of his country, which he appeared to have carefully studied, and alluding to the ancient limits of the Ethiopian empire, complained bitterly of the encroachments of the Mahometans. He said that last year * he had sent General K. with letters to her Majesty, in which he had informed her of his coronation as Emperor of Ethiopia, and complained of the encroachments of the Khedive's troops on his dominions, begging England, as a Christian power, to remonstrate with the Khedive on the subject. The letters he had just

* 1872.

received from Her Majesty and Lord Granville, congratulated him on his coronation, and stated that the British Government recognised him with pleasure as the Emperor of Ethiopia, adding that her Majesty had been pleased to approve the appointment of an Abyssinian consul in London.*

These friendly sentiments, the king said, had given him great joy, and he had ordered a copy of her Majesty's letter to him to be placed in the principal churches of his country, that his people might learn to love the English. "But with regard to the encroachments of the Egyptians," his Majesty continued, "your Government informs me that they have questioned the Khedive, and that he has answered that he has *not* taken any land from Ethiopia, and has *no* intention of taking any in the future, so they think my fears must be unfounded. Now what Ismael Pasha (the Khedive) has said to your Government is false. He told me that the frontier of his country was the Mareb, and now he has taken, beyond the Mareb, the countries of Halhal, Kayekh-barea, Tsellim-barea, Bogos, Taander, Henbub, Mennsa, Ailet, Asgede-bukgala, Zula, Tora, Semhali, Amphilla, and all the land from the highlands to the sea, called Hamasen. These he has taken from me, and all that now remains to me of Hamasen is that part which is situated on the highlands. Moreover, all the world knows that the Shangalla country is mine. After Mr. Powell was murdered by the Shangallas, his

* Mr. Henry S. King, 65, Cornhill.

brother went to Ismael Pasha to ask for assistance to avenge his death, but Ismael Pasha said he could not give it, as the murder was not committed in his country, and when Mr. Powell's brother came to me, I said the blood of the murdered man is my blood, and I sent a strong army, and punished the Shangallas for the murder; yet now Ismael Pasha says that country is his. Also there is a land behind Gondar, called Wakhni, formerly the residence of the sons of the kings of Ethiopia, which Ismael Pasha now claims to be his frontier, and has occupied with his troops. He has besides taken my subject, named Sheik Jumar, who was my governor of Metemma, and has had him chained and flogged for several days, and then sent to Egypt; while his soldiers have plundered the country that paid me tribute. My friends, I will tell you another thing; there is a great convent, called Waldubba, where many monks and priests teach the people the gospel and faith of Christ, and pray for all the world. The Shangallas came out to shed their blood, and refused to pay me tribute. Now, is there not a law that enables a king to punish men that disobey him, and refuse to pay their just tribute? The apostles, St. Paul, and the book of the law throughout the world, allow that there is. So I sent troops to punish these rebels, but Ismael Pasha wrote to me, saying, 'Send me the chief you have sent against the Shangallas, that I may punish him, for he has killed *my* people.' Thus does he ever craftily seek to raise a quarrel with me, and advance his troops into my country, and take it from me, compelling the people to abandon their faith, and placing my *shoums* in chains. Judge then if I am not oppressed! Ismael Pasha does these things because he is ambitious of worldly greatness, and wishes to damage Christianity, and establish Mahomedanism in Ethiopia, and make us his slaves, and the slaves of the devil. He has taken Zula and Amphilla bay, which were mine, and charges a duty, equal to double its market value, on all merchandise exported from my country. Thus am I encompassed on all sides by the Mahometans, who allow me no port or outlet by which I may communicate with other nations, and advance the prosperity and civilization of my kingdom. Oh! my friends, I pray you, let this be known in your country, and how much we desire a port, that we may hold intercourse with other nations. But," continued the king—and here his eyes flashed with the true expression of a soldier—" I will fight to the last if so it *must* be, but I do not wish that the blood of thousands should be shed, if the intervention of the European powers can prevent it. Let them determine the true frontiers of my country, and by their decision I am content to abide."

Few people could have helped being favourably impressed by the earnest and straightforward manner of the king. The isolation of which he so pathetically complained, has indeed been the bane of the vast country over which he rules. Encompassed by the Mahometan Arabs of the plains, this strange Christian empire of tropical Africa has remained for ages cut off from the outer world, like an enchanted island, and a thousand years have scarcely changed the customs or dress of its people. It is true that the Ethiopians have themselves partly caused this isolation, for, being surrounded by enemies, they have ever been suspicious of admitting strangers into their country, and still more suspicious of letting them return from it. But an active and intelligent mind like that of king Yohannes at once sees the danger of such a position, and there are few sacrifices the present king would not make to break through the blockade which hems him in. Nor have his fears concerning the intentions of the Egyptians proved unfounded. While I was in Abyssinia, the Khedive's troops were gradually closing round the country, and few pains were taken to conceal their real object, which was neither more nor less than the subjugation of Ethiopia.

A short time ago I was told by an officer, who was formerly in the Khedive's service, that when we were leaving Cairo, the vice-regal government actually contemplated sending him with us, ostensibly to facilitate our journey through the Soudan, but *really* to reconnoitre the frontiers of Ethiopia under cover of our shooting party. The idea was however abandoned, and it is as well that it was so, for we should hardly have cared to enact the *rôle* so kindly prepared for us.

We now know that the breech-loaders and Gatling guns of the Khedive have failed to subdue the courage of the Abyssinian mountaineers in their rocky strongholds, but I certainly think it a pity that, after the Magdala campaign, when the roads and railways were all there, England did not at least *try* the success of establishing a colony and developing the resources of this fine country and people, instead of abandoning them to their fate, after causing the death of their king. I firmly believe that the advancement of civilization and commerce, to say nothing of Christianity, would be materially assisted were we even *now* to arbitrate between Egypt and Abyssinia, and secure to the latter the means, so long withheld from her, of transporting her produce to the shores of the Red Sea, and communicating with other countries.

Our interview with the king lasted an hour, and before we left, his Majesty introduced us to his uncle Dedjatch Area, who had been imprisoned on a mountain for fourteen years by Theodorus, and released by the English, and therefore naturally expressed a very friendly feeling towards our countrymen. We afterwards rode out to a little church near the camp to see the funeral of one of our *naphteñus* who had died. All the Abyssinians are in the habit of taking monthly doses of *kousso* to check the horrible disease engendered by eating raw meat, but the medicine is so powerful, that it sometimes proves more dangerous than the malady. This poor fellow had taken his dose of *kousso* in the morning, and before twelve hours had elapsed he was dead from weakness. We found his body laid in an open shell near the church door, surrounded by white-robed priests singing the Psalms of David, while his comrades sat in picturesque groups under the fine old trees that grew near the sacred building. The contrast of the dead soldier lying so calm and still while all around was life and animation was very striking.

When we returned to our hut, the king's secretary brought us some of the correspondence that had passed between his Majesty and the Khedive, in order that we might judge for ourselves of the correctness of the statements we had heard in the morning. We were also visited by Basha Nigso, the king's treasurer, who evidently thought himself a very great chief, and said he was going to his province to raise a body of 10,000 horse, a statement we thought it as well to take with a grain of salt. McKelvie came in, and was commissioned by K. to ride to Gondar and make some purchases at the market there. As there were rumours of robbers on the road, McKelvie begged a few cartridges, which I gave him. The weather was still very stormy, so at night we stabled our horses in the large tent which we had brought with us from Cairo.

April 30th.—We were just sitting down to breakfast, when who should darken our little doorway but good Father Louis de Gonzague, the missionary. He said he had come on from Adowa with his own mules, as Ras Barrioü had treated him just as badly as he had done us. How the worthy Father, who was anything but a feather weight, ever managed to clamber over those prodigious mountains of the Semyen I do not know. However, here he was, with his three black gun-bearers, and we were delighted to see him. He told us that when he left Adowa Captain R. was still there with the remainder of our baggage, and *still* vainly endeavouring to procure porters. It was fortunate that R. had a large stock of patience, a most desirable quality in this country. We made Father Louis breakfast with us, and established him in one of the tents we had vacated. It looked strange to see his gentle face and long white robes among the rude skin-clad warriors of the camp. Yet sometimes a bright gleam would break through the usually placid and tempered expression of the Father's eyes, for he had not always been a missionary. Indeed he confessed that,

"In his hot youth,"

he had been destined for a soldier's career, but, as he said reverently, raising his broad-brimmed hat, *L'homme propose et Dieu dispose, Monsieur.*

The weather continued wretchedly wet and miserable. I rode out alone to a church, a few miles from the camp, where still stood the ruins of a tower built by the Portuguese. Being in a destructive mood, I slew one of the beautiful little green love parrots that here abound, and skinned it while taking shelter in the old tower from a tremendous thunder-storm. I remarked here, as I had often done before, with what taste and care the Portuguese always collected the most beautiful of the Abyssinian trees and planted them round their buildings. The old settlers made careful provision for a long stay in the country, judging by their planting those sweet scented cedars, some of which have not yet done growing, though three hundred years have passed since their seeds were laid in the ground. I imagine these stern Portuguese adventurers were not bad fellows, and they were certainly civilising the country very rapidly, when their fatal mania for trying to introduce the "blessed Inquisition" made it too hot to hold them.

Had they gone on as they began, Ethiopia would have been a very great country before this time; but the brief interval of improvement extended over less than half a century, so what wonder that, when the Portuguese disappeared from the scene, the country relapsed back into the state of barbarism it had been in for ages.

As I stood listening dreamily to the wind moaning among the trees, I could almost fancy I saw the stiff old señhors with their long noses and longer rapiers sticking out behind them like corking pins, what ever those are, as they perambulated solemnly up and down by the church instructing the natives in the art of building, and crossing themselves devoutly whenever they yawned or sneezed, or otherwise departed from the grave decorum of their demeanour. Presently I rubbed my eyes, for there in the darkest part of the grove there positively were figures moving noiselessly about with long swords sticking out like corking pins behind them, but suddenly I heard a short grating laugh, and one of my grave señhors bounded in a most undignified way at least ten feet from the ground and cleverly twisting the end of his sword round the bough of a tree, hung head downwards suspended by it, while his companions clambered hand over hand up the long creepers that depended from the branches, and made faces at him; then there was a great chattering and barking, and off they all scampered chasing one another round and round the little church, and holding on to each other's tails in the most ludicrous way imaginable. I should think there must have been upwards of sixty monkeys, and though they took refuge in the tops of the trees when I came forth, they still continued their gambols up there, and I verily believe most of them lived *in* the old church, for they appeared to come out from under its thatched roof, and, as the country round about was open, I cannot otherwise account for their appearing so suddenly.

While I was riding, my brother had been to visit the king, to whom he presented one of Reilly's revolvers with a plated barrel and ivory handle. The king in taking it said—with a grace that might have done credit to the first gentleman of Europe—"The most acceptable present you can make me, Baron, is your arrival at my camp." This was a very pretty compliment for Central Ethiopia, but the Abyssinians are by no means deficient in wit. C. also introduced Father Louis to his Majesty, who questioned the Father closely as to why he had only a Christian name, and the object of his journey, but he received him graciously, and sent him a better tent than the one we had been able to lend him. All night the rain fell in torrents.

CHAPTER XX.

WE PREPARE TO VISIT LAKE TZANA.

May 1*st.*—Was cold and tempestuous, the rain falling as if Lake Tzana had gone up into the clouds, and then thought better of it. May-day in the tropics—I wonder if I shall ever see a really fine May-day! Surely, within 13° of the equator one might have hoped for something more cheerful than this. But in Ethiopia the seasons do not follow the European order, and May and June herald the commencement of the Abyssinian wet season, or winter time. The king received no one this morning, as he had been taking *kousso*. I spent several hours re-writing the lost part of my diary, with the assistance of C.'s notes, which he kindly lent me. It being now too late to go shooting on the Takazze, C. and I had decided to make an expedition to the great lake Tzana, and the king had promised that the letters concerning the abolition of the slave-trade should be ready by the time we returned. I decided to give the king my big elephant rifle, as it was the only thing of any value I had with me, and I knew *he* could easily get the ammunition for it, which had been abandoned with our other heavy baggage. This rifle was a good piece of workmanship, but it kicked so tremendously with eight drams of powder and a five-ounce bullet, that it always required some moral courage to discharge it. However, the maker had thoughtfully provided it with a hair trigger, which saved one from the mental agony of a long steady pull, and generally prevented any hesitation at the last moment, by abruptly letting it off before one knew what was going to happen. When I fired this piece before cleaning it, we were amused to see our gallant guard of *naphteñus* duck down as if they expected to be blown away. I afterwards gave the rifle to our native boys to oil, but they began scouring off the browning with sand-paper, taking it for rust; so I was reduced to following " Punch's " advice, " When you want a thing done, do it yourself." Our stock of shirts had been lamentably diminished by all our losses, and we set the boys to make some new ones of native cotton, but the thunder-storms were so violent that they soon gave up their task, saying they could not work in such weather; indeed it was often nearly dark, and we spent the day miserably enough in our hut, continually discovering new leaks in the roof.

There was a market held twice a week near the king's enclosure, where we obtained such necessaries as cotton cloth, grain, pepper, coffee, &c., and, as a dollar is a large sum in Abyssinia, we had to lay in a good supply of small change, *i.e.*, blocks of salt weighing one pound each, twelve of which—if I remember right—went to the dollar. Never did capital dissolve so rapidly; whenever it was very wet, our cherished stock of money would melt slowly away before our eyes, till nothing but a small pool of salt water remained where once had been a goodly pile of pence.

The king, ever careful of his guests, had sent two days before to Lake Tzana for some fish, which was duly brought us by a couple of horsemen in the afternoon. These fish were very gorgeous in colour, and strange in shape, but their great merit was that they had scarcely any bones, and were excellent eating. Father Louis came, and complained that one of his Shoa servants had been robbed. A half naked *naphteña*, seeing the lad walking about the camp in a good *kuarie*, had taken it from him *vi et armis*, on the usual principle of the Abyssinian *militaire*, that might constitutes right. If the lad had cried out *Abiet! Abiet!* as the natives generally do when attacked, he would have collected a crowd round him, and the *naphteña* might have been recognised, and afterwards punished, but the boy's missionary education had taught him to suffer injury meekly, and he did.

May 2nd.—K. was summoned to attend the king at half-past five in the morning, which appears to be the fashionable hour for royal levees in Abyssinia. This was indeed a *levée*, as it roused poor K. out of his bed. When he reached the king, he found him hard at work, delivering judgment on all cases that were brought before him, so he determined to repeat his visit later, and promised me that he would at the same time present his Majesty with my elephant rifle, and also, if possible, borrow from him a gun and a few cartridges for our expedition to Lake Tzana, as I was now destitute of ammunition, which was all the more provoking that there were some thousands of loaded cartridges lying in the boxes abandoned on the road behind us. Maderakal paid us a visit, and we had a long talk with him and K. on the political state and prospects of the country. He also told us some reminiscences of his youth.

He had been one of several native boys that the French scientific expedition, sent to Abyssinia by Louis Philippe's government, proposed to take back with them to France. It is well known how few of the members of this ill-fated expedition lived to return, and all the boys except Maderakal ran away before they reached the shores of the Red Sea. Maderakal, however, accompanied Lefèvre to Paris, where he was kindly received, and his portrait, as a boy, published in Lefèvre's great book. He told us that when he first landed, I think it was at Marseilles, and saw the people rolling about in carriages, he thought they were devils, and jumped into the sea, declaring that he would *swim* home to his own country.* However, habit is second

---

* Young Abyssinia is less impressionable. My brother brought a native boy to Europe with him on his return. This lad followed him to the station at Suez, and saw the express train move off, but beyond a sardonic grin which spread slowly over his dusky face, he evinced neither surprise nor fear.

CH. XX. *We Prepare to Visit Lake Tzana.* 53

nature, and he soon got accustomed to these strange things, and afterwards went to England, where he learnt to speak the language before, at his own urgent request, he was sent back to his native mountains.

It has been asserted by some writers that the love of country is strongest among the natives of mountainous districts, and this might seem to corroborate the fact; but I afterwards ascertained that the Arabs of the desert possess just as strong an infatuation for their sandy plains, so that I imagine the love of the fatherland is pretty equally divided between the children of the mountain, the desert, the moor, and the forest. Even the natives of Londinum do not utterly detest their November fogs, and were it not for this all-wise law of nature one portion of mankind would assuredly be much less happy than the other.

Maderakal had been in the service of King Theodorus up to the time of that despotic monarch's death, and he related how he used to tremble whenever the late king began to lash himself into one of his ungovernable fits of fury; but Maderakal, like many of Theodorus's former servants, appeared to entertain a sincere affection for his old master, and there seems to be little doubt that Theodorus possessed many of the characteristics of a great man. He was ambitious, brave, intelligent, determined, prompt to execute his designs, and had some chivalrous ideas; but, a deep drinker, accustomed to indulge without restraint in every licence, and the possessor of absolute power, he did not know what it was to control his passions. At one moment he was cruel in the extreme, and the next, generous to a fault. He possessed in a high degree that peculiar power, given to so few, of commanding men, but unfortunately he had no Diogenes near him to ask if he was not ashamed to be master of so much, when he was not even master of himself. There is small doubt that as he grew older he became partially insane, and on the slightest provocation he would lash himself into such terrible passions that the Abyssinians could only compare them to the paroxysms of the black panther, an animal popularly supposed by the natives to be of so choleric a disposition that it will actually die of rage. Maderakal told us how, in his calmer moments, Theodorus would say to him, " My friend, I do not wish to harm you, so when you see me getting angry, run, run for your life, for I do not know what I may do to you,"—advice he often repeated to his favourites. There was once a brave old officer, now dead, whose favourite dictum used to be, " If a woman once gets her eye upon you, sir, there's nothing for it but to take refuge in instant flight, *instant* flight, sir." The same sound advice might have been given to the unlucky subject of King Theodorus on whom the royal eyes chanced to fall in a moment of anger, for nothing but instant flight could save him.

Like his successor, Theodorus was exceedingly proficient in all martial and athletic sports, and he thought that innocent blood might be spared, and his quarrel with England satisfactorily settled, by a single combat between himself and the British General. This was an idea likely rather to astonish an officer of the modern school. I wonder what Moltke would have said to such a proposition? Perhaps Prince Bismarck would not so much have minded, but it is not everybody combines mental power with such physical proportions as those of Prince Otto.* To Theodorus's semi-barbarous mind, however, it appeared that princes were responsible for their own quarrels, and ought to fight them out themselves, instead of making their subjects do it for them, and it never occurred to him to shrink from the responsibility. But he did not know that all kings are not absolute, and therefore could hardly be called on to turn themselves into public champions.

Maderakal spoke French and English fairly well. Murcher, the other interpreter, spoke English and Hindustanee; for he had been in India. He had also accompanied Powell's brother on the expedition sent by Prince Kassa to punish the Shangallas, and recover Powell's remains, and he had some interesting details to relate of the murder.

Powell appears to have been a very courageous man, and a splendid shot. He had wounded an elephant, and gone forward with his wife and son to follow up the tracks, leaving his Alsatian servant at a mountain village to procure corn. This man got into a row with the *shoum* about some native girl, and in the quarrel shot the *shoum* dead. It is supposed the

* I believe that, many years ago, Prince Bismarck, when a University student, did fight a duel, in which he cut off the nose of the future Archbishop of Mayence.

natives were already incensed against him, and indeed all white men, on account of a previous exploit of his, to which I have before alluded, so they killed him. But this was only the beginning of the tragedy, it was now determined that the whole of the white party should be sacrificed, for the natives feared Powell might come back to revenge his servant's death, and they therefore sent on word that Powell and his family must be slain.

Poor Powell was laying outside his tent one hot night, and his wife and son were inside, when a party of Shangallas crept up, and threw a shower of spears, one of which transfixed Powell through the side. Powell was disabled, but he got his revolver from under his pillow, and shot the man who had wounded him in the arm, by which means he was afterwards identified. Meanwhile Mrs. Powell, on hearing her husband's cry, rushed out with the rifles, and stood at bay over him. I was told that all through the weary day this brave English lady defended her wounded husband and kept the Shangallas from him, but at sunset, seeing the agony he was in for want of water, she went for a moment to a stream to get some, and when she returned it is supposed, she found her husband and her child both dead. Then, and not till then, her brave heart failed her, and she lay down beside the father and the child, and died of sheer exhaustion and grief, for it is not known that she was actually wounded. When Powell's brother came to establish the proof of his death, and avenge it, he found the skeletons of the husband and wife, but that of the child was never discovered, and it is not positively known whether it was killed, or sold into slavery, though the probability is that it perished with its parents. I do not know if all the details of this story are correct, but I give it as I heard it in the country.

When Maderakal left us we rode to the top of the hills that overlook Lake Tzana. It was always a beautiful and refreshing sight to gaze on the green fields of the fertile vale of Dembea, stretching from the foot of the mountains like an emerald carpet to the borders of the vast expanse of water more than forty miles long by thirty broad, that glittered on the horizon till it was gradually lost to view in the distant sky line. Some of the wooded valleys running down towards the lake between the spurs of the mountains were very beautiful, and we saw both partridges and antelopes in the bush.

On returning to our tent we found K. just come from his audience with the king, to whom he had presented my elephant rifle. It was a more powerful piece than any the king possessed, and he appeared very pleased with it. As usual, he measured the size of the bore with his fingers, and then patting the rifle, said significantly in English—of which he has picked up a few words—" Man lie down, elephant lie down," meaning that when it was discharged the elephant and the hunter would be mutually rolled over. His Majesty, on hearing that I had no ammunition remaining and could therefore not use my guns, ordered one of his chiefs to give me a breech-loading rifle and fifty cartridges which had been presented to his Majesty by Mr.

Powell's brother. A gun is the possession an Abyssinian holds most dear, and the chief replied that the rifle in question had been given to his father by his Majesty— "And is a rifle the *only* thing I gave him?" said the king, with a look that was not to be mistaken. Indeed he had given to the father the country over which the son now ruled. However, to console the chief, K. promised he should have in exchange a very handsome double-barrelled fowling-piece by one of our best English makers, which, being a muzzle-loader, would be more useful to him than the breech-loader, for which he could not procure ammunition when his fifty cartridges were expended, as the Egyptians strictly interdict the passage of ammunition into Abyssinia, and the natives are therefore compelled to make their own powder, a good deal of which goes a very little way; but this is rather fortunate than otherwise, as many of their guns are almost as weak as their powder. McKelvie, on his return from Gondar, told me that when he made use of the cartridges I had given him, the nipples of his gun were blown bodily out, the said gun being of Birmingham manufacture, especially intended for African exportation. Considering the frequent African campaigns we get involved in, it is perhaps fortunate for our soldiers that some of our exporters deal in such articles, though, how a man with a conscience can trust a fellow-creature with a gun that cost eight and sixpence, I cannot understand; yet I believe some of these guns *are* turned out wholesale at that price, and I suppose a profit is made out of them.

CH. XX. *We Prepare to Visit Lake Tzana.* 59

May 3rd.—K. had another interview with the king and brought me the rifle and cartridges his Majesty had promised me. I consider it a wonderful feat of diplomacy to have extracted a gun from an African prince. It was settled that we were to start for Lake Tzana on Monday, the 5th, stay there five days, and return to Ambachara for the letters, after which the king promised to consent to my beginning the homeward journey, though he did not at all like letting me go so soon. African princes are rather proud of having a white man at their court, and they look upon it as a personal insult if he wishes to depart.

At 10 A.M. we heard that his Majesty had gone to play the martial game of *goaks*, so we mounted our horses and rode out to see it. The royal party was assembled on a long level piece of turf near the church where the poor fellow who had died of taking *kousso* was buried. The ground was kept clear by a number of the king's *naphteñas*, armed with long guns gaily decorated with jackal's tails, and there was a large crowd of natives dressed in their crimson and white *kuaries* standing around to see the sport. The effect of this multitude, clad entirely in two colours, was very brilliant and striking. King Yohannes wore a plain *kuarie* and loose white trowsers, his head and feet were bare, and he rode with the ordinary big-toe stirrups of the country. His hair was carefully plaited, and in his right hand he carried two long straight sticks which are used in the game of *goaks* to represent javelins. The royal charger was a superb milk-white Arab far above the average size, a present from the Khedive of Egypt. The high-peaked Turkish saddle was of purple velvet, richly embroidered with silver, with which precious metal the king's shield—which he carried in his left hand—and the bridle and breastplate of his horse were also profusely adorned. I need hardly say that the glittering white and silver, relieved by the crimson stripe of the *kuarie*, and the darker purple of the saddlecloth, contrasted splendidly, and set off to great advantage the clear bronze colour of the king's face. Though perhaps more simply clad than any of his chiefs, he looked every inch a king as he sat firmly and gracefully on his beautiful Arab steed. All the chiefs were provided with two long sticks like their sovereign, besides which they were armed with their silver-mounted swords and shields. Ras Warenia wore round his neck the splendid black panther skin which he had received from his royal master, and the bridles and breastplates of most of the horses were studded with plates and bosses of solid silver.

The game of *goaks* somewhat resembles the ancient exercise of the *djereed* as practised by the Moors when they still used the shield. One of the chiefs would dash forward hotly pursued by two others, who hurled their javelins at him with great dexterity, the fugitive alternately guarding his back, breast, and side with his buffalo-hide target, as he presented them to his adversaries. Sometimes he would continue flying from them till they had expended all their shafts, and sometimes he would double back upon them with lightning quick-

CH. XX. *We Prepare to Visit Lake Tzana.*

ness, hurling in his turn a javelin at his pursuers. The horsemanship, as a rule, was exceedingly good, equal to anything I have seen at an Andalusian *tentadero*,* and it was marvellous to see the rapidity with which the small Abyssinian horses would double round at full gallop. Owing to the strain of the cruel ring bits, most of their mouths were dripping with foam and blood, and the ground soon become so slippery with the trampling of their hoofs, that there were not a few tumbles. However, nobody appeared to be hurt, though it must be no easy thing to get clear of the native wooden saddles, which have a sharp peak in front nearly a foot high. Sometimes a chief galloped round brandishing his long sickle-shaped sword, and displaying what the French would call the *haute école* of horsemanship. Ras Warenia, who is considered the best rider in Amhara, certainly sat his horse with wonderful grace, though a stout and heavy man, but, as a rule, it was the king's fortune to

"Stand forth distinguished from the circling crowd,
For him who farthest sends the winged reed;"

for the swiftness of his Arab horse gave him a superiority over the others whenever he chose to dash into the *mêlée*, which he frequently did with great spirit, looking very grand on his white steed, with his white robes blowing in the wind, as he shot through the crowd of horsemen like an arrow, and singled out some chief for attack,

* At the Spanish *tentaderos* the wild bull is overthrown with a lance, a feat that requires no mean horsemanship.

laughing gaily as his javelin caught him in some part which he had not been quick enough to guard with his shield. Between the pauses in the game the children of the various chiefs also tried their puny hands at the mimic warfare, sturdily riding their horses, and throwing their javelins, like their elders, while the *gasha-zagries*, or esquires, ran over the ground picking up the fallen javelins of their masters.

On returning to our hut I set to work to clean my new rifle. It was a 12-bore double-barrel of Westley-Richards' best make, but was dreadfully dirty and rusty, and the late owner had succeeded in breaking part of the mechanism for closing the breech. However, I soon got it into working order, and despatched the gun that had been promised in exchange. In the afternoon, C. and I rode out to one of the park-like glades in the woods to try the shooting, and were well satisfied with the result. As we returned through the camp, we remarked with astonishment how unwarlike was its appearance. Here was an army of probably forty thousand men, and yet the camp seemed chiefly peopled by women and naked infants, who were everywhere to be seen in all the various stages, from crawling on all fours to walking as men should, with their faces uplifted to heaven. The innocent prattle of children and the merry laughter of young girls softened the stern preparatives of war, and made it hard to realize that we were in the lines of an invading host.

When an Abyssinian soldier goes on the march, he takes his wife and family with him, and, during the halts, enjoys the pleasures of domestic life; but it must not be supposed from this that the men are effeminate, or the women useless; indeed they carry a great portion of the necessary baggage, cook and wash for their husband, draw water, &c., and to a great extent prevent the army being accompanied by the worst class of camp followers. Every man in Abyssinia knows how to build his own hut in an incredibly short space of time; and the men brought into the field by each chief, as soon as the king halts, build their bell-shaped reed huts in good order round the hut of their leader, which is of larger dimensions and surrounded by palisades, the cavalry lodging their horses in their own huts, as I have before described, that is, of course, when the halt is to be of any duration. For mere bivouacking, the men make shelters of branches, and some of the chiefs have tents—a white cotton one for the warm weather, and a black camel's-hair one for the rain. Each chief knows the exact distance he must be from the king's tent, so the camp is very rapidly formed, and soon presents the appearance of an enormous village. In one point, however, the Abyssinian camps are very deficient—no attempt is made to preserve cleanliness. It has been said that a man rarely sees more than one dead donkey in his lifetime, but here donkeys that had been used for carrying baggage were to be seen lying by the score in every stage of putrefaction, and the filth and offal of the camp was never removed.

The soldiers fight under their chiefs with little organization. K. succeeded in getting about two thousand of the king's *naphteñas* into some sort of discipline, but he never could keep them steadily at drill for any length of time, as the men said they would rather be put to death at once than work so hard. The king has only a few brass cannon. He succeeded in getting a battery of English rockets which were placed under charge of the Swiss Louis, but the powder became so dry that the rockets burst, doing more harm to those who tried to fire them than to the enemy, and when Louis attempted to damp them he only managed to render them utterly useless. Louis was now about to quit the king's service, and had prepared a grand farewell speech, beginning: " All powerful Ethiop, now happily Emperor of these mighty dominions; for two years have I fought beside your Majesty, and contributed to the glory of your conquests, but now my sacred duty to my country calls me home ! " &c., &c., &c. ; and on fine evenings he was to be seen wandering about the camp getting up this bombastic speech by heart with the appropriate gesticulations, and reflecting pleasantly on the reward the king would give him. He was a vain, foolish man, and had, I was told, always been more trouble than service to King Yohannes. Among other events, Mustafa was in so detestable a humour this day that we had to promise him an application of the *giraff* by the king's own flogger if he did not amend his ways.

May 4*th*.—We had slept little, for the weather had been tempestuous, the fleas more voracious, and the wind and rain more penetrating than usual. In the morning I found the piece of cotton-cloth stretched above my bed, hanging within a foot of my face, and, raising my hand, immediately emptied on my devoted head nearly a gallon of rain water that had collected in it during the night. K. was suffering agonies from rheumatism, but later in the day went to see the king. We had a visit from Basha Tesemma, a captain of *naphteñas*, who was to accompany us to the lake on the morrow. C. was desirous of procuring some cartridges for his 12-bore Devisme, and by solemnly promising that when our baggage arrived the loan should be repaid threefold, he extracted a few with great difficulty. One chief said he had thirty unloaded cartridges, which, for the sake of friendship, he would give us if C. would promise to return him the same number full; C. promised, but when he received them they proved to be old cartridge cases that had been already fired off. Such is friendship!

During our afternoon ride we came on the carcase of a dead horse with two large hawks sitting on it. C. killed them both with one shot, and the natives ran down to secure them for food, yet these people think a goose an unclean animal, perhaps that is because they are geese themselves.

The greater part of the evening was devoted to the casting of bullets for the expedition which C. and I were to make next morning.

CHAPTER XXI.

THE GREAT LAKE.

May 5th.—At nine o'clock our baggage mules were packed and standing in front of the hut. The king had appointed fifty *naphteñas* to accompany us, under Basha Tesemma, and one of his attendants, called Alegas, who could speak a little English, being of English origin on the paternal side, though born in Abyssinia of a native mother. Before starting we bid adieu to King Johannes, whom we found sitting on his judgment-seat, a high throne erected in the open air behind the camp. A great crowd of people and attendants stood in a circle round him, and at the foot of the throne were two *Agafarees*, and the executioners ready to execute each sentence as soon as it issued from the royal lips. The ground was wet with blood, a man having just been flogged with the *giraff*, or hippopotamus-hide whip, a terrible instrument, with a plaited thong twelve feet long. His majesty always sits in judgment fasting, and, like the kings of the old romances, is ready to redress the wrongs of all who come to beg justice at his hands, whether they be chief or peasant, his word being final, and the punishment of the offender at once meted out to him. As has been before stated, the fundamental principle of all Abyssinian justice is the Mosaic law, an eye for an eye, and a tooth for a tooth.

Bowing to the Ethiopian sovereign, whose throne was high above our heads, C. and I left this grim scene, and rode W.S.W. for Lake Tzana. We passed within a few hours' march of some hot springs, lying south of Ambachara, which are much resorted to by sick chieftains, and, growing in a sheltered valley, we noticed some large *kousso* trees, with their acacia-like leaves and drooping pink blossoms, from which the medicine is made. We also saw many specimens of *shivti*, the pepper-like seed of which serves the Abyssinians instead of soap, as it makes a lather when ground into powder and mixed with water. Alegas declared that limes, bananas, grape-vines, and apple-trees grew here in abundance, and he also pointed out to us a weed that grows by the banks of streams, and is of so poisonous a nature that it proves instantly fatal to horses and cows, who, strangely enough, are always eager to eat it. It is curious how many terrible forms of death lurk in the midst of the beautifully luxuriant animal and vegetable life of tropical Africa; but here everything is exaggerated. The sun blinds the eye and scorches the brain, the scent of the flowers is so powerful as to become noxious, and the perfect muscular development of the wild denizens of the forest renders them only more dangerous. The gifts lavished by nature on uncultivated Africa are like the gift of beauty to a woman whose mind is unregulated—a fatal possession.

Alegas told us that the king was much pleased with my elephant rifle, and had taken it out with him on horseback, and fired it with one hand, much to the wonderment and admiration of his courtiers. I believe that when his majesty did this he was astute enough to place only a small charge in the rifle, with plenty of wadding; after which he had it loaded with the full charge, and gave it to one of his chiefs, bidding him perform a similar feat. The luckless chief dared not disobey, and, as might be expected, was sent spinning off his horse by the recoil. These rude practical jokes appear to be a favourite amusement of Abyssinian princes. Theodorus was a great hand at them, and woe to the chieftain who demurred at being made the royal butt, for it is almost as dangerous a pastime to play with sovereigns of Ethiopia as with the king of the African forests.

Apropos of Theodorus, Alegas gave us an account of a fight he once had with the people of Mitraha, an island on Lake Tzana. The people of Mitraha had revolted, and when they heard that the king was coming against them, their wise men met in council and said: "Let us collect all the canoes, and haul them on to our island, for then the king's wrath will be unable to reach us;" and when they saw that they had completely cut off the communication with the main land, they laughed and pointed the finger of scorn at the royal despot, who stood grinding his teeth on the shore. Theodorus heard their laughter wafted faintly across the lake, and he waxed so terribly wroth that it was with difficulty his attendants could keep him from plunging, there and then, into the water, and swimming across to chastise the insolent islanders in person. He at once despatched swift messengers to

Massowah for carpenters skilled in constructing boats, and, like the ancient Roman general, organised a swimming legion, with which he attacked the island in force, vowing vengeance on all who should fall into his hands. Some of the islanders escaped in their boats, but Theodorus captured about forty of them, among whom were many women and children, and he had them all shut up in a house, without regard to age or sex, and set fire to the house, so that they might be roasted alive; and the people of Lake Tzana remember, even to the third generation, never again to raise the anger of their king.

We had to make our way on foot down a very steep hill, the plains of Dembria being more than three hundred feet below Ambachara. The bush on either side of the path was full of dog-faced baboons, and we saw some red buck. On a hill before us stood the village of Amba Mariam, and on another hill were the ruins of an old Portuguese palace. At the bottom of the descent we crossed a river called Arno Garno, flowing S.S.W. to the lake, and here we met a number of girls carrying pats of fresh butter nicely wrapped up in leaves; before we could interfere, our *naphteñas* rushed forward and possessed themselves of the butter, which they clapped on their heads, where it soon melted in the sun, and trickled down their necks and faces, to their great satisfaction. It is considered quite *comme il faut* in Ethiopia to have half a pound of butter on the top of your head; and, in default of butter, raw fat, previously masticated until it has become soft and malleable, is used as a dressing for the hair.

At 2.30 P.M. we reached a village, and entered the principal hut. Some eggs were brought us by an old woman, but previous experience had taught us always to test Abyssinian eggs in water before cooking them; and when we tried these they all floated to the surface —a sure sign they were bad. Some guinea-fowls' eggs were next produced, but they all contained partially-developed chickens, so we had to turn our attention to the fowls that were running about the village, while the old woman hobbled off to get a supply of milk, *tef*, and *tella* for our attendants. The *naphteñas* soon captured us a brace of chickens, and, having begged the loan of my hunting-knife, chopped off their heads at one blow. Incredible though it may appear, I solemnly declare that those chickens' heads remained for several seconds rolling their eyes, and gasping on the ground, while the headless bodies ran round and round, one of them positively going out at the door. After a brief space the bodies naturally became rather uncertain in their movements without their heads, and after turning one or two somersaults, as if in search of those appendages, rolled over and died.

I have a vague recollection of once reading a horrible story of the French revolution, in which an executioner, on being asked if decapitated people retain any life, replies, "Ah, Monsieur, I see *you* have never looked in the basket as I have done, when the freshly-severed heads lie heaped together; why, I have to get a new basket every fortnight, for by that time the bottom of the old one is *bitten through*."

I do not venture to theorize about human heads, but certainly these chickens had the strange vitality I have described; and should any of my readers doubt the fact, and care to try the experiment, I believe they can easily obtain ocular proof of its truth, unless English chickens are much less vivacious than African ones, which is hardly likely.

Basha Tesemma made a hearty feast off sour milk and fermenting *tef*, the old woman first rolling the *tef* into a ball in her hands, and then stuffing it affectionately into his mouth. I trust the meal agreed with him. The stragglers of our party having by this time come up, we pushed forward again towards the lake, passing large flocks of guinea-fowl on the way. We had the greatest difficulty to prevent our *naphteñas* taking a zig-zag route, from village to village, in order that they might indulge their plundering proclivities; and we were positively forced to *drive* the Basha in front of us to make him keep the straight road. I may here mention that the Basha was got up regardless of expense, in a gorgeous striped-silk robe, and mounted on a white horse—the favourite colour for steeds here. At his side strode an old man, the chief of this part of Dembea, who was deputed to act as our guide and caterer.

Most of our followers committed small peculations on such natives as passed, when we did not chance to be in sight, and one man captured from a village a stick of a kind much esteemed here. It was cut from a tree that bears a flower like a large orange-blossom, but with three times the scent, and the wood of which is so hard and heavy, that it is said shepherds have been known to kill lions with sticks made of it.

In Abyssinia it is thought a great feat to slay a lion, but, strangely enough, we were told that the shepherds of the mountains not unfrequently drive lions from their flocks with nothing but these sticks. Perhaps the lions found in the mountains are a small kind, though I certainly once heard in Norway of a woman who attacked with her broomstick a large brown bear, that had seized on her pig, and gave it such a vigorous thrashing, that the astonished bruin was glad to beat a retreat and abandon its prey. Happily such very stalwart Amazons are rare among womankind.

As we neared the lake, Basha Tesemma made a desperate effort to inveigle us into a halting at a little hamlet nestling among some low wooded hills, but I drove him ruthlessly down to a small bay, opposite the memorable island of Mitraha, and

"—— nigh upon that hour,
When the heron forgets his melancholy,
Sets down his other leg, and stretching, dreams
Of goodly supper in the distant pool——"

we found ourselves standing by that vast sheet of water which the Abyssinians say is the home of the King of the Demons, who rises through the waves when invoked by magical incantations.

The last rays of the sinking sun threw a mellow light upon the scene; to our right a tangled jungle hung over the lake, which laved the drooping boughs of the trees. The water here was shallow, and rippled gently in on the narrow shingly beach with a soothing murmur; two or three tiny canoes, made of rushes, were drawn up on the bank, and about thirty yards from the shore a solitary heron stood motionless on one leg, watching intently for the passing fish; not half a mile beyond was the little island of Mitraha, with its conical houses, nestling among groves of trees. Perhaps on this very spot stood Theodorus when he vowed his terrible vengeance against its inhabitants.

Alegas begged the loan of my gun, which was loaded with ball, and shot the heron dead. A Wito, one of the curious race of hippopotamus hunters who dwell in this region, approached, and, throwing off the strip of cotton cloth which formed his only covering, plunged into the lake and brought the bird to land. These Wito men have a very peculiar type of face. Their foreheads are extraordinarily retreating, and the outer corners of their eyes and eyebrows slope upwards, like those of the typical Mephistopheles; their sharp aquiline noses curve over the upper lip like a beak, and their chins are prodigiously long. Their ears end in a point like those of the ancient satyrs, and their hair, which they wear unplaited, is short and woolly. A more diabolical cast of countenance it would be hard to imagine, but I believe they are a harmless race, and live principally on the flesh of hippopotami, which they kill with poisoned spears. They believe that the spirits of some people go to God, while others graze on the plains round Lake Tzana in the form of cows; but they do not seem to have any form of worship or religion. They dwell in tiny conical huts made of reeds from the lake, which are hardly large enough for a man to stand upright in; and when they marry they simply swear to take the woman "*Yohannes y mute*" ("By the king's death"), the usual way of ratifying *any* promise in Abyssinia. But the Wito women—some of whom are very beautiful—will not marry a Wito brave until he has proved himself a man by slaying a hippopotamus with his own hand. They do not mix with the rest of the Abyssinians, and appear to be a distinct, probably an aboriginal race. They cultivate no arts but the simple one of hunting, and seem to be quite contented with their lot in this "happy valley." Perhaps

"Thought would destroy their paradise,"

as the poet Gray says.

Mustafa and the baggage mules were nowhere to be seen, so we despatched a *naphteña* in search of them, and having picketed the horses, prepared to dine off what we had in our haversacks. The *shoum* of a neighbouring village had orders to provide food for the king's *naphteñas*, but did not do so. We therefore gave the men permission to procure a cow for themselves next day. Bruce says the kings of Abyssinia give a village to a stranger to supply him with food. This custom is still maintained, but each village is not supposed to be laid under this burden for more than three days at a time, unless the *shoum* behaves badly, in which case the stranger may prolong his stay as a punishment.*

* See Appendix, note G.

In the evening Alegas related how he once came upon seven lions in a forest, but managed to effect his escape unperceived. We slept for two hours, when Mustafa at last arrived with the tent, after much wandering; and not a little frightened at having missed his way in so wild a country, for, though he trusted implicitly in our power to protect him, he knew that, being an Egyptian, he was looked on as an enemy, and did not love to find himself alone. When all our people were asleep, C. and I strolled down by the lake to look for hippos, as the Wito had told us they usually came on shore at night to eat the grass, but we saw none. Tzana looked lovely as the Larian lake by moonlight, but in the jungle hard-by we could hear at intervals the growling of a leopard, breaking the quiet stillness of the night.

May 6th.—We were up at daybreak, and walked by the shore towards a headland that we saw on our right. The beautiful trees and creepers of the jungle were reflected in the water as in a vast mirror; further on were some great grey rocks, and beyond these we came to a long reach of grass running down to the water's-edge, as smooth and green as an English lawn. Geese, spoonbills, black swans, and every variety of duck abounded here, and paid no heed to our approach, for they were unacquainted with the sound of a gun. C. shot a fine black swan, and I a brace of woodcock, which were also plentiful. Presently the noses of two large hippopotami appeared above the waters of the lake, but out of range from the land; however a canoe loaded with cotton was rounding the headland, so we hailed it, and after some parley, induced the natives to bring their load to shore, and carry us on their shoulders to the canoe, which, being little more than a large bundle of rushes, floated very low in the water. Alegas was to have accompanied us as interpreter, but, like Bob Acres, his courage was rapidly oozing out at the ends of his fingers, and failed him at the last moment. He said the *Goumarie** were sometimes very bold in their own element, and would take it into their heads to attack a canoe, and crunch it up, men and all, between their enormous jaws; so we left him behind, and took the canoe as near to the hippos as we could get the natives to venture. On our approach, the huge beasts disappeared under the water, but one of them coming up again to breathe about thirty yards off, I fired a shot with my twelve-bore Westley-Richards, which struck him on the neck with a dull thud, and at once sent him down again. The other then rose, on which C. fired with his Devisme, but rather too high. They did not re-appear after this, so we returned to shore, and walked on to the headland, where C. bagged a brace of guinea-fowl, of which there were great numbers among the bushes.

On the way back, we noticed that the ground was deeply indented with the foot-prints of hippopotami and wild pigs. We were examining these, when our gun-bearers were suddenly charged in rear by a trucu-

---

* *Goumarie*, Abyssinian for hippopotamus.

lent-looking bullock which was grazing on the plains, and which rapidly put them to flight. Shortly afterwards we encountered our friend the Wito, who had come to tell us that he had seen two hippos asleep on a rock in the lake. We therefore dismissed the noisy *naphteñas*, and followed him silently to the spot he indicated. Only the black noses of the hippos were visible, near a reef of rock some distance from the land; but a second Wito had brought his canoe round, and in this I embarked, first taking off my boots, and making all secure for a capsize, as the tiny craft was not more than ten feet long, and could barely hold the Wito and myself. These Wito canoes are of charmingly simple construction. A narrow mat of long rushes is tied together at each end, and distended in the centre with a bundle of reeds. On this bundle kneels the Wito, who paddles his frail bark with a long stick, which has no blade attached to it. When the canoe is dry it floats pretty lightly, but the water soon filters through the rushes, and the canoe sinks lower and lower, till it hardly rises above the surface of the lake; and, being nearly round, of course the least motion is liable to capsize it. Indeed, these boats bear a strong resemblance to the vessel on which the primeval navigator made his first voyage, which tradition tells us was simply a log floating upon the water.

A fresh breeze had sprung up, and the little canoe danced about on the rising wavelets like an egg shell; however, the Wito managed it with great dexterity, and we soon got near the hippos, one of whom disappeared as we approached. I fired at the other, and, as before, heard the bullet strike the thick hide of his neck, causing him to plunge at once beneath the waters of the lake. I then landed on the rock, and fired again as he rose to breathe, with just the same result, the echoes of my rifle, I fear, sadly disturbing the solemn meditations of a flock of pelicans who were floating tranquilly by.

In the day time the hippopotami show as little as possible of their heads above the water, and their skulls and hides are so tremendously thick that an ordinary lead bullet makes no impression on them. There is, however, one small spot behind the ear where a bullet will penetrate, though having no previous experience of this sport, we had not yet discovered its true position.

When I regained the shore, we lunched off partridge's eggs roasted on a fire of dried cactus-leaves, which burned very brightly, as if impregnated with turpentine. The Wito showed us his hippopotamus lance, the point of which was carefully enveloped in a bamboo sheath; the stick of the lance was fully twelve feet long, and into one end was inserted a piece of iron with a small sharp barbed point dipped in poison. The Wito cautioned us not to examine this point too closely, as he said the *smell* even of the poison in which it had been dipped was hurtful. The Wito poison is vegetable, and I believe is prepared by boiling down a plant that grows by the lake, but we could not

The Great Lake.

learn the exact way of making it, as the Witos were very reserved on this subject. That the poison is powerful is certain, for a hippopotamus generally dies within two hours of receiving a scratch from a poisoned spear. The mode of hunting the hippos is as follows: The Wito huntsman hides himself at nightfall among the bushes on the margin of Lake Tzana, near some spot where the hippopotami are accustomed to come on shore to make their midnight feast of grass and young twigs. Care must be taken that the wind is blowing off the lake, for the hippos have very keen scent, and being much more courageous at night than they are in the daytime, will charge down on the hunter if they scent him; their enormous weight and size rendering them very dangerous, though their movements are somewhat unwieldy. As soon as the Wito sees the hippos come out of the water, he poises his spear, and as they pass his hiding-place, throws it so as to strike one of them behind the fore leg, where the fold of the flesh renders the hide less hard ;· the small barbed point sticks firmly in, and the brittle shaft of the spear is at once broken off by the movements of the huge animal, who immediately takes to the water, and soon dies from the effects of the poisoned wound. Some hours after death, the body floats to the surface of the lake, and is hauled on shore by the first party of Witos who may chance to see it, and though it is sometimes found twenty miles from where it was killed, word is always sent to the Wito who slew it, as each spear-head has a mark to indicate whom it belongs to, and there is honour among these hunters.

It is said that the Wito poison does not injure the flesh of the hippopotamus, and the skin having been cut off for whips and shields, the meat is divided by these people for food, its taste, though rather coarse, being by no means disagreeable. The head of the hippo is then immersed in the lake till the tusks are loosened, these tusks being estimated in the country at a value, in barter, of about one dollar the set. Some of the Witos, we were told, make rudely carved bracelets and anklets of the ivory, but I never saw any of this work myself.

As the neighbouring villages still refused to let the *naphteñas* have any food, they dispersed to forage for themselves, and captured a cow, which they slew, and eat raw as usual. In the afternoon, some of the contumacious *shoums* were brought before us, and, on their still continuing refractory, we had them placed in chains, and ordered them to be taken to Ambachara next day, for the King to dispose of them as he thought fit. They now humbly begged to be forgiven, and declared that they would be all that was good and virtuous in the future if we would only set them free; so, on their solemnly promising to send in a supply of grain, we pardoned them, and restored them to liberty; but of course they only took advantage of this to slip over to the island of Mitraha, and we never saw them more, for we did not wish to raise the enmity of the natives by attempting their re-capture. Indeed, I thought it a wise precaution to force Basha Tesema always to have a certain number of his roving *naphteñas* on guard at the camp, by telling him, from time to time, that I should require him to parade them, and, if I did not find all present, would send him and his men back to the king, and have nothing more to do with them; a prospect the poor Basha looked forward to with unmitigated horror, as he well knew what kind of reception his Royal Master would give him if he returned without us. Indeed, he took to following us everywhere so closely, that he became almost as great a bore as a certain escort of bersaglieri that I remember once accompanied us to Pæstum, in the days when brigandage was rife.

Our party was a large one, the day was splendid, and the old Greek temples, standing in lonely grandeur, with the dark blue sea behind them, more than realized all our anticipations; but when, after luncheon, we strolled away in couples to enjoy the beauties of the scene, according to our various fancies, the too conscientious sergeant of our escort, told off a private to follow each couple at six paces distance, with a loaded rifle, for General Desjardin had cautioned him on no account to lose sight of his charges, and the brave fellow obeyed the *consigne* to the letter, quite oblivious of the fact that two is company and three is none. Not a moment could we escape from the vigilant eyes of the grim sentries, who stood behind us, and a few promising flirtations were nipped in the bud, while we all had an uncomfortable feeling, as if *we* were malefactors, and the escort our gaolers. However, to return to the Basha : we ordered him to guard the tent, and not *us*, and then strolled away to enjoy the luxury of a bathe in the lake, for this part of Tzana seemed to be free from crocodiles, though they abound in many of the Abyssinian rivers. After a glorious swim, C. and I proceeded to the little jungle, in which I had heard a leopard growling during the night, and where the Wito had assured us we were certain to find one. We, therefore, plunged into the thickest of the undergrowth, regardless of the thorns that guarded every tree, shrub, and creeper, with the exciting prospect of disturbing the leopard, at any moment, from its lair, or seeing it crouching on one of the great overhanging boughs of the trees ; but though we traversed the jungle in every direction, and our course through it might have been traced by the fragments of our clothing that adorned its brambles, our perseverance, like virtue, had to be its own reward, and we returned to our tent without having encountered the leopard.

When the moon rose over the waters, we started on another quest after hippopotami, but this also resulted in "no find."

May 7*th* was a wet morning. We decided to explore the lake in a southerly direction, so, after writing to K., and striking the tent, we mounted our horses, and cantered along the shore, past two lovely little bays, swarming with gaily coloured waterfowl of every kind. C. rode to the top of a wooded hill, where he found a number of wild geese perched in a tree, like crows.

Alegas said that when Theodorus burned Mitralia, a young girl escaped to the foot of this hill, by swimming from the island to the shore. We presently came to a small river called the Keman, which appeared too deep to be easily forded; but one of the Witos waded into the lake, and showed us a bar of sand that crossed the mouth of the river at some distance from the land, by following which we were enabled to reach the other side without swimming our horses. Beyond the Keman, we traversed a level expanse of green sward, overshadowed by some noble trees, that looked very like a bit of scenery from an English park. Deeply indented in the wet earth by the water's edge were the fresh foot-prints of a full grown lion, who must have been here to drink, the Witos averred, not three hours before. C. shot a duck of the muscovy kind, and not long afterwards we noticed the heads of a large female hippo and her young calf peering at us from the lake. They say these creatures are attracted by the sound of a gun, which excites their curiosity, even when they are under water; I suppose the concussion of the air is perceptible to them. Izaac Walton declared that no true follower of "the gentle craft" should speak near a stream, as it disturbs the fish.

There being no canoes in sight, we dismounted, slung a couple of extra cartridges round our necks, and waded into the lake, holding our rifles above our heads. The hippos, doubtless thinking themselves secure in their own element, did not attempt to go away; but I noticed that the careful mother hippo shifted her position as we approached, and placed her own body between her calf and us. When we had got as near as the depth of the water would permit, I fired, whereat she rose out of the water, and opened her gigantic jaws to their full extent, as if she would like to swallow us whole. C. at this moment fired a Pertuiset explosive shell right into her mouth, which caused her to spring round, and for a moment we thought she was going to charge ; but a shot from my second barrel made her turn again, and plunging under the waters of the lake, she disappeared from sight, taking her young one with her. We had hoped by distracting the cow's attention to get a shot at the calf, whose more tender hide would not have resisted our bullets, and whose flesh would have been delicate eating; but so strong was the maternal instinct in the brave old mother hippo, that she never for an instant ceased to shield her child, and even when, enraged by our shots, she exposed herself out of the water, she never permitted the calf to show more than his black nozzle above the surface.

On regaining the shore, I shot another muscovy duck, and we rode to a small Abyssinian village a short distance inland. Here we saw the funeral of a poor fellow, who had been burnt alive ; his hut having caught fire while he was asleep in it. A crowd of natives were sitting round the body, but rose to their feet as we passed. C. and I breakfasted in an empty hut, and then went for a long walk southwards, round the lake. We forded the river Arno

Garno,* which runs into the lake near this village; and, after wandering through some thin copses of mimosa trees, reached the shore opposite two rocks called "the sisters" or "stones of friendship," which rise side by side out of the water, looking a little like the Faro Leoni at Capri. Ducks, surrounded by broods of precocious ducklings, who could already gaze at the African sun without blinking, though but a few hours emerged from their shells; graceful spoonbills, black and white ibis, swans, flamingos, grave-looking pelicans, speckled geese, and, in short, all sorts of waterfowl, whose names I am not sufficiently learned in ornithology to enumerate, floated tranquilly on the water, or stood meditatively on one leg, among the shallows, in all the bravery of goodly plumage, taking little notice of the strangers who had invaded their territory; for the Witos have no guns, and the birds of Lake Tzana have not yet learned to look on the approach of man with dread. Indeed, it was difficult to realize that all these birds were wild, and that we were not wandering in some Jardin d'acclimatation, where long habit had rendered the different specimens tame.

A sharp shower drove us to seek shelter, which we obtained in a natural summer house, formed by a network of creepers, which had twined themselves round a graceful mimosa tree. Near it we noticed the footprints of a leopard, that had come down here to drink; and towards dusk, as we were returning, we saw three

---

* So called, because the two streams, Arno and Garno, run into it.

hippos, a bull, cow, and calf, swimming in the lake, not far from the mouth of Arno Garno. We waded towards them, greatly to the excitement of a crowd of natives, who had collected on the shore; but the water being deep, we could only get within fifty yards, at which distance we both fired at the bull, who was between us and the others. He at once went down, and did not appear again; but the cow and calf swam away out of range, the mother being careful all the time to screen her child. When we returned to land, some of the natives promised to watch for the body of the hippo that had gone down, and bring it in should it float to the surface, as these animals always sink for a couple of hours when they are killed in the water. Our gun-bearers having now brought our horses to meet us, we rode back to the village, where our tent presently arrived, and we lay down to snatch a few hours' sleep before starting to hunt by moonlight.

At 8.30 P.M., Alegas came to tell us that a hyena was prowling round the tent, with designs on our cattle. We, therefore, took our guns and sallied out, Alegas drawing his great curved sword to be ready for the encounter.

I have seen the hyena described in Professor Wilson's "Narrative of Discovery and Adventure in Africa," in thrilling language, as "not the strongest, but the most ferocious and untamable of all the beasts of prey;" and we learn from the same source that "these creatures, by moving in numerous bands, achieve what is beyond the single strength of the greater animals;

they burst with mighty inroad into cities, and have even carried by storm fortified enclosures." If such be the case, Heaven help the traveller in a canvas tent! but I fear these creatures little merit so high an encomium on their valour. Laughing hyenas, of the largest kind, swarm by thousands in Abyssinia, and nightly prowl round the camp of the traveller; but I never heard of their making a united attack, nor, so far as my personal experience goes, have I ever found them other than the most cowardly of animals.

Why will writers always exagerate the terrible? Perhaps, however, it has the effect of inducing a love of adventure in our youth. I remember that ever since I was a child I longed to follow the wanderings of the adventurous Bruce, and the imaginary Rolando; and if I had known that I should do so, and yet not meet with a single adventure, I might never have gone to Africa. *Mais, revenons à nos moutons*— The hyena we were in search of, as usual, flitted away like a ghost the moment it caught sight of us. So we summoned the two Wito hunters, and proceeded to the borders of the lake, the hour being near when hippopotami were wont to come on shore. Alegas gave us the cheering intelligence, en route, that the *goumarie* were very bold at night, and would charge at the flash of a rifle the moment it was fired. He also declared that they would sometimes take two or three men at a time in their enormous jaws, carry them away into the lake, and sink with them to the bottom until they were drowned. I find, after this story, an entry in my diary as follows :—"I begin to think Alegas rather a romancer." When we reached the edge of the water, we removed our boots and glided silently along in our stockings, as the Witos said it was absolutely necessary to make no noise. We saw the nose of one hippo far out in the lake ; but it afforded an insufficient mark, and we continued our way without firing at it. At last the Witos declared that it was no use going further, as they knew the coast and the habits of the *goumarie*, and were sure we should see no more. However, though ready to admit that they *ought* to know all about it, we preferred following our own instincts, and ordered them to go on, which they very unwillingly did. After again wading through the Arno Garno, we crept among the mimosa trees, our Witos leading the way with their long spears in their hand, as they said that if there were any *goumarie* about they would perceive them long before we should. But we had hardly walked a hundred yards, when suddenly there was a cracking of branches, the trees in front of us parted asunder, and a huge black mass appeared rushing down upon us with short angry snorts, like a railway engine letting off steam. Our native hunters had got, without perceiving it, between the wind and a hippopotamus that was grazing on land, and which, finding its retreat to the lake cut off, had made up its mind to charge. The attack was so sudden that we found ourselves running as hard as we could before we well knew what we were running for ; and the valiant Witos, who had been the first to turn, passed us like

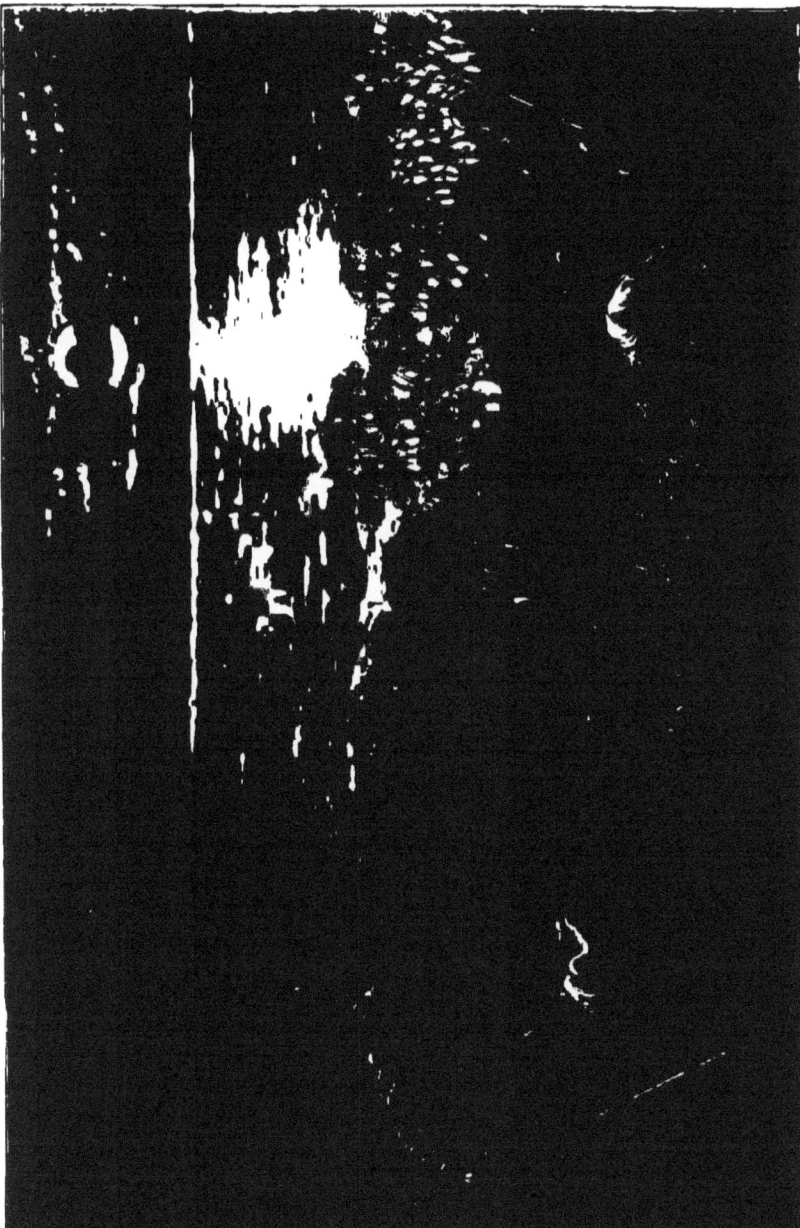

A WICKED HIPPO.

The Great Lake.

lightning and never stopped till they reached the river. *Sauve qui peut* was the first instinct with everybody, yet we could not help feeling that there was something rather ludicrous in thus being suddenly hunted by the very beast we had come to hunt. However, it is no joke to be caught by an irate hippopotamus; so as soon as I could pull myself up, I faced round and got a rapid shot at our pursuer; and its way to the lake being now clear, and the first fury of its charge expended, it turned aside and plunged into the water.

After this little incident, we decided to trust no more to the sagacity and courage of our Witos; but, in future, to lead the way ourselves.

We presently descried the black back of another hippo appearing above the surface of the lake, but it remained so motionless, that the Witos said it must be a stone, and offered to go forwards to reconnoitre. We, however, bid them lie quiet where they were; and, creeping cautiously past the mimosas, the fallen thorns of which pierced our stockinged feet most unmercifully, crouched down behind two little bushes that grew close by the water's edge, to watch.

An hour passed: the moon rose slowly, casting a broad path of light across the lake, and turning to silver the feathery foliage of the mimosas that grew by its shores. The birds were all asleep, not even the flight of an owl disturbing the stillness; for owls are rare in Abyssinia. Our two Witos contemplated pityingly, and with ill-disguised impatience, the weakness of mind that induced us to continue watching what they still declared to be a stone; and we ourselves were getting tired of our position, for the bushes which screened us were so small that we dared not move; when suddenly the waters parted with a mighty splash, and a splendid hippopotamus emerged from the waves and walked slowly towards us, its enormous body showing clear and dark in the bright moonlight. A forehead shot was the only one possible; so we pointed our rifles and waited till it should come to close quarters. When it was within twenty yards of us, C. fired a Pertuiset shell, right between its eyes, which exploded with a bright flash as it struck. I followed this immediately with a conical bullet, from my 12-bore, aimed at the same spot; and the next moment the great beast rolled completely over, and we flattered ourselves that we had got it. But it recovered its feet again, and rushed splashing and stumbling back towards the deep water, waking the sleeping echoes of the night with its bellowings. When, afterwards, the Witos found the body, it had drifted a considerable distance round the shore of the lake; but they honestly brought us the teeth and part of the hide, which was more than an inch in thickness. We saw no more hippos this night, and only regained our tent an hour before daylight.

CHAPTER XXII.

SPORT ON THE LAKE CONTINUED.—OUR RETURN TO
AMBACHARA.

May 8th.—At 9 a.m. we were in the saddle and rode towards our old camp to see if any hippos were taking their *siesta* by the stones where we had seen them sleeping before. Ambachara and all the mountains were enveloped in dense rain clouds; but here in this favoured valley of Dembea, the weather was lovely and the wind blew off the water as fresh and fragrant as a sea-breeze. A heavy surf was running in on the shore, sparkling merrily in the sunlight as it laved the green grass, which extended like a lawn to the water's edge, and tumbled in a long line of white breakers over the bar at the mouth of the Keman, and the rocks beyond. There were no hippos at the stones, but we saw two opposite the dry bed of a stream where, from the number of their foot-prints, they were evidently accustomed to land. Hippopotami walk on the tips of their toes, and make very deep foot-prints, their weight being enormous, owing to the fact that their bones, like those of the elephant, are solid all through. I need hardly say that the full-grown hippopotami living wild in lake Tzana are giants compared to the specimens that have been brought alive to Europe.

The two hippos we had seen from the shore disappeared before we could wade out to them; however, we enjoyed a swim in the lake, and while dressing, I made a discovery which illustrates one of the worst miseries of human life in Abyssinia. I found that hidden in every seam of my flannel shirt lurked hundreds of a kind of white lice, so small and transparent that it was hardly possible to see them without a magnifying glass; yet this shirt was washed regularly every day. It was the last flannel shirt that remained to me of all my stock; but I placed a big stone in it, and consigned it to the depths of the lake then and there, determining that in future I would only wear cotton—a material I should recommend to Abyssinian travellers in preference to flannel.

C. bagged a fine goose, and I shot a duck with my rifle. We were obliged to have these birds cooked at once, as the climate of lake Tzana had the peculiar property of causing all the game we shot to spoil in a few hours, like meat struck by lightning, so that we could not keep anything from one day to the next. I never clearly understood the reason of this phenomenon, for in other parts of Abyssinia, where the weather was much warmer, our game would always keep through the night.

When we returned to the camp, the *naphteñas* were clamouring for food, having, as before, been unable to procure any in the villages. The *Shoums*, as I have related, had all disappeared to Mitralia; so we summoned the villagers, and asked them to let the men have a cow; but they refused to do so, though there were several herds of cattle grazing, half wild, on the plains. Towards these we, therefore, walked, rifle in hand, followed by a crowd of natives, gestulating wildly with their spears. C. singled out a fat cow, and having with some difficulty got within forty yards of it, fired at the white spot on its forehead. The effect of the shot was instantaneous, and the beast sunk gently forwards on its knees and died without a groan. The villagers at once yelled out that this cow was the fattest of the lot, and belonged to the priest. "Very well," said the Basha, "why did you not let us have another when we asked for it?" The *naphteñas* now rushed forwards with their curved swords, and in an incredibly short time all but the skeleton of the cow had disappeared from sight. As for ourselves, we were so fatigued with hunting all night as well as riding all day, that we quite forgot dinner, and slept in the tent till 10 p.m., when the Witos came to accompany us in quest of hippos; but though we made a pilgrimage of three hours in our stockings round the shores of the lake, we did not find any.

May 9th.—This morning we made the Witos practise throwing spears at a small piece of matting stuck on a stick, which they struck with great dexterity at thirty yards. Alegas distinguished himself by casting the spear furthest, though thirty yards was the longest range at which he could make *good* practice. The Abyssinian horsemen, however, can throw farther when at a gallop, as their lances are lighter than those used by men on foot, and the impetus of the horse helps them.

When about to throw the spear, the Abyssinians poise it accurately in the centre, keeping the fore-arm perpendicular, the elbow close to the side, the head thrown back, and the weight of the body on the right foot; they then give to the spear a quivering motion throughout its length, and rapidly springing forwards on the left foot, send it hurtling through the air with such force that it will often transfix a buffalo-hide shield.

Mustafa being again in a most detestable and hopeless humour this day, we gave him a second fatherly warning, that if he did not improve he must be beaten, which would be his punishment; while if he did improve, he should not be beaten, which would be his reward. Whether he appreciated all the beauty and simplicity of this system I do not know, for we mounted our horses and rode out to continue our explorations round the east side of the lake.

We traversed a wide belt of alluvial plain, stretching between the foot of the mountains and the shore; this plain was now dried and cracked by the sun, but in a couple of months, when the rains had fallen, it would be covered by the waters of Lake Tzana, which yearly endow it with a wonderful fertility.* One of our Wito guides proudly pointed out to us the spot where he had speared a hippopotamus, and thus qualified himself,

---

* The villagers who dwell on the plain, shift their *Dii penates* to other villages on the hills during the wet season.

like a true knight, to win his lady's favour. The shore, as usual, teemed with strange aquatic birds, one of which—a beautiful milk-white spoonbill—C. shot as a specimen. A long ride brought us to a promontory, on which stood a little village, and from this point we got an extensive view along the eastern shores of the lake; the country as far as the eye could reach preserved always the same characteristics as that we had already ridden through, being a fine fertile valley, dotted with woods and mimosa bushes, bounded to the east by ranges of mountains, and to the west by the waters of Lake Tzana. To the S.W. the faint outline of the island of Daka was visible, apparently floating in the air and enjoying an isolation almost as complete as that of Gulliver's flying island; for the frail native canoes can only venture out there in the calmest of weather, and, even then, it is quite a long voyage to reach it, little less adventurous than crossing the channel in a Boyton dress.

We turned our horse's heads, and rode back to a cluster of tiny extinguisher-shaped huts, made of reeds, which we had noticed near the border of the lake: this was a Wito village. A gentle Wito girl came out and offered us milk in a *zanañia*—a kind of gourd—prettily ornamented with basket-work. There was something inexpressibly beautiful and attractive about this girl that I do not know how to describe. The grave, almost pathetic look in her large dark eyes, the delicate and sensitive lines of her forehead and eyebrows, the exquisite chiselling of her nose and chin, and the rare purity and sweetness in the expression of her mouth, combined to make her appear one of those rare types of womanhood, in whom the physical beauty of the frame seems only the natural accompaniment of the still more beautiful mind that dwells within—like a priceless gem encased in a fair casket. We not unfrequently see the beautiful casket empty, or the beautiful gem concealed beneath a rough covering; but the spiritual look that lighted up this girl's face seemed to indicate that, here, both gem and casket were together, and yet she was the daughter of a race who, from time immemorial, have adhered to a savage life. She knew no religion, and perhaps had no ambition higher than one day to keep the hut of some hunter more skilled than the rest in spearing the hippopotamus, the pursuit of which animal —little more wild than themselves—had been the one aim and object in life of her father and brothers, and all those of her tribe, who had gone before her, as far as the memory of man could reach. Still, somehow, the wonderful look of soul, thought, and feeling, that lived in her face when she raised her eyes, made one forget everything except that she was a fitting type of fairest womanhood in that fair land where the sun loves to dwell, and lends a wondrous beauty, through the magic of his rays, to every created thing. Her small hands and arched feet might have served as a study to a sculptor, and a bright glow of health shone through the dark transparency of her skin; her black hair was plaited in the Abyssinian fashion, and her lithe girlish figure had a wild grace and beauty all its own, which her coarse shirt of native cotton, confined by a leather thong at the waist, and open at the breast, covered, but did not conceal. There was a modest dignity and gentleness in her bearing as she stood waiting for us to drink the milk, with her great black eyes lifted up towards us, that made us fear to ask her to stand as a model, lest it should frighten or pain her; so we humbly begged for more milk, and strove to transfer the outline of her beauty to our note books while she brought it, but our efforts to reduce to black and white the charm of her expression were all in vain, and I think we must each have drunk more than a gallon of milk during the attempt. Could we possibly have drunk *another* gallon, and had an excuse for staying half an hour longer, I am not sure that I should not have had serious thoughts of asking King Yohannes to give me the province of Dembea, and making the beautiful Wito my queen.

As we were riding homewards over the plain we saw a herd of antelopes, and gave chase to them, to try the speed of our cattle. All horses have a natural love for hunting, and ours entered into the chase heart and soul, following every swerve and movement of the flying herd, leaping lightly over the crevices and irregularities in the ground, and wheeling round with lightning quickness, of their own accord, whenever the antelopes, hard pressed, tried to double back. The more we galloped, the better our plucky little steeds went, which is usually the case with Abyssinian horses, which always require to be warm before they will display their real quality. For a long time we kept so close to the antelopes that had we been provided with lances we could have speared them with ease. I tried firing my heavy Westly Richards rifle with one hand, but did not try again, as the experiment nearly landed me on my back in the dust. At last the antelopes gained the hills, and we pulled up, but not until we had enjoyed forty minutes run at a pace that one rarely sees with any but the Exmoor stag-hounds.

Returning to the Arno Garno, we dismissed our attendants, and rode towards our former camp to look for hippos. Near the Keman we encountered the old chief who had accompanied us from Ambachara, gently urging on with his spear a peasant who was walking before him with a little jar of honey. The old man said it was the only way he could get the villagers to pay their tithes. Being unsuccessful in our search for hippos, we practised shooting at a hippopotamus' skull that lay on the shore, and were afterwards on the point of plunging into the lake for a swim, when a huge hippo—who I suppose had been attracted by the firing—suddenly poked his nose out of the water just below the rock on which we were standing. I did not much appreciate the pleasure of bathing with him, so seized my rifle and shot him in the head, after which he disappeared. Our startled horses had broken loose, but we presently overtook them and rode home by the light of the newly-risen moon. As we neared the camp we were greeted with loud shouts from Alegas and the *naphteñas*, who, alarmed at our long absence, were starting in search of us.

Our Return to Ambachara.

At 2.30 A.M. we attached white paper sights to our rifles,* and waking the Witos, issued forth again to look for hippos. This was to be our last expedition, as it was now time that I should return to Ambachara for the king's letters, and start on my homeward journey. The night was cold, for lake Tzana lies at an elevation of no less than six thousand two hundred and seventy feet above the level of the sea, and is in fact the great reservoir of the rapid Blue Nile, which, bubbling up from its source only a few days' march from the western shore, flows into the lake and out again on the eastern side, carrying down with it every year to the main trunk of the Nile at Khartum, a wealth of water from the lofty reservoir of the Abyssinian mountains, which floods the plains of lower Egypt, and causes their fertility.

We forded Arno Garno, and stole along the shore in our stockings. Presently we heard the snort of a hippo, and could just discern the dark outline of its body where it stood grazing on a patch of grass some thirty yards before us. We tried to get nearer, but the cracking of a dead branch gave it the alarm, and away it dashed, bending the mimosa trees right and left in its course. Another hippo, which we had not perceived, followed, and I had just time to put a bullet into the centre of its flank as it rushed past. We ran down to the shore to try to get another shot, but they were already off into the deep water, the last one bellowing

* By this means we were able to take a fair aim at night.

loudly. Some time afterwards we saw their noses above the lake, nearer land, and lay down to watch them.

My eyes were now much affected by the mists of the lake, and the constant exposure to the baneful rays of the moon, which in this country frequently produce ophthalmia. However, by a perpetual use of laudanum, both internally and externally, I had hitherto been able to keep the disease from becoming very serious.

The moon went down, and darkness closed around, yet still the hippos showed no disposition to move, so C. and I decided to wade towards them, and walked into the lake as far as we could go without swimming, only to find that they had disappeared; however, on turning round, we saw them again to our right, looming above the water like two great rocks. It being too dark to take any aim, we determined to attack them at close quarters, and approached to within ten yards of them. The water now reached our arm-pits, and I could feel the spray which the hippos occasionally blew from their nostrils. We fired four shots in rapid succession, and there was a tremendous commotion in the water, but the bright flashes of our rifles made the darkness appear so much more profound, that we could not see what happened, except that the hippos had gone down, so we left the Witos to watch for the bodies, with directions to bring to us at the king's camp the teeth and heads of any they should find, which they afterwards did. We heard another hippo snorting near us as we re-forded the Arno Garno, but had not succeeded in finding it when we beheld

> "The ruby red clouds in the east
> Float like islands upon the sea,"

and in a few minutes it was broad daylight.

May 10*th*.—When we reached the tent I had a couple of mules saddled, and mounting one myself, and placing a *naphteña* on the other as guide, started for Ambachara, leaving C. to follow more leisurely with the baggage and servants. There were gazelles on the plain, and birds in the bush, but I pressed on as hard as I could for the king's camp, without turning to the right or left. We soon gained the foot of the highlands, and passed below the dark battlemented ruins of an old palace, built for King Facil by the Portuguese settlers, which stands, like an eagle's nest, on an eminence commanding a wide view of the plain and lake. Among the flowers that grew by the way-side were some white lilies, the delicate beauty of which struck me much ; the prettiest variety had a broad purple stripe down the centre of the leaf, and quite scented the air with its fragrance. I got a farewell look at Tzana from the top of a steep hill that separates the highlands from the vale, and about noon, after five hours' hard riding, reached the royal camp, where, to my chagrin and disappointment, I learnt that K. had been ill, and the king's letters to the English government were not even begun. I had promised to be back in England in August, and now determined finally to fix a day for my departure, and adhere to it, hoping that when the king saw I was really leaving, he would get the letters ready. McKelvie presently called, and sat in the smoky hut all the afternoon, talking about traits of native character, while K. lay beside us on his bed of stones, suffering from an acute attack of rheumatism, which had utterly prostrated him.

The Abyssinians are very quick witted, and are rarely at a loss for an answer. McKelvie told me that a thief at Gondar, once went into the market, and sat down by a man who had several blocks of salt, which, as I have said, represents money in Abyssinia. The thief watched till the man turned his head away to talk to a friend, and then appropriated the salt to himself, and hid it under his *kuarie,* or blanket, with the intention of slipping quietly off when he could do so unremarked. But the owner of the salt discovered his loss almost immediately, and began to cry out loudly about it, so as to collect a great crowd round him. "Ah!" said the thief, calmly, lifting up the fold of his *kuarie,* so as to display the property he had stolen, "you should have kept *your* salt hidden under your *kuarie* as I have done *mine,* there are so many dishonest people about;" and with this good advice he covered up the salt again, and walked slowly away with it. The same thief, being caught at last and brought before Theodorus, the king asked him why he stole? "Steal," replied he, "that is to rob people secretly of their property, but I do not do so; what I take I take before their faces, and if they let me do that, surely your majesty cannot call it stealing;" and Theodorus, who loved a clever rejoinder, let him go. If I remember right, however, this thief went on "taking things before people's faces," to such an extent that Theodorus had at last to have his right hand and left foot cut off, which, as the king grimly remarked, would stop this thieving for the future. But, on the contrary, as soon as his wounds were healed, he went on stealing worse than ever, for now nobody suspected him of being able to steal, and he therefore did it with impunity. M‘Kelvie said that Theodorus was often very generous, and had been known to take a poor man into his palace, give him a thousand dollars, and then turn him out at the back door, bidding him not to tell any one.

Late in the evening C. and Alegas arrived alone, all the *naphteñas* and servants having remained behind on the road. The Basha, it is true, although very tired, had offered to remain with C., but one of his *naphteñas* had taken compassion on him, and acted as guide in his place till he was sent to look for an antelope that Alegas had shot, after which he also disappeared, and C. and Alegas were left to find their way to Ambachara as best they could, which was very badly, for they had lost themselves more than once among the intricacies of the hills.

May 11th, Sunday.—I copy textually from my diary, " This morning I have been preparing for my journey, I see the king will not let me leave till Tuesday, he is however very anxious that we should be comfortable while we are here. The other day he asked Maderakal if he thought we should be vexed at his not having sent us tea and sugar, 'for,' said he, 'you know I have none to give them.' K. attends the king every day. Yesterday the king asked him jokingly if he could tell fortunes, and bid him tell that of Dedjatch

Teffery, knowing that K. would say he had plenty of money, some of which the king probably wanted to get, as this chief has the character of being very avaricious, and never pays his tribute punctually. K. looked at Dedjatch Teffery's hand, and said he was a rich man, and that he had escaped death four times, and would escape it again, as he knew how to run away. This greatly discomposed the worthy Dedjatch, who was formerly a partisan of Gobasie, and, at the defeat of that chief by the present king, ran away and took refuge in a church, which gave him the right of sanctuary. To escape from this church he had a goat killed, and smearing himself over with the blood, placed himself on a stretcher, and made some of his people carry him forth, lamenting loudly. Prince Kassa's soldiers saw the stretcher, and asked who was on it, but they were told it was only a poor wounded soldier who was being taken to his own village to die, and seeing the body covered with blood they let it pass. Some days afterwards the people of Tigre got wind of the trick, and overtaking the party with the stretcher, demanded to examine the wounds of the soldier they were carrying. The Dedjatch in a weak voice said that they should do so, merely begging that his own people should uncover his wounds, and telling them to hold up their *kuaries* round him while they stripped his body. The moment he was thus concealed, he slipped off the stretcher, and made a boy, who had really received a wound in the shoulder, lie down in his place; he then wrapped a white cloth round his head after the manner of the turbans worn by the priests, and thus disguised, walked through the throng telling his beads."

I find no entry in my diary of what the Dedjatch's fourth escape was, but all his cunning does not seem to have enabled him to cheat the skeleton and the scythe a fifth time, for in May, 1875, I received news from Abyssinia telling me that poor Dedjatch Teffery was no more.

"The king asked K. yesterday why the Turks were strong, and the Abyssinians, who are Christians, weak? He supposed it was because they had sinned so much. K. said it was because they were not all united. The king's eyes filled with tears, and rising from his seat he retired to his tent, saying he was weary. To-day he is full of warlike ardour, and wishes to fight the Turks if the European Powers will not interfere to stop their encroachments. K. has been to him twice, and he is now writing his letters to the English Government."

"I rode out with C. this afternoon, and gathered some fine mushrooms. When Sir W. G., in a chance conversation, showed me how to distinguish the edible kinds, I little thought the knowledge would prove useful in Abyssinia. Unfortunately I have lost my field glass; I took it out of my holster to make room for the mushrooms, and it must have become detached from the sling while I was jumping my horse over one of the enclosures in the camp; rather a dear price to pay for a dish of mushrooms."

On returning, we found a celebrated Abyssinian

doctor at our hut, who had extracted from the king's neck a bullet, which had been there for nine years. His system was simply to make a small incision over the place where the bullet was supposed to lodge, into which he then rubbed some medicine of so powerful a character, that he declared it would make the bullet work its way to the surface, and roll out from the wound of its own accord, without any mechanical aid at all. However, nothing would induce him to divulge the nature of the medicine he employed. K. said it was perfectly true that this man had frequently extracted bullets in the most wonderful manner, and, as K. had often declared that he had two musket balls still lodged in his own body, we suggested that he should let the doctor perform on him, in our presence, for the benefit of science, on the *fiat experimentum in corpore vili* principle. K., however, did not appear to regard the matter from the same point of view, and said he had become so accustomed to his bullets, that he would rather keep them. We were told that the doctor sometimes sucked the bullet out through a hollow reed which he applied to the wound, but everybody agreed in saying that he extracted bullets without using any probes or instruments. We also heard a wonderful story how he had brought hundreds of worms out of a man's head by anointing his ears and nostrils with a certain ointment.

Maderakal visited us, and, hearing of the loss of my field glass, said that he would send a priest through the camp in the morning with bell, book, and candle, to excommunicate anybody who should find it and not return it to me. This is how they recover lost property in Abyssinia. *Maledictus sit ubicunque fuerit, sive in domo, sive in agro, sive in via, sive in semitâ, sive in silvâ, sive in aquâ, sive in ecclesiâ, &c., &c.*, as the Roman Church would say—Like the poor little jackdaw of Rheims, the finder of my glass was to be followed by the curses of the Church wherever he went, and whatever he did, until he restored it. What an awful position to place a man in! There is no advertising medium in Ethiopia, and he might keep the glass for an indefinite time without ever knowing the awful fate that was pursuing him. Indeed, the glass has not been returned to me *yet*,—let us hope it was never found. The Ancient Egyptians are said to have had an ingenious way of recovering stolen property, but surely it was nothing to this! *

We spent the evening reading a packet of letters and papers which had found its way to us from the coast. It was a great pleasure to get news from home. R., we learnt, had at last left Adowa with the baggage, and, as I had now positively fixed my departure for Tuesday, we sent McKelvie back to meet him, and

---

* When an Egyptian thief determined to steal anything, he went to the priest and inscribed his name, and after having stolen the thing, carried it to the priest, to whom the person robbed also repaired, and received back his property, on paying one-third of its value, which went to the thief.—*Encyclopædia Londinensis, Art. Egypt.*

bring on the big medicine chest with all speed, that I might renew my supply of quinine. The night was bitterly cold, the wet season having now fairly begun in the mountains.

CHAPTER XXIII.

I BID ADIEU TO THE KING—ARRIVAL AT THE CITY
OF GONDAR.

May 12*th.*—The king sent for K. at 5 A.M. this morning. He returned bringing the letters that his Majesty had received from the Queen, Lord Granville, and the Khedive. The Khedive had apparently solemnly denied to the British Government all intention of encroaching on Abyssinia, and had made out a plausible story about the necessity of protecting his frontier, &c. Of course it is almost impossible to decide who is in the right and who in the wrong in the frontier raids which take place in so wild a country; but the fact of the gradual and systematic occupation by Egyptian troops of districts formerly belonging to Abyssinia, speaks pretty strongly of itself; and assuredly these same border raids, which Egypt professes to deplore in so long-suffering a tone, must prove rather profitable, when each one is followed by some fresh annexation of territory. Moreover, these feuds are favourable to the slave trade, and I have heard it asserted that the Mahometans are to blame for encouraging them. Certainly there is evidence to point to such a conclusion, for I afterwards saw many Abyssinian slaves in Egypt and Arabia, but curiously enough I do not remember ever seeing an Arab employed as a slave by the Abyssinians.

The king's scribes were busy all day writing draughts of the letters for the English Government. We lent them our tent, as it was the only place where a cabinet council could be held undisturbed by the curiosity and importunity of the chiefs and courtiers who attend the king. His Majesty's advisers, of course, gave all sorts of conflicting advice, and some strongly opposed his putting an end to the purchase and sale of slaves. The king put off to the last moment committing himself positively to this step, and wanted me to stay longer at his camp, but I adhered to my determination to leave on the morrow, and declared positively that unless the king bound himself to put down the slave trade in the letters he was then writing to the British Government I would not take them with me.

K. went again to the king, and was much troubled at the continual presence in the council of a chief who he had reason to know was in the pay of the Egyptians. When the secretaries left off work—which they were only too glad to do on the first pretext—nothing had been settled, and the letters were still unwritten. It is always the same story throughout the East! Everything except *death* is put off till the morrow.

May 13th.—K. was again called before sunrise to attend his Majesty; meanwhile, I began to have my baggage packed for departure. C. had agreed to accompany me as far as Gondar, after which he intended staying some time longer with the king, and then returning to Massowah through Abyssinia, when the rains should have fallen. As I was pressed for time, I had decided to make my way to Khartoum across the plains of the Soudan and Upper Nubia, which, though said to be frightfully hot at this season, could be traversed more rapidly than the mountains of Abyssinia, of which I had already sufficient experience. The baggage from Adowa not having yet arrived, I determined to abandon it entirely, and the only difficulty that now remained to be overcome was the want of money, for one of my boxes of Maria Teresa dollars had been abandoned with the other things our porters had deserted near Guddofelassic. Fortunately, the king was desirous of transmitting money to his newly appointed consul in London, and on our giving him cheques for £200, ordered his treasurer to count us out a thousand silver dollars, which were placed in a *kuarie* and borne to our hut by a party of servants and *naphteñas* with great state. As may be supposed, the king had never seen a cheque before, and when K. explained to him that it was an order for his consul to receive a thousand dollars in gold from our treasure keepers, he asked where the seal was, for in Ethiopia all documents are sealed instead of signed, as is the usual custom throughout the East. K., with ready wit, pointed out the embossed penny stamp on the cheque, and the king was satisfied. The thousand dollars, which were no small weight, having been piled on the bed, two of the treasurer's servants sat down and began to count them over before us. One of these youths had quite a Venetian type of head, and looked in his long striped silk robe, like a figure out of a picture by Paul Veronese. K. went twice to the king, whom he found busy dictating his letters to his secretary. I asked if he had written the clause about the slave trade, but he had not made up his mind to do that yet.

At 9 A.M. we thought it prudent to get the mules packed, and Mustafa and some of the boys sent forwards to Gondar with the baggage, as the king was unwilling to let me go without his letters; and I was determined not to take them unless he kept his promise regarding the slaves, and at the last moment the native servants might get frightened and not dare to leave the camp without the royal permission.

At 10 A.M. Maderakal came, followed by some of the king's pages, leading a beautiful cream-coloured horse, fully caparisoned in the Abyssinian fashion, the head stall and breastplate being profusely ornamented with plates and bosses of solid silver. This was a present from his Majesty, who also sent me one of his shields, richly ornamented with silver work, a pair of the light spears or javelins, with which Abyssinian horsemen are armed, and a mule, with a curiously worked saddle of scarlet and green leather, which is called in Abyssinia "the golden saddle," and can only be conferred by the king, who permits none under the rank of Dedjatchmatch to use it.

Maderakal said that king Yohannes was now in his

Arrival at the City of Gondar.

banquet hall, whither I at once repaired to thank him; the horse, mule, shield, and spears being brought into the hall after me. His Majesty received me graciously, but his face darkened visibly when I told him that I must take that opportunity of bidding him adieu, as I had duties in the service of my own Sovereign which would render it impossible for me to postpone my departure beyond that day; that to reach my country in time I should now have to travel day and night without pause or rest, and that I had delayed leaving him till the last moment in the hope that I should have been able to take charge of his letters as he had requested, and had trusted they would contain the pledges regarding the suppression of the slave trade, which he had promised me. I then bowed, and withdrew with my brother from the royal presence, amid a profound silence, all the chiefs who were grouped round the throne looking uneasily at the king, as they must have been wont to look at the dreaded Theodorus when anything thwarted him. The chief whom K. believed to be in the pay of Egypt stood craning his neck forwards as far as he dared, with an expression of curiosity on his features which was ludicrous in its intensity, as he strove in vain to catch what passed, for Maderakal had spoken in a very low voice while translating my adieu.

Dedjatch Area, the king's uncle, followed us to the outer enclosure, and making us sit down on some stones, said with great solemnity that he had a favour to beg before we left. "Oh, chief!" we said, "what is it that you desire?" and he replied that it was some antidyspeptic pills. It appeared that when the English delivered him from the mountain on which he had been imprisoned for fourteen years by Theodorus, an army surgeon rendered his happiness complete by giving him some antidyspeptic pills which, as long as they lasted, enabled him to enjoy the good things of this world; but that now they were all gone, he was a martyr to heartburn. C. promised him the pills, and left him happy. It is not always that happiness is so easily bestowed.

We returned to our hut, and bid the *naphteñas* hold themselves ready for departure, but I still lingered in the hope that the king would bring his letters to a satisfactory conclusion. At last Maderakal brought me one of them, and translated it. His Majesty, in this letter, pleaded for the arbitration of the English Government between himself and Egypt, but he had not made up his mind to pledge himself to the abolition of the slave trade, as he had promised me he would; and I therefore sent back the letter, and refused to take charge of it unless this promise was kept, for I had now seen enough of the Abyssinians to know that spoken words might be soon forgotten, while whatever was written was to them as the laws of the Medes and Persians, and that if the king once pledged his word in a written document issued under his great seal, he would hold himself bound by it, when required to do so, as by a solemn treaty.

Though the king's hour for holding audience was over, I now determined to go to him, and make one last effort to induce him to take the important step he had promised; but Maderakal was very reluctant to venture into the royal presence any more, and declared that his Majesty was in a dangerous humour at my having forced him, by my departure, to decide one way or the other; and that as he was an absolutely despotic sovereign, it was not safe to cross him. K., however, volunteered to accompany me, and we walked up together to the king's enclosure. I had just succeeded in re-capturing the unwilling Maderakal, who had slipped away, when we were nearly run over by a crowd of terrified courtiers, all rushing from the king's house at full speed, and streaming down the hill in every direction. The private secretary dashed past us with pens and papers flying in the wind, nor ever stopped till he reached our hut. With frightened faces and disordered robes, the whole of the royal household were escaping from the king's presence as if from Satan himself; and when we asked the cause of all this, we were told that his Ethiopic Majesty was in a furious rage, and flogging people right and left. He had just had a man's hand chopped off for stealing a gun, next he had caused one of his great chiefs to be flogged before him with the *giraff*; and had now despatched a *gashazagry* post haste for a *new* hippopotamus hide whip with which to continue his castigations. Everybody who could, had taken to flight, for no one knew on whom the anger of the princely despot might be vented next, and they implored us, as they rushed past, not to go near him. Under these circumstances we thought it wisest to keep away, and returned to the hut, where we found Maderakal, who had made good his escape at the first appearance of the panic. Barran Barras Tachu, the chief of Chelga, who had previously been appointed to accompany me to the Abyssinian frontier, now came and asked when we wished to leave, apparently deeming it wise to get away as soon as possible; but I decided to remain in the camp till midnight, having promised the king to wait till the expiration of the day for his letters, and therefore ordered him to be ready when the moon should rise. He complained that the road was very bad, but we laughed at his fears, and dismissed him with a caution not to talk about our departure, lest in the present temper of the king it should be imprudent. Though I was resolved to leave that night, as I had informed the king that I should do so, I told K. I would remain at Gondar till the 16th, in case the king, when he found that I had kept *my* word, and was really gone, should make up his mind to keep *his*, and forward me the letters he had promised, in which case I would still take them with me to England.

After dinner we cleared the hut, and set to work to assist K. in preparing the draught of a letter, embodying the clause about the slave trade, which he was to offer for the king's approval on the morrow.

As the evening wore on, the rain came down in torrents, and a violent storm of thunder and lightning shook the mountains, making the prospect of a night ride anything but cheerful. However, at midnight, when our writing was completed, feeling that I had now done all I could, I shook hands with K., and prepared to start for Gondar, accompanied by C. and the *naphteñas*.

The men were in good spirits, considering the weather, for we had supplied them liberally with tedge, but the horses were in a wretched plight, and frightened at the lightning. As I was leaving the camp against the king's wishes, I determined to leave the horse he had given me behind, so, taking the faithful bay which I had ridden from Adowa by the bridle, I bid good-bye to Ambachara.

The rain still continued to pour down as it only does in these latitudes, and the night was pitch dark, except when a lurid flash blinded us for a moment, making our terrified nags start and tremble. Not a light was to be seen in the camp, and, except our immediate attendants, not a soul was aware of our departure. For a long time we were obliged to walk by our horses' heads, as the ground was like soap, and they were in danger of slipping down every moment; but, at last, after a great deal of sliding and splashing, we got clear of the sleeping host, and rode silently and wretchedly for two or three hours W.N.W., till we came to the top of a steep hill, leading down to an extensive plateau. The track that we followed—for path there was none—was literally knee deep in mud, through which men and horses rolled and slid promiscuously, occasionally catching in the bushes that grew on the hill side, but quite unable to control their movements, or regulate the speed of their descent.

At the bottom of the hill was something very like an Irish bog, and here we mounted our horses, and trusted to Providence and their intelligence to get us through it, which they did, though not without frequently glisading twenty feet at a time, and occasionally splashing up to their girths in water. We forded one or two small rivers, and felt our way through some woods, which were said to be inhabited by *shouftas*, or robbers, from whose attacks, however, our escort of *naphteñas* rendered us quite safe. We were sick and ill with wet, cold, and fatigue, and it was with no small pleasure that we beheld the first warm rays of light appearing in the East.

May 14*th*.—When the sun rose at six o'clock, we discovered that our progress through the darkness had been so slow that we were only half way to Gondar. Everybody was still asleep in a village through which we passed, but riding across the plain before us we espied, to our astonishment, a European on a mule. This proved to be the Swiss Lewis whom I have before mentioned. He told us that he had carried out his intention of leaving the king's service, and had delivered his famous speech beginning "All powerful Ethiop! now happily Emperor of these mighty dominions. For two years have I, &c., &c;" but it seems the king had failed to appreciate it, and had merely ordered him to receive 100 dollars to pay his journey out of the country. The rage of Lewis at this treatment was the best comment possible on the professions of devotion with which only a short time before he had

CH. XXIII. *Arrival at the City of Gondar.* 119

so profusely adorned his famous discourse, and he now declared that he would be revenged, for he knew all the passes of the mountains, and would go to the Governor of Massowah and betray the King of Abyssinia into his power. "I will prove to Munzinger Pasha," said he, in conclusion, "that I know Abyssinia, for King Yohannes has bestowed upon me the full dress of an Abyssinian warrior, and it is in this costume that I will present myself at the Egyptian divan." As the French missionary afterwards remarked to my brother, they would probably take him for a monkey, and I believe they did, at least I subsequently heard that he did not produce quite the impression he had intended, the Egyptian officials wisely deeming that a man who was willing to betray his first master might betray his second.

Poor Lewis! he was always trying to produce a dramatic effect, and always failing. We left him still vowing vengeance, and rode across a cultivated plain till 11 A.M., when we at length came in sight of the city of Gondar, grandly situated on a hill, with the lofty table-lands of the Woggera rising behind it like a vast amphitheatre. A river lay before us spanned by an old Portuguese bridge with five arches. It is strange that the Abyssinians do not know how to build bridges when they have had this model before them for three hundred years. The river wound backwards and forwards across the plain below Gondar in such a way that it was necessary to cross it several times before we could approach the heights on which the city stands. We saw many women of the country drawing water, who had mostly short rounded figures, good-natured faces, and were much lighter in colour than the people of Tigre. We had now been marching for more than eleven hours without a halt, and all our people, with the exception of one indefatigable *naphteña*, were out of sight. As we began to ascend towards the city, however, we met our baggage mules under the charge of Mustafa and our native servants, who, though they had left Ambachara thirteen hours before us, had only just arrived, having taken refuge in a wayside village from the storm of the previous night. We now clambered up a rocky ascent to a level plateau covered with grass, which commanded a fine view of Gondar, and here we pitched the tent and picketed the beasts. When the chief of Chelga at last arrived, he proposed we should lodge in the house of the Governor of Gondar, to whom we had a letter from the king, but remembering our previous experience of Abyssinian houses we decided to stay where we were, and truly from our elevated position we enjoyed a magnificent prospect not devoid of romantic interest.

Before us to the north, stood the capital of Ethiopia, perched on a spur of grey rock, and divided into two quarters, one Christian, and the other Mahometan, while behind, like a mighty wall, rose the heights of the vast table-lands of the Woggera, stretching away to the distant mountains of the Semyen. On our left "Debra Tzai," the mountain of the sun, over the rugged crest of which I must pass to reach Chelga, cast a dark shadow across the plain, while behind us the fertile

CH. XXIII. *Arrival at the City of Gondar.* 121

vales of Dembea extended to the S. W., encircling the demon-haunted lake Tzana, now glistening in the sunlight like burnished steel. We could see the towers of the magnificent castle which the hands of cunning Indian architects raised here as if by enchantment in the heart of the mountains of Ethiopia, dominating the Christian quarter of this strange city, where, we were told, that on moonlight nights, spotted leopards might be seen clambering over the thatched roofs of the houses like cats. In the subterranean vaults of the ancient castle were said to lurk flying dragons, and gigantic rats, as large as bull dogs, who, perhaps, are hunted by the leopard cats in the still hours of the night, and the country around teemed with weird and fantastic legends. Here had dwelt that terrible lady, Gouxa Herrut, who preserved her beauty by drinking the blood of young children; here still lived Christopholos, the Greek magician, of whom I shall have occasion to speak later. In the country that lies between Gondar, Chelga, and the Woggera, dwelt the superstitious Kumants, who yet adhere to the ancient traditions of the Magi, worshipping fire, and bowing to big trees and the moon. To the N.N.E., were the fierce people of Jiratan, who have tails, and are cannibals that devour one another. Of more distant tribes, like the Beni Temash, who have human bodies and crocodiles' heads; the swarthy diggers of copper of the Fertit country, south of Darfour, who file their teeth like ogres, and their near neighbours, the Beni Kelb, the male portion of whom are dogs, and the female lovely women; I cannot speak without entering on a wide field of mingled truth and fiction which would take a volume to itself. I will only mention that in the East there are firm believers in the Beni Kelb, and female slaves reputed to have come from that country fetch a very high price. The traveller who visits the Beni Kelb, is said to be kindly received by the dogs, who go forth to find him food, which is prepared by the hands of their fair helpmates, but woe to the traveller should he trifle with the affections of a Beni Kelb maiden, for his hosts, the dogs, will then set upon him and devour him.*

In the afternoon we went to explore the ruins of the castle of Gondar. Our path followed the side of a deep and rugged ravine overlooking the Mahometan or *Kouffou*† part of the city, as Alegas called it, which lay below us, and extended up to the Christian quarter on the hill; from this upper town it was separated by a small running stream, which we were obliged to cross. Loose stones were lying about everywhere, and the houses were in no way different from the usual Abyssinian model, being round in form, built without mortar, and covered with conical thatched roofs. They were all huddled together in inextricable, though very picturesque, confusion, each man having apparently constructed his dwelling where fancy dictated, and with the first stones that came to hand. We entered a large open space or square, where we saw a crowd of natives sitting under the shade

* See Mansfield Parkyns.
† *Kouffou*, bad or wicked.

of a big tree. At our approach they all rose to their feet, and our *naphteñas* having halted, the Governor of Gondar, a handsome man of about fifty, whose head —contrary to the usual Abyssinian custom—was covered with a red *tarboush*, came forth to meet us. After a few salutations, the whole party surrounded us, and set off at a rapid pace for the castle. It would be as hopeless to expect an Abyssinian crowd to abstain from following one, as to expect flies to keep from a jar of treacle!

Presently we saw before us a great square keep or donjon, rising from a large and picturesque pile of buildings surrounded by beautiful trees. This was the palace of the kings of Ethiopia. The sky behind it was magnificent, dark purple, with copper-coloured thunder clouds, which seemed to touch the top of the mountains.

As we advanced, we perceived what a splendid building this palace, or rather castle, was. Lofty towers, and battlemented walls and terraces, rose above the foliage in all directions. We passed by a great tree whose gnarled and twisted roots stood fifteen feet out of the ground, supporting the trunk on a sort of natural summer house, and entering a gate under a tower in the castle-wall we found ourselves within the interior court, now all overgrown with grass and weeds. The castle itself consisted of a large and irregular block of buildings piled picturesquely round an immense square keep, of considerable height; there were four smaller round towers at the corners of this keep, and big beams of blackened wood that had once on a time supported balconies, were still to be seen projecting from the walls below the windows. In every crack and crevice, lovely tropical creepers had taken root, clinging round the ruins like a green garment.

Ascending a lofty flight of steps we entered the great hall, which was dark and spacious; the old gates and shutters still remained, but were fast falling into decay, and we seemed to hear—

> "The sound of time long passed
> Still murmuring o'er us in the lofty void
> Of these dark arches, like the lingering voices
> Of those who long within their graves have slept."

From the windows there was a grand view of the distant lake Tzana, rendered more than ordinarily beautiful by the magnificent sunset-sky that now lit up the whole scene and threw a ruddy glow over the ruins. We passed through many corridors and vaulted chambers, and ascended to a terrace above the great hall, but we could not gain the summit of the keep, as the flying wooden staircase, which had formerly existed outside it, had rotted away. We were astonished at every turn by the beauty and picturesqueness of the piles of buildings that clustered round the great tower of the castle, and by the grand solidity of the masonry. Long battlemented walls stretched into the distance, and scattered over various parts of the park-like grounds and deserted gardens were groups of beautiful towers, decorated with fanciful tracery in red stone, which gave them a semi-Moorish appearance. Indeed, I at first took the red stone ornamentation for brick-work. The

Arrival at the City of Gondar.

palace had evidently been designed by the old Portuguese adventurers on the plan of a mediæval stronghold, but the Indian workmen they had employed had given to it a fantastic character all its own, and everywhere the gorgeous foliage of the creeping plants, hung in graceful festoons from tower and battlement as if tenderly striving to hide the rents that time had made even in these massive walls.

As we gazed from a lofty window in the keep at the deepening tints of the stormy sky strange night birds dashed out from the recesses of the inner chambers, and sweeping close past our heads, sailed away on outspread wings into the twilight. An *Achcoco*, one of the gigantic tribe of Abyssinian rats, fully two feet long, emerged from some subterranean dungeon and scampered along the crumbling wall : here and there, in the deep shades of the passages leading to the underground chambers of the castle, we could hear a rustling amongst the dead leaves, probably caused by some of the leopards that abound among these ruins, and sally forth when the veil of night has fallen upon the earth. In fact, the whole scene reminded one of some weird legendary castle of romance, and it was hard to realize that the old Portuguese settlers had reared this vast edifice only for the semi-savage monarchs of Ethiopia, and that it had never been peopled by doughty knights and fair ladies. Certainly the little band of adventurers who came to Abyssinia under the brave Cristobel da Gama in the sixteenth century, left a noble and lasting monument behind them in the palace they built at Gondar.

We stood for a long time on the castle terrace watching the storm-clouds gather, like a host of winged genii, over the dark range of highlands before us. At one moment the sky was all purple and burnished copper, with rain falling in the distance; then it became glorious with crimson and gold, as the sinking sun threw a farewell glow over Gondar, and again it changed to a dark sombre green, illuminated by vivid flashes of violet lightning, which from time to time revealed the gleaming surface of the distant lake, while the deep roll of thunder echoed all around, shaking the old ruins, and reverberating through the empty vaults and passages of the castle till they resounded as if they had been built of the sonorous marble of Campanini.

What Milton would have called 'Cimmerian darkness' had closed around when we began to retrace our steps, and heavy drops of rain were already beginning to fall. We could only stumble our way along the rocky path that traversed the side of the ravine by the help of the bright flashes of lightning that almost blinded us every other minute, while the mingled roar of thunder and rushing water, prevented us from hearing our own voices. Soon after we reached home the rain began to descend in earnest, and even the double roof of our tent was quite inadequate to keep out the torrents of water which poured down upon it like a second deluge, bidding fair to float us bodily into the swollen stream below, while every now and then fierce gusts of wind whistled through the straining cords, and flash after flash of lightning, following one another in

Arrival at the City of Gondar.

rapid succession, cast a lurid and fitful light over the ruins of the ancient town. We could hear the frightened horses and mules plunging madly as they pulled at their tether ropes, but there was no one to watch them now, for guards, servants, and porters had all fled to the town for shelter, and we were as solitary on the isolated bluff of rock where our tent was pitched, as if we had been encamped in the desert of Sahara. However, there was little to fear from man or beast. On such a night as this, the most ravenous hyena, or daring leopard, would prefer the darkness and safety of his lair to the lightning and tempest outside ; and as for man, though he sometimes emulates the cruelty of a beast of prey, he rarely equals him in courage when bent on an evil purpose. So having lighted a fire *inside* the tent, for the fire outside had been long since extinguished, we cooked a hasty meal and proceeded to the calm enjoyment of our pipes, after which we lay down on our soaking carpets, and were soon as sound asleep as if we had been lying on beds of down, instead of in a pool of mud and rain-water three or four inches deep.

May 15th.—When we opened our eyes in the morning the weather had not changed for the better, and the city of Gondar was only dimly visible through the mass of falling water. Everything was soaking wet, and, as it was impossible to light a fire, we had to send Mustafa to cook our breakfast in the town.

About mid-day two visitors made their way to us in spite of the weather. One was an Assyrian merchant, who had come to Gondar from the Soudan to trade, but having had his goods seized by Ras Warenia, then absolute master of Amhara, was now waiting for King Yohannes to redress his wrongs. The other was a Greek, called Christopholos, who had been twice put in chains by Prince Kassa, for aiding and abetting the rebel chief Gobasie, in whose ranks he had fought, armed with an enormous elephant gun that dealt destruction on all who came within its range. He was now living at Gondar, ostensibly as a gunsmith, an art beyond the skill of the Abyssinians; but it was whispered throughout this part of Ethiopia that he was really a magician, most of whose time was passed in studying the black art, and, as it afterwards appeared, popular report for once spoke true. But notwithstanding the strange and sinister rumours we had heard about this man, we were quite unprepared for his extraordinary appearance. Looking at him from a distance, and watching his swift sure step, his lithe agile figure, and the almost cat-like activity of his movements as he sprang from stone to stone of the rocky path, you would have said he was in the very prime of youth and strength, but when you saw his face you seemed to be in the presence of a man over whose head at least a hundred years had passed, and it was not a little startling to behold the young shoulders thus surmounted by a haggard, wan visage, through which the death's head showed so conspicuously.

There are stories of people whose hair has turned white in a single night, and Christopholos, with his stricken, blasted look, might well have passed for one of them. His face was perfectly colourless, a dead mat white, and the low, narrow forehead was furrowed as if by the cares of centuries. The teeth were slightly projecting, and there were two little hard lines at the corners of the thin lips, that made you instinctively feel that this man might be cruel, with a ferocious cruelty like that of the feline races, that increases in intensity as it is indulged. His hair hung in long locks over his neck from under a black cap, but it was perfectly bleached, as were his eyebrows, beard, and moustache; his nose was sharp and aquiline, with the skin tightly drawn over it, while, at either side, the small, red, deep-set eyes sparkled like live coals, giving a peculiar air of fire and energy to the worn and battered mask in which they were set; however, beyond a certain look of latent fierceness, and of some *past passions* that had left an indelible mark on his features, there was little in the countenance of the Greek necromancer to betray his actual thoughts, just as his appearance gave not the slightest clue to his real age, which might have been anything between thirty and a hundred. He was dressed in a blouse of black cotton, confined at the waist by a black leather belt, supporting a brace of revolvers, which he wore behind him, so as to be ready at need to either hand; he spoke Italian fluently, and expressed himself with some grace, saying that he hoped we would come to his house, and offering to be our guide through the ruins of the castle when next we wished to see them. As nothing could be more dreary than our soaking tent, we gladly accepted this offer, and accompanied him back to his dwelling, which was in the Christian quarter of Gondar, and more comfortable than the houses we had hitherto seen. I noticed two Ethiopian crosses carved in wood nailed against the wall, one of which he gave me, seeing I was struck by its peculiar form. He also sent a slave in search of skins and native silver work, as we had expressed a desire to purchase some. In the meanwhile we examined a few books that he had, all of which were full of magical signs and formulæ traced on the blank leaves, but he seemed unwilling to talk of magic, though he showed us a large collection of drugs and poisons, some—if he was to be credited—possessing most marvellous properties. Presently the slave returned, bringing a number of quaint silver ornaments, prettily worked in filigree. There was a pair of anklets to which were hung numbers of little pendants, that tinkled like bells, and there were chains supporting silver boxes for charms or relics, to be worn on the breast and back, for charms are much esteemed in Abyssinia, and even the horses and mules are generally adorned with a necklace of little leather bags containing spells against various misfortunes.

Working silver and leather seem to be the two elegant arts the Abyssinians possess, and I believe they learned the art of working silver originally from some Armenians, who came to Gondar, and were detained there by the Ethiopian sovereigns, who were jealous of letting such ingenious people leave the country. It is not, however, easy to buy much of this silver work, unless some lady happens to wish to sell her trinkets, as the silversmiths only make things to order, and take a very long time about it. When an Abyssinian lady wishes for a set of ornaments, she sends to the smith the necessary weight of silver in dollars, and gives him half as many dollars again for his work. Thus a pair of anklets, containing twelve dollars weight of silver, are worth eighteen dollars. The silver of the old Austrian Maria Theresa dollars, which is the only silver used in Abyssinia, is not very pure, and most of the filigree work of the country is somewhat rude and coarse, though I have seen some chains that were beautifully fine and supple.

We bought several ornaments, and received a visit from the Governor of Gondar, after which we started on another excursion to the castle. The Greek pointed out to us, en route, a building said to be the tomb of Sultan Facil's horse, and we went into an old church, called Sultan Facil's Church, which was now being repaired. There were frescoes on the walls like those we had seen in the cathedral at Axum, and we were much struck by the portraits of a couple of the kings of Ethiopia, Iynsiau Negous and Kesukeyasu Negous, painted on panels covered with cotton-cloth. The two monarchs were depicted sitting on their thrones, wearing the great crown of Ethiopia, and attended by two very small men, holding two very large umbrellas over their heads, while at the feet of one was a man in chains, probably somebody the king had overcome ; but whether intended for a rebel chief or the devil, I do not know. We also saw a sketch on parchment of a Virgin and Child, by a modern Abyssinian artist, which, though very quaint, was much better than I should have expected. In the yard of the church was the tomb of Consul Plowden * (Basha Plowden, as the Abyssinians call him), a little hut built of stones, in which an old priest now lives.

As we made our way to the castle, which stands on an elevated tract of ground behind the city of Gondar, Christopholos related wonderful stories of horned dragons, and other dreadful beasts that he had sometimes encountered among the ruins. These stories were much on a par with Tedlar's tales of the flying snakes of the Walkit, and a monstrous serpent, thirty cubits long, that is said to inhabit the shores of Lake Tzana, but which we had fortunately not come across. However, Christopholos spoke with the strongest conviction, and appeared really to believe that dragons did dwell in the subterraneous vaults of the castle. Perhaps he had seen in the dusk of the evening one of the gigantic race of African lizards, called, I think, *Iguano*, which are ugly enough to frighten anybody.

We entered the castle through some of the lower chambers: these were nearly dark, and numbers of frightened bats flitted past us as we made our way up a narrow flight of red-stone steps into the great hall, on the walls of which we remarked some Indian or Moorish designs, and the cross of Solomon often

* Plowden was speared in the time of Theodorus.

CH. XXIII. Arrival at the City of Gondar.

repeated. In front of the windows was a big tree, on which Sultan Facil, for whom, the Abyssinians say, this castle was built, used to hang his prisoners; and in a chamber of one of the round towers we found, clinging to the rafters, a family of some thousands of bats that had multiplied there undisturbed, and now covered the entire roof of the chamber, filling it with a mysterious noise. We afterwards passed out on a flat terrace, the pavement of which was pierced with round holes, large enough to admit the body of a man; these communicated with a subterranean dungeon below, wherein pointed stakes were placed, on which prisoners thrown down these *oubliettes* used to be impaled. In the centre of the castle green grew a curious tree, with clusters of spear-shaped leaves, radiating like stars from a stout stem: it is called *Berbera*, by the natives, who declare that it only grows in this country, and has great medicinal virtues, among others, that of making fish drunk and insensible, if its leaves be soaked in the waters of a stream.

As we passed out of the principal block of building we encountered a second of the gigantic Abyssinian rats, called *achcoco*; it was as large as a badger. We also saw the stables where of old the kings of Abyssinia kept their lions.

Scattered through the grounds that surround the original castle, are several smaller palaces erected at different dates, one of these, called the Ladies' Palace, is charmingly ornamented with red stone work in the Moorish style, and the very flowers and trees that grow wild about it seem to have a more graceful beauty than those elsewhere ; here the jasmine spreads a pleasant fragrance around, and the echo of the voices of the beautiful Ethiopians, who once trod these deserted walks, seems still to float softly through the air, while it is on the pink walls of this palace that the last rays of the sun always appear to linger longest before it sinks in the west.

> " You may break, you may ruin, the vase if you will,
> But the scent of the roses will cling round it still."

One of the buildings commanded our admiration from the great height of its fine arched roof. Here and there, the Portuguese had introduced reminiscences of the Moorish ruins in Portugal, while on the floor of one of the halls we noticed a rude and grotesque carving of a lion, a goat, a man smoking, and some flowers. We saw a pretty palace that had been built for an Abyssinian queen, named Muntuav, and remarked that the masonry, even where intended as ornamental, was always exceedingly strong and massive, while the introduction of round towers at various points gave a castellated effect to the whole group of buildings which covered a very large space of ground.

King Theodorus set fire to the palace of Gondar when he thought the British troops were coming to invade Abyssinia from the Egyptian side ; he is also said to have had forty thousand head of cattle slain in Amhara, which, putrifying, caused a plague in the country.

At some distance from the other buildings stood the palace of Ras Michael. This was a more modern erection, built in imitation of the old Portuguese edifice by native workmen. It was the first attempt I had seen on the part of the Abyssinians to follow the architectural models of the Portuguese; and though the masonry was rude, it was solid, and showed that it is more idleness than want of ability that has made the Abyssinians neglect architecture, as they neglect agriculture, and almost all other civilised arts. Perhaps, too, the necessity of having constantly to defend their mountains against the attacks of enemies, has had something to do with the disdain in which they hold all pursuits except those of war and the chase.

Before returning we went to see a new church that had just been built. . The whole of the walls, from floor to roof, were covered with paintings in distemper, like those we had seen at Axum, proving that the art of painting has not quite died out in Abyssinia, though it is much neglected. The colours were brilliant, and there was a Byzantine character about the way in which several subjects were introduced into one panel, but the surroundings of the sacred personages were decidedly Ethiopian. One group depicted our Lord drinking *tedge* with the Virgin Mariam, while St. Peter sat nursing his bottle in the background. Another painting represented Mahomet being dragged off his famous white Arab mare by the devil; a third showed Sultan Facil regally attired, with a saint's nimbus about his head; and there was a very awful picture of a big blue devil, with blue horns, white teeth, and round red eyes, eating up little black men, supposed to be sinners, while the good people going to heaven had all beautiful white skins. When we returned to the Greek magician's house we learned that there were no skins of wild beasts now for sale in Gondar, as the king had bought up all he could a short time previously, to have them converted into *lemds*, the fur tippets which he confers on the chiefs whom he wishes to honour. The value of a lion's skin in Gondar was about fifteen dollars. Darkness having now set in, we invited Christopholos to dine with us in our tent, whither we proceeded on some mules he had procured. After dinner we purposely led the conversation to the subject of magic, and, as the evening wore on, I began to talk of the powers of the Cabala and other spells that I had read of in old books. This induced Christopholos to drop his reserve, and at last he confessed that his principal object in coming to see us, was to know if we had brought a divining-rod with us, as he believed there was gold to be found in the neighbourhood, and had hoped we might have one to lend him. I replied gravely, that unfortunately we had omitted to include a divining-rod among our baggage, but that if the common hazel grew in the country, he could make one for himself by following the prescribed formula. This led to a further discussion on the science of necromancy, into which he entered with the greatest interest and enthusiasm, and there seemed little doubt that he really believed in the black art, and his own powers as a magician. He declared that by taking the fat of bears and wolves, tempering it with the blood of men or serpents, and mixing the whole with a certain herb that grew in the country, a candle could be made, which, when lighted, would conjure up a phantom host of armed men, who would appear to surround the holder of the light; he also said that he knew of a certain medicine which would render one perfectly invisible, and seriously averred that his old chief, Gobasie, had used it, and that it was through the possession of some such drug that the redoubtable Aba Kassié had always been able to make his escape, even when most securely chained and guarded. He told us of an ointment that made one's limbs so supple that one could withdraw them from the tightest fetters, and of another that would render iron as soft as wax, so that it could be broken with the greatest ease. I asked if he knew how to make the potent ointment that enabled the Abyssinian doctor, we had seen at the king's camp, to extract bullets without surgical aid, but he confessed that this was a secret he had not yet been able to discover, though he hoped soon to do so, and knew of a drug that was better still, as it would preserve one from bullets altogether. He, moreover, declared that he had actually attempted most of the spells he had spoken of, and could give us ocular proof of their potency if we allowed him time to prepare them. The hours passed quickly in such conversation, and it was late before our strange guest left us, to prepare ourselves by sleep for the fatigues of the morrow.

CHAPTER XXIV.

THE RIDE TO THE FRONTIER.

May 16*th*.—Not a trace of the storm remained. The tropical sun had spread its glamour over the land, and though the swollen river still rushed madly over the grey rocks, its spray glistened with the varied colours of the rainbow, and the air was sweet with the fragrance of flowers, and gay with the song of birds and the hum of insects. Our tent, too, no longer stood deserted and alone; the Governor of Gondar, Christopholos the Magician, Barran Barras Tachu the chief of Tchelga, and many others were waiting outside to see me; for to-day I had decided to start on my homeward journey through those great plains of the Soudan and Upper Nubia which lay between me and Khartum on the White Nile.

I had been told that the deserts of Upper Nubia would be a sort of Gehennum on earth at this time of the year, as the rains had not yet fallen, and for nine months the thirsty sand had been baking under the rays of the African sun. But I preferred taking this route, as I hoped to travel faster over the plains on a camel, than I could through the interminable and roadless mountains of Abyssinia; and I had now tarried so long at the Court of King Johannes, that I had no time to lose if I wished to reach England at the time my duty required. Moreover, I was anxious to arrive at Wakhni, the frontier village of Abyssinia, before the next market-day, in order that I might join the merchants returning to Galabat through the forests which form a sort of debateable land between the Abyssinian and Egyptian territory, and which were said to be overrun by fierce and predatory tribes, owning allegiance to neither country, and much addicted to plundering small parties.

It did not take long to prepare for my departure. C. having decided to remain in the highlands of Abyssinia till after the approaching rainy season, I was thenceforward to be alone; and I therefore left with him the tent and baggage, determining to take with me only what was absolutely necessary for the homeward journey. A bag of flour, another of coffee, some pieces of native cloth, a hundred cartridges for my Westley-Richards rifle, and rather more than seven hundred dollars in silver, composed the principal part of my luggage, which was packed on four mules.

While I was busy with these preparations I was honoured by the visit of a dirty old man, who announced himself as the Sheik of the Mahometan quarter of Gondar, and brought me a long straight sword, of the kind used by the Hamran Arabs, which he *said* was a present, though when I offered him in return a very beautiful necklace of Turin beads—the only trinket I had left—he expressed a wish for something more;

and when I accordingly gave him a couple of dollars, and imagined I had got rid of him, he presently re-appeared, to say he had noticed among my things a new red *tarboush*, and lifting from the folds of his turban a very old greasy cap, offered to exchange with me, always for the sake of *friendship*. This was too much for my patience, and I bid him begone, and Allah be with him!

I felt disappointed and vexed that I had not received the letters the king had promised me, for all my efforts of the last three weeks now appeared to have been thrown away. McKelvie, too, who we had hoped would by this time have overtaken us with the medicine-chest, had not arrived; so that I was unable even to provide myself with drugs in case of illness.

However, before the sun was high in the heavens we were all in the saddle, and riding down the ravine leading to the river that flows below Gondar. As we approached it we saw a young maiden bathing herself in its sparkling waters, quite unconscious of our gay cavalcade; but when our horses entered the stream she heard the jingling of the harness, and, looking round for a moment, with her big black eyes wide open, bounded lightly away among the rocks, like a frightened Diana.

Christopholos and my Abyssinian friends now bade me good-bye, but C. rode with me up the rocky ascent of "the mountain of the sun," at the other side of the river. We had almost gained the top, and I was taking a last look at the old palace of "the King of

Kings," and the grey stone houses of the Ethiopian capital, which in all human probability I should never see again, when we perceived two horsemen following us at full gallop, their horses all covered with foam and mud, as if they had ridden through the night. One of these horsemen was evidently from the king's camp, and carried something white in his hand, which he waived over his head; while the other was the Governor of Gondar, in his silk dress, apparently mounted on the horse the king had given me, and which I had left behind at Ambachara, for I could see the silver harness glittering in the sunlight.

There was no doubt now that a message had arrived from his Ethiopic Majesty, and one of importance, as the governor was bringing it in person. We immediately halted our party, and waited the advent of the messengers with some anxiety; for after the explosion of royal anger I had witnessed at Ambachara, I was not quite sure what the king's message might portend, though I was determined, if necessary, to resist any attempt to detain me longer in the country.

Our suspense, however, was not of long duration; the panting horses soon gained the top of the mountain path, and, leaping from the saddle, the Governor of Gondar threw himself at my feet, and handed me a sealed packet. I tore it open, and, to my great relief, found it contained the letters from the king to Lord Granville, promising solemnly, if the English Government wished it, to use every means to abolish the slave-trade in Ethiopia. This was extremely cheering, for I knew that the king would consider his sealed and written promise to the Government as binding, and with a very little encouragement from the Foreign Office, would do much to check the slave-trade in this part of Africa; all the more that the Abyssinian slave-traders, being Mahometans, he did not regard them with favour. In addition to these letters, there was a note from K., who told me the king, as soon as he found I was *really* gone, had despatched the letters to follow me with all haste, and had already issued orders about the laws to be enforced against slave-dealing.

It appeared that the horsemen who brought the despatches had ridden hard all night, but had only reached Gondar as the governor was returning from bidding me adieu. My new horse, notwithstanding the forty miles he had traversed, was looking full of fire, and I was very glad to get him, as my poor bay had been very hard worked of late, and was falling out of condition.

It was now time for C. to leave me, so, exchanging a long shake of the hand, we said farewell, and parted: he to return to the king's court at Ambachara, where he wished to stay some time longer, and I to continue my solitary journey northward through the Nubian deserts.

I felt very sad as our two little parties lost sight of one another in the distance, for who could tell if we should meet again, or either of us ever reach home at all? Does not Asrael, the Angel of Death, who, according to Eastern tradition, sits on high, chronicling in his eternal book the names of those who are born, every instant raise his hand also to blot out the name of some one who has lived his allotted time, and must die? Life, which at all times is uncertain, seems doubly so in Africa, where the wanderer has to encounter a treacherous climate, a warlike and uncivilised people, and forests teeming with large game. A traveller will do well, however, not to let such gloomy thoughts occupy his mind. As Sir Samuel Baker says: "In this country any grief of mind will ensure an attack of fever, to which all are more or less predisposed during the unhealthy season." But I believe the great secret of health in *all* countries, is to encourage cheerfulness in oneself and others.

I was now alone on my homeward journey, without even an interpreter, through whom I could make myself understood by my attendants, for Mustafa only spoke Arabic, and Alegas had remained with C. However, before starting I had asked Barran Barras Tachu, whose name, by the way, was pronounced like a sneeze, how long it would take to reach Tchelga, and on his coolly replying five or six days, I had explained to him that I did not wish to go from village to village to indulge the plundering propensities of his *naphteñas*, and that he must manage to reach Tchelga that night, or I would send him back to the king. We therefore rode briskly forwards in a nearly straight line W.S.W., across a level table-land that gradually merged into undulating hills, covered with scanty bush.

Presently Mustafa came up beside me and said:

"You know that Greek, sar, who came to your tent?"

"You mean Christopholos, Mustafa?"

"Yes, sar; I know his face when I see him, sar: he live once in Cairo. He live for six years in the same house with an Italian, near the Turkish bazaar, and he profess to be his very good friend, and eat with him every day, sar; but after six years he find out where this man keep his money, and at supper he give him wine, and they drink together, and when his friend the Italian fall asleep, he take a knife and cut off his head, and throw it out of the window into the yard; and then he take the money and go away, leaving the body upstairs on the table. I know him at once, sar, for I was in Cairo when that happen."

"Well, Mustafa, it seems I have had a murderer to dine with me; but why did you not tell me this before?"

"I not dare, sar. You see his eye—he never forgive anybody—he kill me if I tell you, sar. I not dare to do so when he was there."

So this was one of the terrible episodes which had left their shadow on the face of Christopholos; certainly the magician was not a pleasant man to have either as a friend or an enemy.

We skirted the country of the Kumants, whom I have before alluded to as worshipping fire, big trees, and the moon. They have anything but a prepossessing type of countenance, their jaws being heavy and projecting, and their foreheads narrow and pointed. I was

The Ride to the Frontier.

told they are worse than the Gallas, who at least remain faithful to their friends; while these people will kill any man, even for a single piece of the common bread of the country. Their mode of gaining a livelihood is, if not strictly honest, ingenious; for they live by carrying wood to Gondar to build houses with, and generally, soon after the house is built, return at night and set it on fire, so as to have to bring fresh wood for its reconstruction: thus they are never without work.

About sunset we forded the famous river Atbara near its head: even here it was a big stream, though very muddy. A short way beyond we came to a little straggling village, which Barran Barras Tachu boldly announced to be Tchelga. I had never seen Tchelga, but I felt convinced that he was deceiving me, and being anxious to arrive at Wakhni on Sunday (it was now Friday), so as to avail myself of the protection of the merchants returning from the market to Galabat, I summoned what Abyssinian I could command, and sternly ordered him to continue the march.

It was quite dark when the barking of a number of savage dogs announced our approach to the true and veritable Tchelga—a large village, composed, in the usual fashion, entirely of round huts, whose extinguisher-shaped roofs were dimly visible against the night sky. Barran Barras Tachu led me into a hut which was apparently used as a storehouse, for it contained some bales of cotton and large earthen jars, like the jars one associates with the story of the Forty Thieves, full of grain. My *naphteñas* captured some fowls, and, cutting off their heads, placed them in a flat dish, with butter and red pepper, to cook. A few pieces of *tef*, a gourd of honey, and a basket lined with hardened cow-dung full of milk, completed the entertainment. I tried to sleep, but sleep was out of the question, for the hut swarmed with all sorts of horrors. I was therefore quite ready to start before daylight next morning.

May 17*th.*—When I summoned my *naphteñas* from their slumbers they held up their feet reproachfully, and said they were footsore with the long march of the previous day. So I gave them all leave to return to Gondar, merely keeping with me my friend Barran Barras Tachu, Mustafa, and three native boys, called Guan Goul, Sinké, and Feynta, who had been my gun-bearers ever since I was at Adowa.

As we rode out of Tchelga I noticed, lying across the path, a beautiful green snake three feet long, which, from the shape of its head, must have been one of the many venomous kinds that abound here. Presently we met the *shoum* of Tchelga, a grey-haired old man, with a long double-edged sword, of the kind used by the Hamran elephant hunters, slung over his shoulder. He saluted his chief, Barran Barras Tachu, with much respect, and at once turned back and accompanied me, with his two servants, a pair of gigantic, bullet-headed negroes, naked to the waist, and armed with Portuguese matchlocks, some three hundred years old, which they appeared to regard with much pride.

We had many thousand feet to descend before we

should be clear of the mountains of Abyssinia, and I pushed on as fast as was possible through a country which was now becoming broken and intersected by deep ravines. My rapid rate of travelling did not, however, suit Barran Barras Tachu, who more than once proposed that we should halt for the day, arguing, with Abyssinian philosophy, that all days were alike, and, as each village we stopped at was bound to supply us with food by the king's order, the more stoppages we made the better. But I was inexorable, and some time afterwards discovered that the worthy Barran Barras Tachu had taken French leave, and abandoned me, though the old *shoum*, with his two negroes, still continued to keep me company.

It was pleasant to watch the flora of the country becoming more luxuriant and beautiful as we gradually descended from the great elevation of the table-lands to the low, warm valleys leading down towards Nubia. I remarked in particular one charming tree, with a red leaf and a yellow flower, growing in clusters like May blossom; and there was another tree, with light green, spade-shaped leaves, and red flowers that hung down from it like scarlet feathers. The ferns and wild flowers, also, that clothed the mountain sides, were as beautiful as they were varied.

We presently entered a little valley possessing wonderful acoustic properties, for one of the *shoum's* people, climbing into a big tree, hailed a village more than half a mile distant on the other side. Shrill voices replied, and some of the villagers came running down the mountain with jars of native beer, which we drank under a lofty *ficus religiosa*, the wide-spreading branches of which afforded us a shelter for our noonday halt.

On resuming our route, we followed for many hours one of the tributaries of the Atbara, which ran along the bottom of the valley, making its way down, through endless ranges of mountains, to the plains. The thunder rolled all day, and the effect of the detonations, as they were echoed back from peak to peak, was very grand. The thunder storms are continual at this time of the year, and the last view I obtained of the highlands of the Woggera showed them dimly looming through the purple clouds, like a great wall stretching between earth and heaven, with incessant flashes of forked lightning playing across it.

About 5 P.M. we came to a wretched little group of huts, where the *shoum* proposed we should sleep, as it was the last village before Wakhni. I, however, decided not to halt till sunset, and told the villagers to send some *tef* after us, for they had none ready when we arrived. The boys and mules were now dead tired, and, as Sinké had fallen sick, I had him placed on my spare horse. Presently we entered a forest, and soon the darkness became so intense that we could not see one another as we rode under the trees; so, on reaching a clear space, where there was a pool of water, we halted and laid down, dinnerless, under the canopy of heaven, taking care to keep near to our beasts, lest the leopards and other wild animals we could hear howling in the woods should carry them off during the night.

May 18*th*.—At sunrise we arose and continued our way through the wood, which was full of blossoming trees, with wonderful creepers hanging in gay festoons from their boughs, literally illustrating a verse satirized by Pope:

> " The groves appeared all dress'd with wreaths of flowers,
> And from their leaves dropp'd aromatic showers."

We presently forded the tributary of the Atbara, and came upon a herd of camels eating the young branches of the mimosa trees. This was a sign that we were fairly beyond the Abyssinian mountains, where the soft-footed camel cannot travel. My native horses were not a little frightened at the sight of such uncouth, long-legged animals, and wanted to run away when the camels lifted up their ugly heads, and roared in the harsh grating notes peculiar to them.

About nine we arrived at Wakhni, which is now the last village on the frontier of Abyssinia, though not long ago Galabat also owed allegiance to the Ethiopian kings, and was governed by an Abyssinian *shoum*. I was told that the general of the Egyptian troops, pursuing a system of gradual encroachment, had even sent officers as far as Wakhni; but these had been recalled a short time before I arrived there.

I gave the *shoum* of the village a letter from King Yohannes, ordering him to help me on my journey, which he promised to do; and as I saw a large party of Arab merchants, who had come to the market, preparing to return to Galabat, I expected to have no difficulty in getting forward that day. Unfortunately, a short time before noon, it began to rain, and the merchants at once declared that they could not begin the journey, though, as they were half naked, and well rubbed over with butter, it was difficult to conceive that they would have been any the worse for a little water. However, so strong was their prejudice against travelling in the wet, that they declared they would remain at Wakhni a week if necessary, and kept as carefully under shelter as if they were afraid their colour might be washed out of them.

I now went to the *shoum*, whom I found reading a letter in Arabic characters, which a horseman had just brought from the direction of Galabat. After reading this letter the *shoum's* manner changed entirely. Before, he had bowed low at sight of the lion on the seal of King Johannes, promised me an escort of spearmen through the bush, and seemed zealous in my service; now, he would only let me have a single attendant as guide, and, though he pretended the road was quite safe, he insisted on being absolved of all responsibility should anything happen to me. I endeavoured to hire some men from the merchants, but they unanimously declared the country between Wakhni and Galabat was infested by robbers and wild beasts, and so dangerous that nothing would induce them to separate from their companions. This made me begin to distrust the good faith of the *shoum*. He knew that I had letters with me from the King of Abyssinia to the English government, and that Egypt always tried to prevent any such communications from reaching Europe, lest they should interfere with her plans of encroachment.* The *shoum* was a Mahometan, and it struck me he might wish to curry favour with the Egyptians by getting hold of my despatches. I was quite alone, with only one gun; the country was unsettled, and nobody was responsible; so that it would not be difficult. Besides, I had with me a large sum of silver, and it seemed strange that, after promising me an escort, he should want me to go without one, and that he should wish me to believe the road was safe when it appeared to be quite the reverse. The more I remarked his manner, the less I liked it, and I decided to leave Wakhni at once, so as, at least, to give him no time for preparation.

Calling my servants, I had the mules loaded, and rode into the forest, determined to make my way through it as best I could; but we had scarcely gone a mile when my native boys—who had shown great uneasiness as they approached the frontier, lest they should be taken by the Egyptians and sold for slaves—were seized with a sudden panic, and all ran away. It was in vain I called to them that I only wanted them to keep me company for twelve hours longer, that they might help to load the mules in the morning, after

---

* The French vice-consul at Massowah assured me that when he first arrived at his post, even the despatches he addressed officially to his government were intercepted, and that it was only by getting the engineer of one of the steamers going up the Red Sea to take charge of duplicate despatches, that he at last managed to communicate with his minister, and force the Egyptian authorities to respect his correspondence.

which they should be free to return. Their fears got the better of their fidelity, and they left me at the very time when I wanted them most. I confess I was disappointed, for I had believed them faithful, and had tried to attach them to me by many little acts of kindness.

Mustafa was the only one who remained—he, honest fellow, would not leave his master, though he was horribly frightened at the prospect of crossing the bush alone; and, indeed our position was helpless enough, for we soon found that four refractory mules were more than we could manage, as the amiable animals kept alternately lying down, slipping off their packs, or wandering into the recesses of the forest, forcing us to leave the beaten track, which we more than once nearly lost.

A very little of this sort of work showed me the hopelessness of attempting to reach Galabat at our present rate of progression, unless we were prepared to spend a month in the woods; so, much to the relief of Mustafa, I turned the horses' heads and rode back to Wakhni, where I decided to try a new scheme.

I sent for the *shoum*, and told him that I did not think it right to expose the king's letters to the risk of being lost, and that therefore, unless he would provide me with an escort, I feared I must send them back to the king, and that I should charge him with their safe delivery. The satisfaction the *shoum* could not help betraying at this announcement went far to confirm my suspicion that his real object was to get the letters into his own hands; so, my servants having returned to their allegiance when they saw me come back to Wakhni, I called them and gave them the letters in the *shoum's* presence, telling them to take two of my mules and return to Ambachara next morning, and that the *shoum* would give them all they required. I then expressed my intention of not starting for Galabat till next day, and retired to an empty hut.

Though I had apparently given my servants the king's letters to take back, I had really substituted in their place a letter in English to C., telling him my suspicions of the *shoum*, and the stratagem I had adopted, and also cautioning him against our mutual friend, Christopholos, the magician of Gondar; nor did even Mustafa know, until he reached Cairo, that I still had the king's letters with me.

My first care, as soon as I was alone, was to exchange the contents of two of my mule packs—one containing dollars and the other hippopotamus' teeth—so that the pack supposed to contain dollars should only contain teeth, and *vice versâ*. While I was making these preparations, I sent Mustafa to try if he could not privately secure the services of one of the camel drivers who had attended the market, by the offer of a liberal reward.

Money is a powerful argument, even in the wilds of Africa, and there presently came to me a wild-looking Hamada Arab, armed with shield and spear, and covered with amulets, who, after some hesitation, agreed to bring his camel to my hut at night, load it with the baggage of the mules I had sent back, and guide me through unfrequented paths of the bush to Galabat, by which means I hoped to frustrate any treachery the *shoum* might be contemplating.

I was sitting in the hut, directing my boys in the construction of a little shelter tent, composed of five spears and some pieces of native cotton, when I was astonished to hear a voice speaking in German, and Mustafa ushered in a European in the dress of an artisan. He said he had landed on the shores of the Red Sea, and made his way to Wakhni from the Soudan, with the intention of entering Abyssinia, and offering his services as a workman to the king. He had no money, no friends, and did not speak a word of anything but German; for which reason Mustafa had brought him to me, as nobody could understand him, or make out what he wanted, where he came from, or whither he was going. The only wonder was, how he had come so far! It seemed, however, that fortune had favoured him, and that he had been passed on from place to place by different parties of merchants till he had at last reached Wakhni. I was, luckily, able to help him another step on his journey, by sending him to Ambachara under the care of my servants, whom I charged to give him one of the mules to ride. Though imperfectly educated, he seemed a very intelligent man, and certainly was possessed of a wonderful amount of pluck and perseverance.

Since my return to Europe, I have learned that he reached Ambachara safely, met C., who presented him to the king, and managed to make a little money; but, in attempting to cross the Sewyen to Adowa, in his usual happy-go-lucky sort of way, he fell into the hands of a band of *shouftas*, or robbers, who stripped him of all he possessed, and left him naked and alone in the midst of the mountains, where he very nearly died miserably of cold and hunger. He, however, subsequently made his way to the sea coast, and joined Count Zichy's hunting expedition in the Bogos.*

When night closed in the rain was still falling, and I tried to get a few hours' sleep, of which I stood in much need. I had determined to delay my departure till after midnight, as I had told the *shoum* I should not leave till the morrow.

* See Appendix, note H.

CHAPTER XXV.

GALABAT AND ITS SLAVE MARKET.

May 19*th*.—About two hours before sunrise, the Hamada Arab, faithful to his promise, made his camel kneel before my hut, and noiselessly loaded it with the packs of the mules I had sent away. I mounted, for the first time, the horse the king had given me, not without difficulty, as he was very restive; and, placing Mustafa on the bay, gave him one of the mules to lead, while I took the other, which, I need not say, carried my precious stock of dollars. In this order we followed the camel and its driver, as they glided, like ghosts, through the sleeping village, and were lost in the shadows of the forest beyond.

No one had seen our departure, except my Abyssinian boys, who came running after me to kiss my hands and knees in a silent farewell. I believe the lads had affection enough to be sorry to part from me, though their devotion was not sufficiently strong to induce them to follow me through the bush.

The night was very dark, and from time to time we had to call to each other, as we could only tell by the sound of our voices if we were still together. Our guide, however, seemed to have an instinct for the road, and wound among the trees, keeping clear of all obstacles with wonderful skill, until the welcome advent of the daylight enabled us to see what we were about.

As the sun rose in the heavens, wreaths of white cloud floated up from the woods, and gathered like a veil round the distant mountain peaks behind us; whilst around stretched hundreds of miles of undulating bush and thorny nabbuk jungle, a tangled mass of glorious African vegetation, decked with sweet-smelling flowers of every colour.

Gradually the heat became intense, and the whole atmosphere vibrated beneath the almost vertical rays of the sun. In the early morning I had seen beautiful birds, of bright cerulean plumage, flitting among the trees like living turquoises, and active, cinnamon-coloured lizards, with blue tails, chasing pretty russet lizardesses, with golden throats, over the glistening quartz stones; but now, in the burning heat, all these were still. The birds ceased to sing; the blue lizard lay basking, motionless, on the rock by the wayside; a pair of tiny gazelles stood gazing at me dreamily with their large black eyes from the shade of some sweet-scented mimosas, among the boughs of which sat a little grey monkey, too overcome by the warmth even to make faces. The green beetles gleamed like emeralds in the dry, yellow grass; and not a sound broke the stillness save the humming of numberless insects among the flowers. It was just such a scene of tropical beauty as Doré has depicted in some of his illustrations to "Atala"; and all one's senses seemed to drink in the sunlight and scents and sounds, with a dreamy satisfaction that was very delightful.

> "There is a pleasure in the pathless woods,
> There is a rapture on the lonely shore,
> There is society where none intrudes——"

Suddenly all such thoughts were put to flight by the strange conduct of my horse, which stopped short and began to shiver, as if stricken with cold. I looked up and saw, not five-and-twenty yards before me, a magnificent spotted leopard slowly walking across the glade, with an easy, undulating motion, intensely suggestive of latent power and agility.

He stood in the full blaze of the sunlight, with his long tail curling and uncurling like the coils of a serpent, and his sleek spotted coat glistening with a thousand rich prismatic tints that are never seen in the caged animals brought to Europe, whose fur soon becomes dull and pale, losing all the lustre and beauty that distinguishes the wild animal in its native country. The leopard had paused nearly in front of me, but he showed no sign of having perceived me, and remained for about ten seconds gazing straight before him, looking very handsome in the pride of his strength and perfect symmetry.

I threw the bridle of my horse, which still trembled violently, over the branch of a tree, and, slipping quietly to the ground, levelled my rifle and fired. I think one's conscience need hardly reproach one for shooting a leopard, yet there was something terrible in the sudden change that now came over the beautiful beast, who a moment before seemed to enjoy life so thoroughly. His hind quarters lay paralyzed on the ground, with the blood slowly trickling from a wound in the back; but he uttered no cry, only, as the smoke floated away, he raised himself with a great effort on his forepaws, and glared round for the enemy who had so swiftly smitten him of his strength, with a diabolical expression of rage I shall never forget. His white teeth gleaming in the sunlight, the skin on his nose and forehead all wrinkled into thick folds, and his powerful claws tearing up the ground, as he drew his breath in short, spasmodic gasps, were so horribly indicative of pain, rage, and impotent ferocity, that a dark shadow seemed to have fallen over the peaceful forest scene, and to have all at once marred its beauty.

I determined to try to give the leopard his *coup-de-grâce* with my long hunting knife, as my terrified horse had broken away, leaving me with only one cartridge, which I wished to reserve in case of future need. But I was mistaken in supposing he was quite paralyzed, and had not calculated on the tenacity with which wild animals, especially those of the feline kind, cling to life. When I reached within half-a-dozen yards of him, he suddenly started up, and with a desperate effort, collected all his strength for a spring; but I suppose his strength gave way, or the pain of his wound cowed his courage at the last moment, for, just as I had made up my mind that an encounter was inevitable, he turned sharply to the left and disappeared down a gully, where the bush grass grew ten feet high. I had instinctively raised my rifle when I saw him about to spring at me, but his abrupt change of direction caused my shot to fly harmlessly past him, which left me without cartridges. However, I went into the bush grass to look for him, a search that had to be conducted with great caution, as the grass was so thick and high that I could not see a yard before me. I searched for some time, but, though I knew he could not be far off, my efforts were unsuccessful; and, perhaps, it was fortunate they were so, for a wounded leopard is no pleasant *vis-à-vis*.

As for Mustafa and the Arab, when they heard my rifle and saw my horse galloping back riderless, with the bridle over its head, they halted and prepared to retrace their steps, exclaiming, with Eastern wisdom: "*BISMILLAH!* why should we go forwards if our master is killed and does not want us?"

We crossed several small streams, and about 2 P.M. forded the Gandowa, a considerable river, which was here divided by a little island. It is a tributary of the Atbara, and the current was so rapid that we narrowly escaped being carried away by it. On the opposite side we halted under a tree for a short rest, and about 3 P.M. continued the march. I felt rather weak, and noticed that streams of blood were trickling down my legs, from numbers of sores that had broken open from the fatigue of riding. These sores were the result of my having lived almost entirely on animal food in Abyssinia, and I was obliged to burn them with lunar caustic every day for three weeks before I could check this inconvenience.

When night closed in we made a meagre supper off some pieces of native bread, and lay down under a tree to sleep till the moon should rise.

I may here mention that it is advisable for a traveller sleeping in the jungle not to lie too near the trunks of the trees, as the snakes collect under the trees at nightfall, and one of them may easily be mistaken for a dead branch, their habit being to lurk where the shade is thickest.

May 20*th*.—When the moon rose we rose too, for the Arab said this part of the forest was infested by wild border tribes, who owed allegiance to no sovereign, and whose only law was that the stronger should plunder the weaker, and I was anxious to get through it as rapidly and secretly as possible. I might have cried out, like Shylock: "Oh, my Christian ducats!" for on them depended my means of traversing the Soudan; and I guarded the mule that carried the valuable burden with unceasing vigilance and no small anxiety.

The night was cloudy, and the moon afforded us but little light, so that our progress was necessarily very slow, and whenever I got a few yards ahead of my two companions the forest echoed with the voice of Mustafa, exclaiming, in the most pathetic accents: "Where are you, Captain? Do not go away, *good* Captain; do not leave us behind!" I noticed he always called me Captain when he was nervous: it seemed to stimulate his courage.

Presently the moon became obscured, but, through a break in the clouds to the east, Ashtaroth, the morning star, rose like a diamond in the violet sky, casting a pale gleam of light across the path. In that instant I caught sight of something dark that bounded noiselessly through the long bush grass to within three yards of my bridle-rein, and the next moment perceived it was a panther, in the very act of crouching for a spring. Luckily, I was riding with my rifle ready cocked in my hand, and, levelling it straight in the animal's face, I fired both barrels in rapid succession; but I had no time to ascertain the fate of the panther, for my new horse, who had never had a gun fired from his back before, no sooner saw the flash than he reared upright, and plunging madly forwards, bolted with me through the jungle at a furious pace, tearing me ruthlessly through the thickest of the tangled growth of trees and creepers, armed with long fish-hook thorns, and causing me to leave, like Black Hassan,—

"A stain on every bush that bore
A fragment of my palampore."

There was nothing for it but to crouch down on the neck of the horse and hold tight. Even the cruel native ring-bit, with which I still rode him, was perfectly powerless to stop his headlong career, though I exerted all my strength; and it was not till I had made a very considerable détour, and was nearly reduced to rags, that I at last struck the track again, where I was presently joined by Mustafa and the

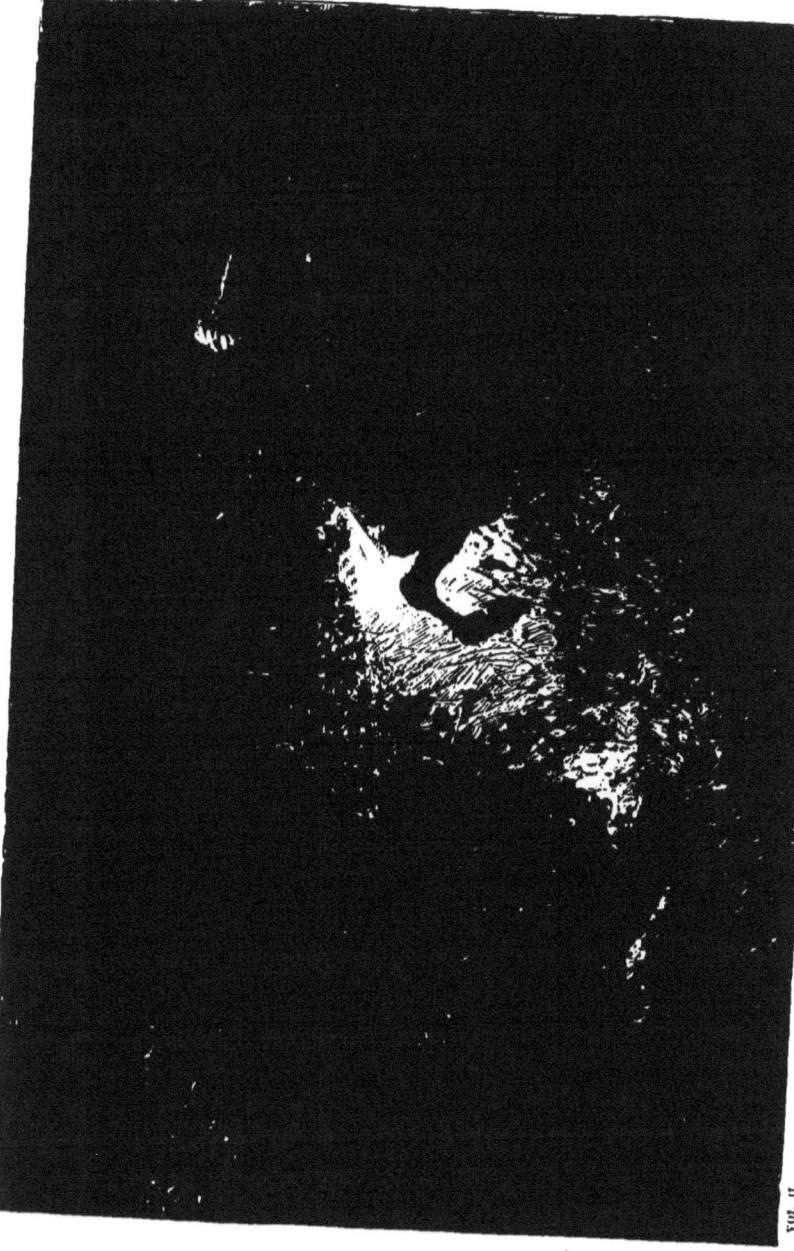

A NIGHT ENCOUNTER.

Arab, who had taken a short cut through the bush to meet me.

About sunrise we heard a hoarse, grating roar among the trees to our right, which sent a peculiar thrill through both men and beasts. We stopped, as if by consent: the Arab looked at Mustafa, Mustafa looked at the Arab, and I looked at them both. The roar was repeated, and the Arab now whispered the word, "*asad*"—lion. As my horse was frightened and would not advance, I tied him to a tree, and, bidding the two men stay with the cattle, followed the direction of the sound on foot; but as I advanced the lion seemed to retire, and then there was silence for some time, after which I suddenly heard his roar behind me. I believe it is a common habit of lions, if they discover that they are being pursued, to make a circle and follow the person who was previously following them. Anyhow, this lion was too wary to let me approach him, though I doubled back several times; and, at last, his roar ceasing altogether, I was forced to abandon the chase.

As we neared the confines of the bush, we came on an encampment of natives, all armed to the teeth, with their horses picketed beside them. They proved to be only a party of merchants, and we rode on without halting, till we reached a stream not half-an-hour's ride from Galabat. Here I was met by a French missionary, of the same order as the young missionary we had seen at Ambachara, who had been released from prison by King Johannes. He said he had heard at Galabat that a white man was coming out of Abyssinia, and as the only white man he knew of there was his brother missionary, he had supposed it must be he, and had come to meet him.

We rode together to Galabat, which is a considerable market town, composed principally of round houses, thatched with conical roofs of grass, after the Abyssinian model. It has a shallow stream, and plenty of green trees growing round it, which give it a pleasant aspect. Behind it is a hill, on which was a camp of Egyptian troops. We crossed the stream which partly encircles the town, and entered the market-place. Being market-day it was full of natives, clad in every variety of the scanty costume of Upper Nubia, and of all shades of colour, from sickly yellow to jet black. Tokrouris, Abyssinians, Arabs, Gallas, and even a few Greek and Armenian traders mingled with woolly-headed negroes from the White Nile; while everywhere camels were being led about, laden with cotton, gum, hides, and other produce of the interior of Africa, much to the terror of my little Abyssinian horses, who could not reconcile themselves to the great height and strange proportions of the "desert ships." Standing in the midst of this noisy crowd, we found the principal merchant of Galabat, a Mahometan Abyssinian, called Jusef, who welcomed me hospitably, and had a tent pitched near his house for my accommodation.

The Egyptian general at Galabat was a Nubian negro, and he was away chastising some refractory tribes of his own colour; but his second in command, in whom I recognised one of the officers who had sailed with us down the

Red Sea on board the Kosseir, presently came and blew up Jusef, or, as he expressed it, "pulled his beard," for not having given him immediate notice of my arrival. This officer was a very little personage when I had last seen him, but here he had developed into a great man, and bullied Jusef unmercifully. His reception of me, however, was almost gushing; and he told me that his Highness the Khedive had given orders that, should C. or myself return from our journey in Abyssinia through the Egyptian Soudan, we were to be furnished with every assistance. At the invitation of my new friend, I rode to the Egyptian camp, which commanded the town. The top of the hill was perfectly level, and the camp was enclosed by a strong stone parapet, with platforms at the four corners for cannon. The round huts of the soldiers were built with the greatest regularity, in long double lines, and everything seemed in excellent order.

I was presented to the Colonel-commandant, a white haired Arab, and, a divan having been placed in the open air, we sat down in state, while a regiment of soldiers, composed entirely of slaves, who had been given the Hobson's choice of serving Ismael Pacha instead of their masters, marched past to the sound of pipe and drum. They performed their evolutions perfectly, and were all clothed in neat cotton uniforms, that contrasted strikingly with their black faces and red caps. While we were smoking, and drinking the inevitable *finjal* of coffee flavoured with cloves, a Nubian band played several Arab and Turkish airs, and then two new Gatling guns, or mitrailleuses, were wheeled up for my inspection. The Egyptian troops were also provided with bronze mountain pieces, and all the men were armed with breech-loading Remington rifles. Before I left, I was shown all round the camp, which was well supplied with food and munitions, was very clean, and certainly in first-rate order. It was evident that every preparation had been made for a war with Abyssinia, should the occasion occur.

My companions, while striving to make a favourable impression on me, also endeavoured quietly to extract what information they could about the movements of King Johannes, the strength of his army, and the state of his country; nor were they a little startled when they learned that I had ridden from his camp at Ambachara in less than six days, and that the force he had with him was so large. They were also unable to understand how I had crossed the bush between Wakhni and Galabat without their knowledge, for they evidently kept a line of scouts on the frontier.

On our way back to Jusef, we called on the chief of irregular cavalry, a magnificently attired individual, with a fine collection of pistols, knives, and yataghans in his sash. The greater part of his men, I was told, were mounted on swift camels, and were employed carrying despatches, or scouring the desert in search of fugitives. The distances they traversed were wonderful, but sometimes their camels died, or were killed, and they never returned.

Jusef, on my return, presented me with a little red monkey, who as yet was only half tame; and, after an

Galabat and its Slave Market.

early supper in the hospitable merchant's house, I retired to my tent for the night.

May 21st.—There are two market days at Galabat, Tuesday and Wednesday, and the town has an important trade in Abyssinian produce, such as bees-wax, coffee, cotton, and hides. In 1862, when Sir Samuel Baker was there, it belonged to the kingdom of Ethiopia, and the distinguished traveller relates how the Sheik Jemma,* on seeing his firman, told him "that this was Abyssinia, and that the firman of the Viceroy of Egypt was a bad introduction, as the Egyptians forced them to pay tribute at the point of the bayonet, although they had no right to enter this country; and that they paid taxes willingly to the King of Abyssinia, as he had a right to exact them." But now I found the Egyptians sole masters of the place, the whole revenue of which they diverted to their own uses. Not content with placing the Abyssinian *shoum* in irons—some people said he had even been unmercifully flogged—they had sent him, though old and infirm, the long and painful journey across the Nubian deserts to Cairo, from which he would probably never return to see his native hills; and the town was now held by a strong force of Egyptian soldiers, quartered in the camp I have described, who—if I might believe the complaints of several merchants—committed whatever outrages they pleased on the defenceless natives. I was told that although the Egyptian

* Evidently the "Shiek Jumar," that the King spoke to me about.

Government had professed to pass laws prohibiting the slave trade, and that Galabat was now entirely occupied by Egyptian soldiers, and under the absolute control of an Egyptian general, I should yet find a public slave-market there, where I should see many Galla and Abyssinian slaves, some of whom were Christians, openly bought and sold. I therefore expressed a desire to Jusef that he should show me the slave market, and he readily agreed to accompany me there, evidently regarding it as one of the sights of the place.

We rode into a large field outside the town, where were a number of long low booths, made very roughly of branches. Each of these booths was divided into several little compartments, the interior of which was hidden from view by curtains of native cloth hung in front of them. The slave merchants sat smoking beside their booths with Arab gravity. We visited them one after the other, and they led us into the different compartments, expatiating on the beauty and merits of their slaves, very much as a dealer shows off his horses. Galla and Abyssinian girls were numerous, and averaged from thirty to seventy dollars. Over the head of each was thrown a piece of cotton cloth, which concealed her features till her turn came to be inspected, when the dealer removed it, like an upholsterer uncovering a chair. They had scarcely any clothing, and sat crowded together in their little cells, with the African sun burning down on the flat roof close above their heads, in an atmosphere which was perfectly stifling.

Galabat and its Slave Market.

Many of these young girls were very beautiful: their colour was often not darker than that of a Spanish gipsy, their features were small and delicate, their forms proportioned like a Greek statue, and their eyes large and lustrous. I have been told that these fair children, for they were little more, who are brought here from the Galla country, Showa, Wooma, and other parts of Abyssinia, are of a gentle and affectionate disposition, and faithful and loving to those who treat them kindly. They did not seem to know Arabic, and their masters made them do what they wished by signs. I heard no weeping or lamentation; but, though they were all so young, I did not see a single smiling face, and their lot seemed a sad one indeed; transported, at the very spring time of life, into a strange country, to be given up body and soul to the highest bidder. I believe they are generally bought by merchants, who send them to Arabia, where, if they be Christians, they are soon made to renounce their faith. Occasionally, it may happen that one of these girls gets into a good harem; but, for one that does, numbers die on the way, from change of climate, change of food—*too often indeed the want of it*—and the long, long journey across the deserts under a broiling sun. They say that all people who live among mountains love their country; and I have often thought how fondly these poor girls must think of the green valleys among their native hills, when, like caged birds, they gaze through their lattices at Jiddah, on the hot sands of Arabia el Hidjaz! Indeed, I afterwards heard, when I was at Jiddah, that one of these fair prisoners had recently flung herself from her window into the street below, preferring death to captivity.

Of the horrors the poor creatures sometimes have to endure from the brutality of the men who capture them, and take them down to the markets of Upper Nubia in regular droves, like so many cattle, I can hardly speak. Even children do not escape, and it is not uncommon to see young girls not more than seven or eight years old suffering from the most horrible diseases. Nor will the traders of Galabat guarantee the health of their slaves, or even allow them to be inspected by a doctor. The mortality among them is simply fearful, and even now it makes my blood boil to think of their fate.

"Not for this,
Was common clay ta'en from the common earth,
Moulded by God, and tempered with the tears
Of angels, to the perfect shape of man!"

I fancy a slave dealer soon forgets that a slave has any feelings. While I was in one of the booths, a beautiful young Galla girl, some seventeen years old, happened to take the fancy of an old man, who might —except so far as beauty was concerned—have very well been her grandfather. The veil was torn from her shoulders by the merchant, and she was made to stand up and display her beauty.

"Light was the form, and darkly delicate
That brow, whereon her native sun had sat,
But had not marr'd."

The customer felt and examined carefully her teeth, feet, hands, and knees, very much as people look at the points of a horse. Then came the haggling about the price, the old octogenarian beating down the merchant, dollar by dollar, though the merchant only asked ten pounds for her, the price of a good mule. All this time the poor girl was looking on with straining eyes, trying to read her fate in the merchant's face, for she could not understand what he was saying. Probably, as there are two market days at Galabat every week for slaves, and this was the second day, she was doomed to be sold, for her owner wanted to get rid of his remaining stock; but they were still cheapening her when I left the stifling booth and stepped forth into the bright sunshine, where a lark, singing high up in the blue heavens, seemed to mock in its freedom a dejected crowd of naked negroes, just arrived from the neighbourhood of the White Nile, who sat huddled together, without distinction of sex or age, and some even with their hands still tied, for they were merely regarded as so many strong animals, to be sold cheap for purposes of labour. But I will not linger longer over the revolting picture.

What can I say of this horrible traffic that has not been said before? It is a blot on the face of the earth, a disgrace to humanity, and a standing reproach to all so-called Christian nations that allow it to exist; but—

"Those gentlemen of England who sit, in Downing Street, at ease,"

cannot see this. It is so hard to realize, when we are

comfortable at home, the sufferings of fellow-creatures five thousand miles away; yet a few vibrations of the telegraph from England to Cairo might work a great change. It is true that "Charity should begin at home," but when by a little exertion of influence we may save from shame, misery, and death, our fellow-creatures abroad, ought we to hesitate?

CHAPTER XXVI.

FROM GALABAT TO KATARIF.

On returning to my tent I was horrified to discover that the white ants had made their way into it, and were attacking my baggage. I had often seen, in Abyssinia, fields covered with the conical hills, from ten to twelve feet high, raised by these creatures, which, at a distance, looked exactly like a native village. The white ants are regularly distributed into labourers, and soldiers, or fighting ants; with others, holding the rank of king and queen, to rule over them. Professor Wilson says, that the queen, when she is about to add to the numbers of the tribe, presents a most extraordinary spectacle, being swelled to greatly beyond her natural dimensions, and producing at each delivery a progeny of many thousands. Terrible stories are related of the destruction caused by the inroads of these ants; who devour everything before them, clothes, leather, wood, and even, it is said, human beings, unless they take refuge in flight. A fallen animal will have its bones picked clean in a wonderfully short space of time; for union is strength, and these small animals become formidable when working in millions. However, I believe they will not attack baggage if it be raised on stones some height above the ground; and, after I had emptied my tent of everything, they soon abandoned it, and went off in search of what they might devour elsewhere.

Jusef showed me over his house, which consisted of several thatched buildings standing in a large enclosure. One was devoted to his harem, the fair inhabitants of which disappeared precipitately behind some curtains as we entered, leaving nothing visible but their small arched feet, and dark eyes peeping out from among the folds. In the outer enclosure were two young camel-leopards, which had just been captured for a German who had come up here to collect animals for the European menageries. I was much struck by the brilliant tints on the skins of these beautiful creatures, so different from their appearance when they have been transported to captivity and our colder skies. As darkness bleaches the colour of most living things, so where the sun's rays are hottest their colour appears to become more brilliant. The camel-leopard, though difficult to capture, is, like the ostrich, easy to transport to Europe, as it supports the journey across the desert better than other animals. Here, in the Soudan, the value of a young camel-leopard was about fifty dollars; but in Europe it would probably fetch five hundred.

Jusef said, that the same German who had bought the camel-leopards had some dromedaries, or *hygeens*, to dispose of, which might suit me, as I had told him I wanted to procure dromedaries on which to make the journey of nearly four hundred miles to Khartum.

Every one knows the story of the three artists—one English, the other French, and the other German,—who were each commissioned to paint a perfect dromedary. And how the Englishman travelled all over the world to inspect personally every dromedary that could be seen; while the Frenchman went to the Jardin des Plantes at Paris, fully convinced that the dromedary there *must* be the finest in the whole world; and the German, never even troubling to look at a dromedary at all, shut himself in his study with a goodly supply of beer, books, and tobacco, and proceeded to evolve out of his own inner consciousness the perfect architype of the dromedary of the future.

I was no judge of a dromedary or camel; and yet it was important to procure good ones, as, at this time of year the plains I should have to traverse were almost destitute of water. So I followed the German's principle, and evolved from my inner consciousness a beautiful standard dromedary by which to judge all that might be shown me. Alas! they fell very short of the standard; indeed, they were not dromedaries at all, two of them being only light trotting camels, while the third was a strong camel suitable for baggage. When I first saw them they were kneeling round a skin full of grain, which they were devouring ravenously; though every now and then they found time to roar and bite at each other with an expression of countenance that was evil in the extreme. The camel preserves the quaintness of the antediluvian animals; and with his long neck and projecting breastbone, always reminds me of some uncouth bird, a cross between the ostrich and the griffin, that has accidently got possessed of four legs.* Besides their natural ugliness, and decidedly bad tempers, the three specimens before me were as thin as skeletons. But there was a certain look of blood and pluck about them, which, judging them as I should a horse, rather pleased me, and I determined to take them, notwithstanding Mustafa's gloomy prophecy that they would die of sheer emaciation before the end of the first day's journey. Fortunately Mustafa was not a prophet in his own country, and these camels afterwards showed powers of endurance that astonished even the Arabs.

I gave in exchange for my three *hygeens* two horses and two mules,—a bad bargain, as a camel at Galabat is only worth thirty dollars (£6), while a good horse will fetch fifty; but I could not take my horses across the desert, and I was willing to let the German have them to exchange with the Arab hunters, for camel-leopards.

The Hamran Arabs, who are the great hunters of this part of the country, are splendid horsemen, and boldly pursue the large game of Africa, armed with no other weapon than their long straight double-edged cross-handled swords, which they wield with so much power and skill that they can ham-string the elephant and rhinoceros, and can cut a man through the

---

* Remains of camels have been found in Europe and Asia, in recent beds of the tertiary epoch, showing its co-existence with the mammoth, giant wood-stag, and cave-bear.

middle of the body, like a carrot, at one blow. These swords are carried in a red leather sheath between the thigh and the saddle, when riding, and slung round the neck when walking. I remember being told by a French general that, during the Franco-Prussian war, he found it advantageous to make his cavalry carry their swords between the leg and the saddle, as the men suffered much from the constant strain on the waist of a heavy sabre. Certainly some improvement might be made on the present regulation belt, which is not only very fatiguing on a long march, but liable to produce permanent injury.

The great test for one of the Arab swords is, if it will cut iron. The Arab, naked to the waist, raises his sword in both hands, and, whirling it round his head, aims a mighty blow at a piece of iron. If the sword makes a cut in the iron, and yet preserves its edge uninjured, it is considered a weapon fit for a Sheik, and is handed down from father to son in a family as a treasure not to be sold at any price. Sheiks and rich Arabs have the handles of their swords and the rings of the scabbard mounted in silver, cunningly worked, and I have even seen verses of the Koran etched on the blade. But an examination of the marks on these swords showed me that the blades all came from Solingen, whence they must be shipped wholesale to the Red Sea. The traders on the coast of the Egyptian Soudan buy them and transport them inland, where the natives mount them with scarlet-leather scabbards, and cross handles of the old

Crusader pattern; the verses of the Koran are also etched in the country, but this is only done at Khartum, where there lives, or lived, an old Arab silversmith skilled in such work.

Having now got camels with which to continue my journey, I rode up to the camp to ask the governor for a guide to Abou Harras, a town on the Blue Nile, about two hundred and eighty miles from Galabat, whither I wished to proceed. The governor at once offered to give me a messenger he was sending to Abou Harras with letters, if I would mount him as far as Katarif, where the Sheik would provide him with a fresh camel. I gladly accepted this offer, and turned homewards to prepare for the journey. In the crowded market-place, on which the sun was blazing down with intense heat, I was astonished to see guns for sale at eight dollars (*thirty-two shillings*) a-piece. What must they have cost in Europe? And yet, cheap though they were, I was told that a slave was not unfrequently exchanged for a gun.

May 22nd.—At 6·30 A.M. my camels were packed, and at 7 my guide made his appearance. He was a Nubian negro, and confessed it was thirteen years since he had been to Abou Harras, but he believed, "*inshálláh*" that he should remember the road. He gave me a letter from the Governor of Galabat to the Arab Sheiks of Katarif and Abou Harras, and it now only remained for me to bid farewell to my kind host Jusef, on whom I bestowed my gold signet-ring, as it was the only thing of value I had left to give

Turning our faces Northwards, we rode past the camp, near which a pair of gigantic Maraboo storks—*Abou seen*, "Father of the teeth," as the Arabs call them, from the formidable proportions of their beaks—were marching with long strides through the fields, performing the meritorious duty of scavengers. These birds present a somewhat heavy and ungainly appearance, but they have such enormous wings that they can soar even higher than the vulture, though *its* flight is so high that it is far beyond the reach of the naked eye when making its circles through the air in search of prey.

The guide rode the spare camel devoted to the baggage, while Mustafa and I were mounted on the two *hygeens*, or trotting camels, which I resolutely kept at a trot, though it required no small amount of fortitude to do so, as the trot of even a *hygeen* produces a sensation that can only be compared to riding on the roof of a bathing-machine being rapidly taken over large boulder stones. However, the walk is little better, as the continual swaying backwards and forwards is intensely fatiguing to the back, and makes some people sick; thus fully illustrating the simile of the camel being the desert ship.

Our road lay through a level country, thickly covered with mimosa trees; and the only people we saw were a few wild-looking Tokrouris, riding on the bare backs of oxen, and armed with wooden clubs, shaped like hatchets. The native name for these weapons is *tombásh*, and they are often thrown at an adversary, though they do not return as the boomerang is said to do. The

Tokrouris also carry curved knives, and spears horribly barbed behind the point, so that they cannot be withdrawn from a wound. They are a very black race of negroes, who originally emigrated to the fertile frontiers of Abyssinia from Darfour, an arid country west of the White Nile, lying principally between the 12th and 15th degrees North latitude. Though a true negro race, their noses are prominent and curved, nor are their ears of less ample proportions; but as if to compensate for her liberality in this respect, Nature has given them very small eyes, which slope upwards, and they wear their hair standing upright on the top of their heads like a mop, which does not give them a prepossessing appearance.

Presently we heard an unmistakable bray, and were overtaken by a fat old man in a voluminous turban, mounted on an active little donkey, which he goaded on with the sharp points of his Turkish slippers, which served him instead of spurs. We interchanged *salaams*, and he introduced himself as a merchant from Khartum, whither he was returning. At his back hung one of the long swords of the country, handsomely mounted in silver; and, seeing that I admired it, he at once begged me to accept it—an offer I was obliged to refuse as I had nothing to give in return. Behind him rode his wives on two camels, guarded by a couple of negroes armed with flint-lock guns.

We passed three small villages, at one of which the old merchant halted; but I continued riding till sunset, when, as it was becoming too dark for us to find our way, we were forced to halt at a small hamlet, called Eggeford, which proved to be almost deserted, on account of the dearth of water. We could therefore obtain nothing for supper beyond the bread we had with us. About nine o'clock the moon rose very brightly, but I lay down under a tree, determined to rest myself and the cattle till sunrise, as the heat of the past day had been intense, and I was weak and ill, the wounds in my legs having broken open again, and the ophthalmia I had caught at the lake being much aggravated by the sun and dust.

May 23rd.—At daybreak we perched ourselves again on our uncouth steeds, and continued the journey; our road lying, like yesterday, through a tract of country thickly covered with mimosas.

These beautiful trees not only please the eye by their graceful appearance, and the sense of smell by the sweet fragrance of their flowers, but they are extremely useful. There is a variety from the bark of which excellent fibre is obtained by the Arabs for the manufacture of ropes, and sacks that serve to hold the gum-arabic which the mimosa also produces. Sir Samuel Baker, in his "Nile Tributaries," alludes to the beautiful effect of the pure crystallized gum-arabic on the stems and branches of the trees, which at one season makes the mimosa bush look like the jewelled garden in the story of Aladdin. Another variety of this tree, the *Acacia Arabica*, produces a fruit used by the Arabs as a medicine for its astringent and tonic qualities, and invaluable also for the tanning of hides; and there is a kind of mimosa, the branches of which are said to bend like those of the sensitive plant when they are touched. Hence Moore, in his "Lalla Rookh," calls it—

"That courteous tree
Which bows to all who seek its canopy."

If you sit down beneath a mimosa when the sun is hot, it will afford you a grateful shelter; but should a rain-cloud approach, the shade will instantly become a mere skeleton shadow, dotted with little patches of light, and you will see the delicate leaves of the mimosa all close, as if by magic, to let the grateful moisture fall round its roots. Such sensibility surely almost amounts to instinct.

There appeared to be little game in the bush, for we only saw two antelopes during the whole day's march. My monkey made his escape at a village where we halted for an hour; but, after an exciting chase, he was recaptured before he could reach the trees. When he saw that his pursuers were gaining on him, he quietly lay down on his back and waited philosophically to be taken.

As the sun sank slowly through a chaotic mass of gold and crimson clouds, and for a moment appeared to rest like a ball of fire on the earth, a melodious voice broke the stillness, calling aloud the praise of "Allah, the Most High!" and we presently saw a young man, mounted on a tall white camel, singing verses from a religious book as he rode through the gloaming. On his head was a handsome *qúfieh*, or handkerchief, of variegated silk; his dress was of fine white cotton, ornamented with innumerable buttons; and at his side hung a long Turkish gun. We exchanged the usual *salaams*, and continued our journey together.

When the darkness of night overspread the landscape, a circle of bright fires blazed into the air round a village in the distance, and I learned from my companion that the natives were burning the bush to clear it. Guiding ourselves by these flames towards the village, which was named Tdoka, we made our camels kneel before a large thatched house, built of branches and plastered with mud, which my new friend invited me to enter. He also insisted on giving up to me his bed, saying that he had seen me with Jusef at Galabat, and that it would be an everlasting shame to him, an Arab, if he allowed a stranger to pass his village without offering him hospitality. Then, telling me that Mustafa and my camels should be well cared for, he left me to the care of his servants, who presently entered bearing an *angarep*, on which was a soft mattrass and pillows covered with spotless white cotton. A carpet was spread on the ground, and, after a slave had offered me a brazen vessel full of clear water in which to wash my hands, I found myself sitting cross-legged before a carved octangular stool, on which reposed a large tray containing a delicious dinner of four courses, comprising flesh, fowl, and vegetables cunningly stewed in the Arab fashion. Two slaves stood by with lighted beeswax tapers, and a bowl of fresh milk, followed by a *finjal* of scented black coffee, completed the luxurious entertainment, which seemed almost like one of the enchanted feasts of the Arabian Nights, after the meagre fare I had been so long accustomed to in Abyssinia. My host now sent to ask if I would receive him, and, after politely inquiring whether I required anything further, told me that he would bear me company on the morrow as far as Katarif, whither it seemed we were both bound.

This night, for the first time in four months, I enjoyed the luxury of sleeping between sheets.

May 24*th*.—It was of no use ordering Mustafa to make my coffee in the morning: my host insisted that, as I was a stranger, it would be an undying shame to him if he did not provide me with *everything;* and I had hardly risen, before the scribe of the village, a hale old man in a white turban and long black robe, came and pressed me to breakfast with him, while the "*gemmalin*," or camels, were being saddled. The repast, like that of yesterday, consisted of various stewed meats and vegetables; and, as soon as it was over, my Amphytrion mounted his donkey and accompanied me to the confines of the village, the ground round about which I noticed was carefully irrigated and cultivated. However, we soon plunged again into a vast tract of bush that extended on all sides as far as the eye could reach, though mimosa trees were somewhat less plentiful than on the preceding day.

At noon, the sun being fearfully hot, we made a short halt, and lunched off some cold meat which my Arab friend had been careful to provide; and then, as we were to pass no water on this day's march, rode far into the night, the bush presenting always the same monotonous and dried-up aspect.

Towards sunset we met an Arab, riding on a trotting camel, who stopped to talk with my companion. He was a handsome young fellow, with beautiful dark eyes, and a long, trailing moustache—a rare adornment here, where the beard seems only to grow when man enters on the fourth decade. On his head was a red *tarboush*, with a silk and gold handkerchief bound round it, one end of which fell over his shoulders; his shirt was of the finest cotton, very wide at the sleeves, and elaborately plaited; over this he wore a long tunic, also of spotless white, decorated with many buttons at the breast and wrists, and confined at the waist by a handsome sash, from the folds of which peeped a long knife or dagger; his loose trowsers were tucked into pointed scarlet-leather boots, very much turned up at the toes; and at the side of his camel saddle, which was covered with black sheep-skin, hung a scarlet leather holster, containing a brace of silver-mounted Turkish pistols. In short, he was an Arab dandy.

Soon after the two young men had parted, we saw some gazelles, but could not get within shot of them. However, my companion shot from the back of his camel a couple of brace of guinea-fowl, which served us for supper. I may here mention, that the best way to cook birds on the march is to skin them, feathers and all; split them open; and, after sprinkling them with red pepper, lay them on the fire. By this means a very good grill may be obtained in less than a quarter of an hour.

About midnight we stopped to rest under a tree, but

I had hardly been asleep an hour before my friend arose and continued his journey, as he wished to be at Katarif early in the morning. I remained where I was till sunrise, when, rousing Mustafa and the letter-carrier, I also proceeded on my way.

May 25th.—After four hours' march we came to a well, with a number of mud tanks round it, which a crowd of nearly naked Arab men and women were employed filling *gratuitously*, for the benefit of the passers-by; this is a capital institution in a country where water is life.

My camels drank eagerly, and we rode on till we reached a village, where they told us that we had taken the wrong road. However, we struck a track leading through the bush towards Katarif; and, about one o'clock, had the pleasure of seeing the conical roofs of the houses of "*Soog Abou Sin*," as it is sometimes called, rising before us.

I had heard that there was a Greek merchant living at Katarif; and, as in Africa hospitality from one white man to another is a matter of course, I enquired my way to his dwelling, and without further ceremony made my camels kneel at his door, and walked into the hut, where I received a very kind welcome.

Katarif, or the market of Abou Sin,* is situated on the border of immense prairies, which, in the rainy season, are covered with long grass, but at this time of the year, after being exposed for eight

* *Soog* means market.

months to a burning sun, were an arid and waterless desert. I was told that, for three days' march, we should find no water on the road; and was therefore anxious to obtain another camel, to carry a supply of water and corn; but it was no easy task to get away from Katarif.

As yet I had been unable to procure any waterskins; and here, after much trouble, I could only get some old ones that were scarcely water-tight. The Sheik also sent word that he could not let me have a camel for two or three days; and even the Greek merchant, with whom I was lodged, declared it was hopeless for me to try to get away sooner. What did it matter? *Bukkara inshállâh*, to-morrow, should Allah will it; or, if not, then, *inshállâh*, the day after that. It was enough to make one fancy, like the mad Lady Elizabeth in Miss Braddon's novel, that "the order of the universe was changed, and time was all to-morrow." I received a visit from my travelling companion of the previous day, and, after giving him a present of some English powder, asked him to accompany me to the Sheik, an aged Arab, whom we met riding on a donkey, for an Arab Sheik thinks it quite the proper thing to ride a donkey, though he may own the most beautiful horses and *hygeens* in the country.

The Sheik dismounted as we approached, and saluting us with a grave *salaam*, repeated his former assertion that he could not let me have a camel. I therefore ordered Mustafa to tell him that, if this was the case, I should leave the letter-carrier behind, so as to keep my third camel for the water-skins, and continue the journey alone, leaving him to be responsible for the non-arrival of the governor of Galabat's messenger to Abou Harras. This was an argument he was not prepared for, and he promised to have a camel ready for me at seven a.m. on the morrow.

May 26*th.*—Seven o'clock on the morrow came, but of course no camel came with it. The Sheik, who knew nothing of maps and compasses, had not kept his promise, believing that it would be impossible for me to go forwards without a guide; however, I soon convinced him of the contrary, by having the water-skins placed on my third camel and preparing to start. My host, the Greek, was almost as bad as the Sheik in trying to delay my departure, and related all sorts of horrible stories about the arid tract of country I was going to cross; but I merely mounted my *hygeen* and bid him farewell. He insisted on accompanying me a short way, in accordance with the Arab usage, and earnestly requested that when I reached England I would forward to the Foreign Office a petition he had prepared, begging that he might be granted the protection of an English passport, as he was entirely at the mercy of the Egyptian troops, and there was no security for property in the Soudan.

We were just starting, when the Sheik begged me to delay a little longer, as the camel was coming; and true enough, a very small child presently appeared, driving a very large camel, but the camel was unprovided with either saddle or driver, which necessitated another delay; and, at last, after waiting vainly till ten o'clock, I determined to put my threat into execution, and, leaving the letter-carrier behind, rode off with Mustafa.

Katarif is only a little Arab town of round grass-huts, but, being on the direct camel route from Cassala to Khartum, on the White Nile, it is of some importance, and boasts of two market-days in a week. This being one of them we had to make our way through a long row of open sheds, made of straw, in many of which the long cross-handled swords of the country were exposed for sale, at one and two dollars apiece. In some sheds squatted half-naked Arabs, selling red-leather scabbards for these swords; while in others such luxuries as beads, perfumery, red pepper, and balls of raw fat for dressing the hair, were to be bought from coffee-coloured Arab women, who would have been pretty if they had not had their faces disfigured by the three long gashes on each cheek, which they here inflict upon themselves as an *ornament;* for the cruel goddess, Fashion, is no less a tyrant in the wilds of Upper Nubia than in the drawing-rooms of Paris!

Besides the ordinary vendors of cotton, grain, gourds, &c., there were numbers of Arab cooks engaged in broiling most savoury cow-steaks in large earthen dishes, which diffused an appetising odour through the air, that caused many a swarthy Tokrouris, riding by with shield and spear on the bare back of his camel, to pause and fortify himself with a meal before entering on the lonely prairie.

Mustafa and I had not left Katarif far behind us

before we were overtaken by the letter-carrier, riding on the sheik's camel, and accompanied by its Arab driver, who, as usual, was forthcoming the moment we were gone. I never could clearly understand what can be the motive that makes both Abyssinians and Arabs have such an inveterate love for putting everything off till the morrow. Perhaps, when they have had more intercourse with Europeans, they *may* at last learn that if a thing must be done it is best to do it at once. There seems little chance of it at present.

An old Spanish legend relates that St. Isidore, who, before he became a saint, was a hopelessly dull boy, one day looked into a well, and, noticing that the marble was worn by the constant friction of the rope, modestly compared his head to the marble, and said to himself, "If a rope by constant rubbing can wear a groove in hard stone, surely constant study ought to make some impression even on *my* mind," whereupon he became a saint. Let us hope that some such beneficial change may one day be worked in the Arabs, only I fear their heads are even harder than that of St. Isidore!

A short ride across a level plain brought us to a little village, where was a well surrounded by a crowd of Arab girls and children, laughing gaily as they drew up the water in pieces of hide attached, at the four corners, to a rope—the only form of bucket known in the country. This was the last well on our road, so we loosened the girths of our camels and let them drink their fill, a privilege they availed themselves of by swelling to an enormous size.

The village was quite a pretty sight, with its round straw huts fenced-in with cane, shaded by palms and other eastern trees; while, lying in the sunshine round the well, reposed peaceful groups of humped oxen, and Roman-nosed sheep with enormous tails, among whom strutted a purple-headed stork, quite tame. But a very different prospect soon met our view, for we now entered the desert, or, more correctly speaking, vast tract of waterless prairie, that lies between Katarif and Abbou Harras, on the Blue Nile.

CHAPTER XXVII.

A CAMEL RIDE ACROSS THE PLAINS.

I COPY textually from my journal: "This desert is not sand, but mud, and nothing meets the eye as far as it can reach but the dead skeleton grass of last rain season, which rises dry and white in the burning sunshine, making the plain look at a distance like a gigantic field of over-ripe corn. The track is worn bare by the feet of camels and strewn with their bones. An unwholesome smell of dead vegetable matter rises from the cracks in the black mud, now all parched and baked, and reflecting back the almost vertical rays of the sun, like heated fire-brick. It is easy to understand how fever, "the pestilence that walketh in darkness and the destruction that wasteth at noonday," lurks on these plains, both when the tropical rains are melting all the decayed vegetable matter of which the mud is composed, and when the sun is boiling the blood in one's veins and the very air one is breathing is at the temperature of a baker's oven.

"Presently we come to the carcase of a camel newly fallen, his head turned towards his journey's end. Poor fellow, he had almost reached it—like how many men! A score of tufted vultures, holding council over him, are the only living things to be seen, besides the great saw-legged locusts, and spotted salamanders of a sickly yellow, apparently born of the mud, which crawl out of every fissure.

"But now we see a lake of clear water, not more than five miles off, and surrounded by trees, whose forms are distinctly visible, reflected in its mirror-like depths. It is only a mirage, though so surprisingly real that even Mustafa, a born Arab, is deceived by it.

"The red sun sets, leaving a broad golden wake over the dry grass, like the path of light it casts on the sea, and as the purple veil of night falls over the desert the sheet lightning lights up the whole horizon, flashing vividly round a dozen different points of the compass at once.

"I am still suffering from ophthalmia and the wounds in my legs, so make a short halt at sunset. But as we are to find no water for three days we cannot afford to tarry more than an hour, and ride steadily forwards again till two in the morning, when we make a second halt, lying down in our clothes beside the camels.

"Occasionally we can see against the starlight sky the dark silhouettes of some Arabs passing on their camels like the shadow figures of a galanty show; but presently a tropical shower—the first of the season—begins to fall, the large drops of which almost hiss as they touch the baking ground, and I take refuge under an ox-hide that I have brought from Galabat, till morning."

May 27*th.*—We rose with the sun and mounted our camels. The Arab riding in front on the Sheik's camel, naked to the waist, with his shield and spear at his side, and his long black hair waving to and fro, looked quite a picture. The negro letter-carrier with his white turban, red sash, and bright blue shirt, at a distance had the appearance of some extraordinary bird of gaudy plumage; but Mustafa was the grandest sight of all: perched on the top of a heterogeneous pile of kettles, carpets, skins, horns, and provision-bags, with my rifle in his hand, and the monkey behind him, which made hideous faces whenever the lurching motion of the camel disturbed its balance, and amused itself by picking out the cotton that served to close the mouths of some bottles of native arrakee, and emptying their contents on the ground, much to the grief and rage of Mustafa, under whose special care I had placed this valuable store of spirit. "I speak to him in Arabic, sar," said Mustafa despairingly, as if the monkey were a fellow mortal, "but he only make fun of me and laugh in my face!"

We now saw before us some great rocks rising like islands from the sea of dead grass, but though every rent and crevice in them was as plainly visible in this clear atmosphere as if they were quite near, it took six hours' hard riding before we reached them. An Arab passed us on a dromedary. He had started from Soog Abou Sin eight hours after us, and ridden all night. Happy man, having no baggage but his sword and shield, he could go fast, while we were condemned to three miles an hour, and even that was a quick pace for a baggage camel.

I was astonished to see an Arab on foot suddenly appear on the plain, but he disappeared as mysteriously as he appeared, and where he came from or whither he went I cannot imagine, as the eye here swept over a level plain in every direction. It was noon when we reached the rocks we had seen in the distance, and turned our beasts loose to get what sustenance they could from the dead herbage. I saw a guinea-fowl among the stones, and from this argued that there *must* be water somewhere, but the Arab declared that he knew of none.

I was vainly seeking some shelter from the sun, which being now directly overhead, produced no shadows, when Mustafa staggered up with mouth and eyes wide open, looking perfectly limp with terror. His dark brown skin had turned to a livid blue, and his flesh was quivering like calves'-foot jelly, with a spasmodic and perfectly involuntary action. I asked him what was the matter, but at first he could only point to a heap of stones, which, when I examined them, presented nothing extraordinary in their appearance. However, at last he explained that he had gone near these stones collecting dry grass and sticks for the fire, when a gigantic cobra, "four yards long," had suddenly reared itself up as high as a man in front of him, and turned him, as he said, all cold in a moment. Though the snake had not bitten him, and had glided away after merely rising up and hissing at him menacingly, there was no doubt of the terrible nervous shock it had produced on him, which was followed by a profound mental and bodily prostration, that left his system unstrung for a long time. He declared he felt quite unable to move from the spot where he was standing when the snake rose up before him, though he fully realised the danger of his position.

In a desert where there is no water, well or ill one cannot tarry; so, after little more than an hour's rest we continued the march, though the sun was now so hot that our water-skins perspired like human beings, and were fast becoming empty through evaporation.

Late at night we reached the base of Mount Sirgain, a mass of rock which we had seen from time to time standing out black against the horizon illuminated by the violet flashes of the lightning, that was playing all around us, as on the previous evening. Every now and then the night wind swept through the skeleton grass with a low moaning sound that reminded one of stormy weather by the sea; and indeed there was something wonderfully deserted and ocean-like in the great plain as seen by the lurid electric light, with the pale dead grass rising and falling in long waves before the force of the wind.

We only halted at the foot of Mount Sirgain for an hour, and rode on again through the night, like restless spirits, till nearly dawn. Once a thunderstorm swept over the desert, and our camels, frightened at the phenomenon, knelt down, and burying their heads in the dust, wanted to stop, but we made them go on, as our water was now nearly all evaporated, and we could not afford to march less than twenty hours in the twenty-four. At last, two hours before sunrise, we lay down to sleep; but, even as we slept, we had to keep one hand on the water-skins, for the Arab declared the hyenas were often rendered so daring by thirst that they would make a dash at a caravan and carry the water-skins bodily off.

May 28*th*.—At daybreak we rose again. All the water had disappeared, the skins which we supposed still contained some proving to be merely distended with hot air. Mustafa, having no water, had the bright inspiration to boil my coffee with arrakee, or white spirit, and presented it to me as usual. I need hardly say he very nearly brought my travels to an abrupt termination. Boiling-hot spirit, with the thermometer at 109° in the shade, and the nearest well far away on the horizon,—ABASANGA!!! as the Abyssinians say.

Nearly all trace of vegetation had now disappeared, and the desert was a dazzling expanse of white sandy soil, very painful to the eyes. Before us on the horizon we could see a level island of rock several miles long, rising above the plain, and looking not unlike Lundy Island, as seen from the Devonshire coast. This was Jebel Araing, where we should find water. The air was so perfectly light and clear that every crack in the rock was distinctly visible, and it appeared impossible that the *Jebel* could be very far off, yet hour succeeded hour of weary marching beneath a burning sun, and the mountain only seemed to recede further before us as we advanced.

The ground was now becoming thickly strewn with the bones of camels that had died before they reached the well,—for it causes a camel considerable suffering to go more than three days without water, and once a camel sinks down from exhaustion he *never* rises again. Our camels being lightly burdened had travelled somewhat faster than the caravans do, but already my poor *hygeen*, who, when he left the wells near Katarif, was distended to an enormous size with water, had become as fine as a greyhound, and I had to be continually tightening the girths. It was painful to feel the poor beast stumbling along over the parched sand, with his head down, his mouth open, and his dull eyes ever fixed wistfully on the distant rock where was the well. Twice he nearly went down, and I knew that if he did so he would not rise again; but he struggled on bravely, though he staggered perceptibly as he dragged himself wearily forwards. My three men were only little black specks on the horizon behind me, for I had ridden ahead, knowing that once at the wells I could send them assistance should any of their camels fall; but now it seemed that my own camel was the one that was about to succumb, and the confounded *Jebel* still looked no nearer than it had done when we started, though we had been marching incessantly for five hours. Fortunately, notwithstanding that I was horribly thirsty, I had been careful to preserve about a quart of water untouched in my leather-bottle or *zemzemir*, and this I now poured into a calabash that hung by my saddle. No sooner did my camel hear the

THE LAST DROP OF WATER.

gurgling sound than he turned his long neck and looked up in my face with such an eager wistful expression in his eyes, that somehow he reminded me of the Ancient Mariner. I bent forwards so that he could reach the calabash, and in a few moments he had drained it dry. It was a very small draught, but every drop seemed to give him new life, and he even broke into a feeble trot, compared to which the action of a cart-horse with all its joints dislocated would have been luxurious.

Presently we reached a few straggling mimosas, then a grove of green trees, among which guinea fowl were running, then we saw a troop of dog-faced baboons, and an Arab woman and her daughter starting away across the desert, heaven knows where! with waterskins on their backs: and at last the murmur of many voices and the roar of hundreds of camels, announced that we had reached the wells.

Almost in the centre of a long range of rocks before us was an immense natural amphitheatre, partially enclosed by perpendicular walls of red granite. An opening at the other side of this amphitheatre formed a natural gate, through which the traveller could gain the desert beyond, and thus avoid making a detour of many miles, for everywhere else the rocks sloped at an angle of $45°$ to a height of some six or eight hundred feet. The desert island, for I can give it no better name, was encircled by a belt of mimosa trees, and in the level sandy bottom of the amphitheatre twenty or thirty deep wells had been dug, out of which a crowd of Arabs, tanned dark as bronze, were busily engaged drawing water, which they poured into little mud reservoirs, surrounded by groups of thirsty camels. Like all the Arabs of these plains, their only clothing consisted of a narrow piece of cotton wrapped round the loins; but their figures had a suppleness, and the movement with which they swung their water-skins up from the wells, a peculiar grace that I had not noticed among any of the other Arab tribes, who, as a rule, are rather angular, and have a hard spare look that reminds one of leather thongs and whipcord. These people, too, had oval faces, and an almost womanly delicacy of feature. They drew up the water from the wells to a sort of rude song, that repeated by many voices swelled into a chorus and produced no unmelodious effect as it was echoed back with variations by the granite walls of the mountain.

Round about the wells, in the blazing sunshine, lay hundreds of camels, cows, and donkeys, which had been brought here when the other wells of the plains had become dry, and the ground was littered with shields, spears, bales of cotton, skins, and other merchandise, the wild-looking owners of which sat under the mimosa trees, waiting till their beasts had quenched their thirst.

The Arab, who, two days before, had passed us on his trotting *hygeen*, presently came and squatted gravely down on one end of my carpet. He was a Shukeriah, very dark, with a somewhat sinister expression of face, and part of his hair standing straight up, like a mop, on the top of his head—after the fashion of the country—while the rest hung round his neck in long woolly ringlets richly adorned with fat. He was of course naked to the waist, and the whole of his personal effects apparently consisted of a giraffe-hide shield, a long straight sword, a heavy spear, and the swift *hygeen* on which he rode. He told Mustafa that he could guide me a short cut across the desert to Abou Harras if I would accompany him, and I agreed to do so when the sun should be somewhat less hot; for, notwithstanding his rather sinister look, that the desert beyond Jebel Araing was said to be infested by predatory Arabs, and that it seemed slightly imprudent to leave the beaten track of the caravans, there was neither deceit nor malice in the man's face, and I determined to trust him.

When our camels had rested and again distended themselves with water, we passed through the natural gate in the rocks, and entered a tract of leafless mimosa bush, peopled by myriads of scarlet locusts, but we soon emerged again on the open desert, which was, if possible, more dreary than the previous one, being now perfectly barren sand and stone, with not even the skeleton of the dead grass of a past season to cheer it. Even the dead grass had been better than nothing, for it *moved*. Here all was motionless!

The sunsets I saw, while crossing these plains, were some of the most beautiful I can remember. A rich golden glow would light up earth and sky as the sun sank behind the horizon, changing the tropical desert into a wondrous Tom Tiddler's ground, the very stones of which seemed moidores, and the sands auriferous dust.

We were marching through the darkness, and I was humming a tune, when presently I heard Mustafa's voice:—" Master, sar, the Bedawee ask you not to sing." " Why ? " " He say there be many bad Arabs about; he not want them to know we are here. Will I give you your rifle, *Captain ?*" " No, Mustafa, I have my revolver; you can hand me my rifle should you hear me fire it." " Very good, sar; but you not leave me, Captain !" " All right, Mustafa." And so we continued moving silently through the night for many hours.

I know nothing more painful than the want of sleep when one is riding a camel. I had been obliged to take frequently small doses of opium for my ophthalmia, and these, together with the little rest I had been able to enjoy since I left Galabat, produced in me a profound desire to sleep: a desire that each hour had been increasing in intensity, till it seemed that the riches of Golconda, had I possessed them, would have been a small price to pay for five hours' calm repose. Several times I had nearly gone off into a doze, when a sudden lurch of the camel reminded me of the insecure nature of my lofty seat, and I woke with a start and a vague idea that I was going over a precipice, just in time to save myself from falling over the camel's head. The silence, the darkness, and the rocking motion all combined to make the necessity of keeping a vigilant lookout—I was riding in front—very trying. However, at last, between two and three in the morning, the Arab said he thought it would be safe to halt, and we made our beasts kneel down in a little hollow that concealed us from view. My camel, who had learned to know me, came shuffling up on his knees and slept beside me, looking in the half-light of the stars like a great boulder stone. I could distinguish the sound of a party of Arabs passing near us in the night, but they did not see us.

May 29th.—We rose as usual with the sun, and keeping the camels at a trot, made a long march before noon. Some of the atmospheric effects on the desert were very curious. The rocky islands we had left in the far distance appeared floating above the surface of the plain like clouds instead of rising from it, and the higher points of Jebel Araing being now only visible, presented the appearance of a series of isolated rocks, while at the same time the air was so beautifully clear that it was impossible to appreciate their distance.

At last we reached a wide tract of mimosa bush, among which scores of camels were roaming at liberty. They were the first living things we had seen since sunrise. Owing to the burning heat the mimosa trees were all dried up and nearly leafless, but they suggested the *idea* of shade, which was pleasant. We presently espied two naked Arab boys, who, after a colloquy with my Shukeriah friend, singled out a camel calf of tender years and drove it towards its mother. The mother stopped to let it suck, and, while it was thus engaged, the boys managed to approach and draw some of her milk into my calabash. The milk was very sweet, and, with a few dried dates that the Shukeriah produced, we made a delightful repast.

The mimosa bush continued very thin and scattered, and the heat was terrible. About one o'clock a hot blast swept across the plain, that literally made us gasp for breath; we could do nothing but halt where it overtook us and lie down for three hours till it had somewhat abated. I have felt the hot breath of the *sirocco* in Italy, and the *levante* in Spain; but, for a real furnace-blast, to make the brain reel and bake up the very marrow in one's bones, I never felt anything to equal this tropical simoom.

At last we were able to continue our way, and presently saw in the distance a line of palms fringing the banks of the Rahad, a tributary of the Atbara; this was a welcome sight.

Two hours after sunset we reached a well seventy feet deep, and as usual surrounded by a crowd of Arabs, one of whom I secured to guide me to the nearest village; for the Shukeriah, as soon as he found we were entering an inhabited region, abruptly bade me adieu, saying that he could accompany me no further, and turning his *hygeen's* head, trotted away across the lonely plain towards the east, where he was soon lost to view in the darkening shadows of the night. Mustafa said he seemed afraid to enter a village; but whatever he was, or wherever he went, he acted loyally by me even to the sharing his little stock of dried dates.

It was late when my new guide led us into his village, a small hamlet consisting only of a few round houses dotted promiscuously about, with cattle sleeping tranquilly near them; not a light was to be seen, and everything was profoundly quiet. I was led to the Sheik's house, and the Sheik roused himself and greeted me. He, like most Sheiks, was an old man, and he said he was very poor, but all that he had was at the stranger's service. "You have the head of a Sultan," said he, courteously, as he sat beside me, and approaching the taper to my face, stroked my beard; "it is for you to command, and all I have is yours." The compliments of the Arabs are of course as worthless as most compliments, and yet the grace with which they deliver them shows a certain refinement; for compliments may be truly called the currency of good society, and well-bred people naturally prefer to say agreeable things to each other to going out of their way to say unpleasant ones. It is just as easy, and much nicer. Indeed, it shows a certain vulgarity of mind to take a pleasure in pointing out painful truths. Suppose your head *be* too big, or your eyes *be* too small, or your legs *be* too short, or your nose *be* too long, the person who reminds you of these uncomfortable defects has probably not got them himself, and is really taking a mean delight in vaunting his own advantages by comparison. It were much more generous of him to tell you that small eyes are just as serviceable as big ones, that big heads—except in the case of idiots—generally denote large minds, that short legs are often more solid than long ones, and that

Julius Cæsar and his Grace the late Duke of Wellington were both remarkable for their noses—but this is a digression.

An *angarep* or Arab bed was prepared for me in the Sheik's own house, a skin of *dhurra* or grain brought for the camels, and a supper laid before me, consisting of a gourd of sour milk and some eggs; the fare was simple, but as the Sheik said, it was all he had to give, and it was offered readily with true Arab grace. In Lower Egypt, where travellers are common, the rights of hospitality have taken the form of a grudging obedience, or a calculating covetousness, very different from the traditional hospitality of the Arabs, which, I am glad to say, still really exists among some of the wild tribes of Upper Nubia.

I slept profoundly, for curiously enough, since we had descended to the Nubian plains, all the manifold varieties of vermin that rendered life a burden and a sorrow in Abyssinia, had completely disappeared. It was too hot even for a flea to exist!

May 30*th*.—An hour before daybreak I roused Mustafa from a heavy slumber and continued the journey. Our route ran parallel with the river Rahad, and the palms which grew beside the water were occasionally visible to our left. We passed three small villages, obtaining at each a guide as far as the next, and at last the white minaret of a mosque rising needle-like before us denoted our approach to Abou Harras, a little town situated on the east bank of the famous Bahr-el-Azerek, or Blue Nile (the ancient Astapus), which here traverses a vast plain of rich brown soil highly adapted for the cultivation of cotton, but, I need hardly say, uncultivated. The best houses in Abou Harras were of the usual round form, though built of stones and inclosed by cane fences, while the common habitations were merely square mud hovels. The Blue Nile was here upwards of five hundred yards wide, and rising rapidly. The water was not blue, but a rich opaque red colour, being highly charged with earth, which it was carrying down from the highlands of Abyssinia, where the rains were already falling. So thick was the water, that even when it was placed in a glass, you could not see through it, but the taste was fresh and pleasant, and it was a grand sight to see the great river hurrying past on its way to fertilise the plains of Egypt.

In the centre of the stream, just opposite Abou Harras, was a white sand bank, each day becoming smaller, and on the dry glistening ridge of this, five or six great crocodiles were basking lazily, while at the further side of the river a graceful cluster of a peculiar kind of palm (*Barassus Æthiopicus*), which I only noticed south of Kartum, afforded shelter to a number of large black birds with long curved beaks, who performed the duty of town scavengers. Not a human being was visible, for it was the hour when all seek refuge from the noontide heat, and the great river seemed to be the only thing moving besides ourselves.

With some difficulty we found the house of a merchant, to whom my Greek host at Katarif had given me a letter, and I was installed in a dark room with very thick walls, which rendered it cool and pleasant. The merchant came and said he would take all that I wanted on his head, graphically placing his hand there, and when the heat had somewhat abated we walked to the banks of the river to look for a boat to convey me down the stream to Khartum, now not more than a hundred and twenty miles distant. There was only one rickety old boat to be had, the owner of which offered to take me for twelve dollars, which he said was the price he would get for carrying a cargo of corn. I agreed to engage the boat on his solemnly promising to start that evening, and obtained from the Egyptian custom-house officer, who came to visit me, the promise of a trustworthy man to take my camels by land to Khartum.

The Arab population of Abou Harras were very dark in colour, and the fashionable dress for both men and women was merely a narrow belt with a long fringe hanging to it, worn round the waist; blue bead necklaces, silver anklets, and little red leather bags containing charms hung to the arm above the elbow, were also in vogue.

As the evening breeze rippled the river I prepared to embark, but of course the boat was not ready, though the owner hoped that *bukkara*, to-morrow, *inshálláh*, should Allah be willing, he might be able to leave. I told him that, *inshálláh*, I should be far on my way before the morrow, and sending for the man from the custom-house, had the camels saddled and continued my journey by land.

We followed the right bank of the Blue Nile, keeping as near it as was possible; but some hours after dark the guide missed his way in a maze of nabbuk trees and mimosas which so hedged us in with their formidable thorns, that, in the darkness, we could find no outlet, and were obliged to lie down under a tree till the morning light should enable us to release ourselves.

May 31*st.*—When I opened my eyes I discovered, about three inches from my nose, a gigantic spider, with a body as big as a walnut and legs in proportion; this awakened me thoroughly. We continued our way through the mimosa bushes, which here formed a kind of jungle, and tore to shreds everything we had about us that was tearable, my Arab mattress in particular suffered severely, and the cotton with which it was stuffed adorned the trees so profusely that they looked as if they were covered with white flowers. The camels too not unfrequently forgot they had riders on their backs, and made desperate efforts to pass under trees that were scarcely lofty enough to clear their humps, and armed with fish-hook thorns of most excruciating strength and sharpness.

Occasionally we caught a glimpse of the river: the wind had risen, and the water was rippled into little waves which, being bright cerulean blue where lighted by the sun, and dark russet red on the shadow side, presented a very strange effect. A pair of enormous butterflies fluttered through the air before us, flirting outrageously, and in many of the trees I noticed great flat nests, occupied by big black and white storks, which did not move, or in the least depart from the grave decorum of their manner as we passed, though our heads often reached within half a foot of them.

Passing a village where the houses, though of the ordinary conical form, were constructed of sun-dried brick, we rode on till we reached an Arab ferry that plied across the river. I determined to cross to the Western side, and joined a dignified Sheik who was standing on the shore with nearly a hundred camels, several donkeys, and a beautiful bay horse, which he wanted taken over.

The ferry was not very large, and as I calculated it would take at least a couple of hours to transport all these, I asked him to let my three camels go with the first boat load, but instead of doing so, he hurried as many of his cattle as he could into the boat and pushed away from the bank, grinning derisively. However, he became grave enough when he perceived that he was covered by my rifle, which I had at once cocked and levelled, and waving frantic signs to me not to fire, he returned to the shore and made room for me.

The embarkation of the camels was a most ludicrous process, as they seemed quite incapable of stepping over the side of the boat themselves, and each of their long legs had to be lifted into it separately by main force. The horse, however, leaped in with a bound that nearly swamped us, and we pushed away, my three camels with their baggage, eight or nine donkeys, the horse, and about twenty Arabs, all packed like herrings, making a good boat-load. The ferry was flat-bottomed and propelled by half-a-dozen Arabs, who stood facing the bows, armed with short paddles, which they dug straight into the water like spades and pulled towards them, singing the while a rather pretty chorus, the burden of which, though occasionally varied, appeared to be *He dey le-he y ho!* the paddles flashing out of the water simultaneously with every ho! At the stern of the boat sat the ferryman, an aged Arab, naked to the waist, hoary as Charon, and armed with a long oar, which he used instead of a rudder to steer the boat, like the old Roman steersmen. There was a considerable breeze, and, when we were in the middle of the river, a large flight of locusts was suddenly blown across it, which came pattering about us by thousands like hail, the air for many hundred yards round being quite dark with them.

After the most ludicrous efforts my camels were at last induced to jump out of the boat and clamber on shore; we followed them, and I went to look at a fleet of five flat-bottomed, one-masted, lateen-rigged barges, that were moored at this side of the river. I hoped to secure one of these to take me to Khartum, but in the first four not a soul was to be seen; however, in the fifth, I espied a Dongolar Arab (who, like all his tribe, had a remarkably villanous cast of countenance) lying on his back, lazily sharpening his long nails with a curved knife. He said he was not the *reïs* or captain; but after a little parley, he agreed to take us down to Khartum, on his own responsibility, for twelve dollars. I therefore sent my camels forwards in charge of the guide, and embarked the baggage.

Of course, when we were ready to start there was a delay. The Arab said he had changed his mind, and we must wait for the *reïs*, who had gone to a neighbouring village, and, *inshállâh*, would return in a day or two. Nor was it till I had threatened to cut the boat loose and navigate it myself, that we at last got under way.

"Sar," remarked Mustafa, with quite a Johnsonian air, "since we leave Massowah, not one of them black fellows in Habash or Nubia have kept his word; they all liars, sar!" for Mustafa, as I have before hinted, though himself two shades darker than the darkest oak wainscoting, affected to look on all "black fellows" with great scorn.

The wind had now fallen as suddenly as it had risen, and the boat drifted slowly down with the current towards Khartum.

CHAPTER XXVIII.

JOURNEY DOWN THE BLUE NILE, AND ARRIVAL AT KHARTUM.

IT was now sixteen days since we had left the capital of Ethiopia, and by dead reckoning we had ridden not less than four hundred and fifty miles. We had only halted once for an entire day, at Galabat, which left fifteen days of continual marching, at the average rate of thirty miles a day; a forced march, considering that I had ridden my own cattle all the way, and was encumbered by baggage. Of course our speed had varied with the nature of the country, and while traversing the great plains between Katarif and Abou Harras, we must have covered at least fifty miles in every twenty-four hours. After riding incessantly day and night across those interminable wastes on a swaying camel, it may be imagined how delightful it was to lie in the shade, under a shelter of matting I had rigged on the quarter-deck of the boat, and to idly watch the bubbles floating down the great " blue river," as it bore us slowly towards the fair Mediterranean sea, still more than a thousand miles away.

There was even something soothing in the very monotony of the brown mud banks past which we glided so smoothly, the outline of which was only broken here and there by a few feathery mimosas, a clump of graceful palms, or a cluster of bright green bushes, dripping into the deep, red-coloured water. The low hum of a *sageer*, or Arab water-wheel, occasionally floated drowsily through the air, and there was a hazy calm and tranquillity about the scene that made this gentle drifting progress down the Nile wonderfully pleasant to a tired man. All the worry and care and toil of the long journey through Ethiopia seemed left behind, and for the moment I felt as if I would ask nothing better than to glide thus smoothly on for ever.

Sometimes we passed white sand-banks covered with storks, herons, and other strange water-birds; I even saw a white bustard, of curiously hydropathic tastes, standing gravely cooling his legs in the water. A little farther on, a couple of lazy crocodiles had a bank all to themselves, and smiled benignly as we went by; I could not help thinking of the verses by the author of " Alice in Wonder-land :"

 " How cheerfully he seems to grin,
 And neatly spreads his claws,
 To welcome little fishes in
 With sweetly smiling jaws."

The Arabs of the Nile country solemnly believe that crocodiles shed tears after they have devoured their victims, and there is certainly a plausible look about the creatures that seems to say—" I would eat you with pleasure, but at the same time I would weep over your untimely fate with the sympathy of a friend "— which, however, would not make them relish the meal the less. I have seen the same sort of expression on some human faces.

Crocodiles have the tongue attached to the lower jaw, so that they can give no distinct cry, but when wounded they make an inarticulate noise, like a dumb person, which is painful to hear. They rarely go far from the river, and when I shot one he turned on his back and rolled rapidly over till he dropped into the water, where he sunk like a stone.

The way my crew navigated the Bahr-el-Azrek was beautifully simple; they just let the boat drift round and round as the current took it, merely pushing it off with a pole, when it grazed a sand bank. Sometimes we went stern foremost, sometimes broad-side on, now in the middle of the stream, now at the side, swinging slowly round till the view seemed a vast revolving panorama.

Towards evening, where the Nile's banks were low, we occasionally saw enormous herds of camels of all ages and sizes, which had come down to drink, and sunset was heralded by the appearance of a wonderful golden haze on the horizon. The water was as smooth and oily as quicksilver, and reflected each tint of the roseate sky so faithfully, that it was difficult to say where the one ended and the other began, while the sun appeared like a red-hot ball, half in the sky and half in the water. A few delicate violet clouds floated lightly overhead, and presently the gold and red mists of sunset changed to a cool greenish gray, as the day died serenely amidst a profound stillness that pervaded both air and water.

Those who have not been in the East can have little

idea of the exquisite blue of the evening sky, where the delicate crescent of the new moon now shone pale and silvery, with one little star near it, as depicted on the flag of Egypt.* Later the shades of night deepened, and the broad blue Nile seemed turned to silver as it lay bathed in the pure white moonlight. In one of its wild gyrations the boat suddenly struck on a sunken rock, and when, with considerable difficulty, we had got her off, and I was preparing to go to sleep, she bumped again on a sand bank at the east side of the river, and stuck hard and fast. The evening wind had risen, but it only blew her further on, so, after several ineffectual efforts, we were fain to leave her where she was till daylight.

June 1st.—At daylight I again tried to get off, but we were jammed under a high mud bank, and unless the wind shifted it seemed likely we might remain there till doomsday.

Besides Mustafa and myself, my crew only consisted of two negro slaves too old to work, and three young Dongolar Arabs, who *would* not work. Mustafa, espying a solitary native on shore, came and begged the loan of my rifle that he might capture him and bring him to assist us; of course I refused to let him use the rifle for any such purpose, so he compromised the matter by seizing my walking stick, and started in pursuit. The man came and gave what help he could, but it was all of no use, our utmost efforts could only move the boat a few yards, and then she stuck again harder than before. I tried to get my crew to assist, but they would not exert

* The Egyptian flag has a crescent and a star for device.

themselves in the least, and when I tried beating one of them, they simply jumped into the water and ran away. Being thus deserted by our crew, Mustafa and I had nothing to do but to make the best of our mud bank, and wait calmly till, *inshállâh!* as the Arabs say, some happy chance should release us from it. Luckily we had some sardines that I had bought of an Armenian at Galabat, and there was no lack of water.

I had been drowsily watching a young crocodile swimming round the boat till I had fallen asleep, when I was roused by a voice, saying, *Taïbîn hawâgah?* * and found a rather good-looking Arab sitting cross-legged beside me. He was the *reïs* or skipper of the boat, who, having heard that I had engaged his men to take me to Khartum, had followed me by land. I soon arranged with him to bring back the crew, for he did not want to lose his money, and the wind being now slightly shifted, we set the sail and managed to get off.

The level mud banks of the river, were, as yesterday, only varied by a few palms and mimosas, while overhead the sky was an unbroken blue, through which the sun blazed without mercy, but my shelter of matting secured me from its rays, and the rising wind fanned our foreheads and filled the great white lateen sail, bearing us steadily onwards. Up here the breeze was young and fragrant from the wooded highlands of Ethiopia. It had been cooled by the tropical rains, and scented by the perfume of the mimosa groves

* A form of greeting.

through which it had wandered, but when it should have crossed the great Nubian desert it would be converted into a burning simoom, wasting and scorching all before it, the hot breath of which might even be felt on the shores of Europe.

One of the two aged black slaves we had on board was called Jack—nobody knew how he had come by the name—and his fate was to do all the work, and be cuffed alternately by every one of the crew. His companion in bondage was an old woman, frightful to behold, who did nothing but grind corn, from morning to night, between two big rough stones, and smoke *ashes out of the fire* in a long pipe. Neither of these poor creatures understood a word of Arabic, and I was amused to see one of the Arabs, when he wanted a knife, pass his finger across his throat, a sign the negro at once understood. The *reïs* had bought both slaves in a lot for forty dollars (£8); but Mustafa said that at the slave market, which is still privately carried on near the Turkish bazaar at Cairo, their age would have made them fail to fetch even that much. I cannot understand why the slave traders ever thought it worth their while to drag the poor old things from their home up the White Nile!

We passed many crocodiles basking in the sun. They looked wonderfully like one's childish ideas of scaly dragons as they dragged themselves slowly along the sand, making a long furrow with their tails.

The sunset was again most lovely, and after dark we again bumped on a sand bank, not far from one of the little Arab villages which occasionally dotted the banks of the river. I sent the crew into the water to try to get the boat off; but we were firmly grounded, and had to wait for daylight.

June 2nd.—We got off at sunrise, though only to run ashore again half a mile further down. The wind was now blowing quite a gale, and forced us hard against the mud bank of the river. The *reïs*, simply remarking that we could not go on till, *inshállâh*, it shifted, composed himself into a comfortable position with the philosophy of a man to whom all days are alike, and who is prepared to sleep for an unlimited time.

I went on shore, but could not see two hundred yards before me for the clouds of sand that were being blown right across the Nile, and which struck my face like a scourge. The waves reflecting the blue sky on the sunny side, and dark red on the other, gave the river a purple tint of such brilliancy that no painter could have copied it faithfully without running serious risk of being called colour-mad by European critics.

The water looked fresh and tempting for a bathe, but I could see the pointed noses of two large crocodiles protruding out of it, near a sand bank not a hundred yards off; however, the Arabs had told me that the crocodiles only attack people in shallow water, and that they never attempt to eat a man swimming out of his depths, so, on the strength of this belief, I determined to risk a swim : for I contemplated sending my men again into the water to tow the boat from under the bank, and it seemed hardly fair to make them do what I would not do myself. I confess that as I prepared for the plunge, a horrible idea *would* suggest itself that even if a black man was safe in deep water, the glistening skin of a white one might perhaps attract the hungry crocodile in the same way that a silver bait attracts fish, reflecting however that the longer I looked at the leap the less I should like it, I dived in and struck out for the middle of the stream. It was delightfully refreshing to cleave one's way through the cool sparkling water of the great river, but the touch of each broken branch or stick that floated past produced a most unpleasant sensation, and, though I can testify in support of the native theory, that the crocodiles did me no harm, I came to the conclusion that their company was not conducive to the full and unalloyed enjoyment of a bath.

By threatening Abdallah, the *reïs*, that if he could not get the boat off, I should leave him and proceed by land, I at length induced him to wake up and exert himself, and after much tugging and pushing to a guttural chorus of *ley le-he ho Abdallah!* we once more got under way.

We passed a shed where some Arabs were building a boat; I had remarked that these Nile boats had no ribs, and now discovered that they were simply constructed of thick planks placed edge to edge and fastened together by very long nails driven slantingwise through them, and yet they do not come to grief more often than our iron-clads!

I think it is a character in one of Dickens's Christmas stories, who remarks that nothing arrives more regularly than dinner-time, while nothing arrives *less* regularly than dinner. I felt this painfully when the dinner hour came, and Mustafa appeared empty-handed to say the provisions were all finished; I even began to debate whether, if the voyage lasted much longer, it would be best to eat the crew or the crocodiles, and decided that it would be fairer to eat the latter, as, had they been hungry, they would probably not have scrupled to eat me.

It fell quite calm towards evening, and I had out the sweeps and made the men row all night. It took two men to work each of these oars, which were thirty-one feet long, and made of several pieces of wood lashed together.

June 3rd—In the morning the men went ashore and towed the boat with a rope. We had nothing now to eat but a little corn, which Mustafa mixed with water and baked; unfortunately I was no cook, and did not know how to make it more palatable. True I had learned from a modern novel, " how to cook an olive," viz. —Put an olive into a lark ; put a lark into a quail ; put a quail into a plover ; put a plover into a partridge ; put a partridge into a pheasant ; put a pheasant into a turkey. First partially roast : then carefully stew until all is thoroughly done down to the olive. Throw away the turkey, the pheasant, the partridge, the plover, the quail, and the lark. Then eat the olive! But this style of cookery was hardly suited to Nubia, and I would recommend travellers not to go there unprovided with a simple cookery book, showing the various ways of cooking eggs, fowls, game, &c. It may prove a valuable companion in moments of ill health when the taste becomes capricious, and raw meat and food swimming in rancid butter are as bad as poison.

At last a breeze rippled the water, and we were able to sail. The crew threw down their tow rope, and, jumping into the river, swam after the boat like porpoises. We passed a *shadoof*, the simple lever, with a counterpoise for drawing up water, which from time immemorial has existed on the banks of the Nile, then we saw a square building on the right, which Abdallah said was the telegraph station of Khartum, and soon after we were moored amid a fleet of lateen-sailed boats, near a row of flat-roofed houses buried in palm trees on the west side of the Nile—we had arrived at Khartum.

I landed, and wended my way through a straggling bazar, where I was accosted by a jovial merchant, who declared that he was the American Vice-Consul, though what his use was, as he only spoke Arabic, and there were no Americans, was a mystery; next I proceeded to the house of the Austrian Vice-Consul, the only resident European official, but this gentleman was asleep, and it was long before I could induce his servants to venture on awaking him. When he did appear he welcomed me civilly, and offered me the hospitality of his house. He was, however, so wasted by fever, that I thought I was hardly justified in troubling him, and repaired to the divan of Ismael

Pacha, the governor of Khartum, and ruler of all this part of the Soudan.

A young Abyssinian slave ushered me into a lofty room, with white-washed walls, in one corner of which sat the Pacha, with his legs crossed on the seat of a spacious arm chair, and his slippers on the ground before him. He was a stout, good-looking young man, and, after gravely saluting me with the motion of the hand to the heart, lips, and forehead, which constitutes the oriental *salaam*,* addressed me in French, which he spoke fluently. He asked me many questions about Abyssinia, and I was astonished to see how little was really known in Egypt of that country, and what wild and exaggerated stories the border Arabs told about it.

Long afterwards, I learned accidentally in the course of a conversation with the Egyptian Minister of War, that no sooner did I leave the divan than the Pacha had every word I had said to him telegraphed to Cairo. I mention this to show how eager the Egyptian government were even then to obtain information about the country they intended to invade, but of course I was careful not to betray in any way the confidence of King Yohannes.

Ismael Pacha was both intelligent and well-informed. On the divan where I was sitting lay several volumes of the *Monde Illustré*, which he had just been reading, and he told me he had been educated at Marseilles.

---

* I believe these motions are intended to convey the impression, that you gather up the dust from under the feet of the person you are saluting, and after pressing it reverently to your heart and your lips, place it on your head.

He had met Sir Samuel Baker when he started on his first expedition, and asked me anxiously if I had heard anything about him, as it was many months since any news of the adventurous traveller had come down the river, and a rumour had been circulated that he was dead. We little thought that, at that very moment, Sir Samel Baker was on the White Nile, only a few days' sail from us.

The Pacha could not conceal his surprise at the short time it had taken me to come from Gondar, and appeared rather startled at realising the fact that the King of Ethiopia's camp was not twenty days' march from Khartum. He was very kind, and placed a house, guard, &c., at my disposal, telling me to ask him for anything I required, and begging my acceptance of a splendid crocodile skin, fourteen feet long, from the Bahr-el-Abiad.

My next visit was to the bazaar, where some little European trifles were to be obtained, which to me seemed quite luxuries. A subtle smell of scent pervaded the air, as it always does Eastern bazaars; and the provision market was very picturesque with its piles of bright yellow and red melons, beside which squatted ebony-coloured negresses from the White Nile, adorned with monstrous silver nose and lip rings.

In the evening I joined the Pacha on the banks of the river, and we sat till a late hour, chatting, smoking, and drinking pale ale like two German students *unter den linden*, only the *linden* were lofty palm trees, the river flowing so smoothly by was the great Blue

Nile, and overhead the stars hung in the sky as large and lustrous as houri's eyes, while the night breeze that gently fanned our faces, had perhaps rippled the Bahr-el-Abiad at its unknown source.

June 4th.—At dawn the Pacha sent me his own horse to ride—a pure Arab from Arabia the holy. I never saw such a beautiful creature, even among the three hundred Arabs in Alli Pacha Shereef's stable. The neck and quarters were as broad and strong as those of a young bullock, the first beautifully arched, with a long silky mane falling on either side; the legs straight and fine; the nose and ears small and delicate as a greyhound's; the corners of the large dark eyes, and the inside of the wide quivering nostrils, a bright pink; and the clean cut hoofs and pasterns as shapely as a lady's foot. The colour of this noble animal was a rich chestnut; and he was caparisoned with a handsome Turkish saddle and bridle of crimson and gold. A bare legged *saïs*, or groom, dressed in blue and scarlet, held the rein, and ran before me, crying to the people to make way, *W'à riglak*, mind your foot! *Yemínak*, go to the right! *W'à, ya gedda*, take care, good man! *W'ái ya bent, dàhrak*, mind your back, my daughter! &c.

I rode beside the river, passed lateen-rigged boats being laden with Indian corn; and murmuring *sageers* worked by drowsy oxen, through cool shady groves of date-palms, and out on a sandy plain leading to the junction of the two Niles; here I laid the reins on my horse's neck and let him go, for no sooner did he feel the hard sand under his feet, than he was longing to be off. Away we sped at a gallop, but such a gallop! the Eastern legend which tells how when Allah had created all the animals, he tempered the lightning with the south wind and made the horse, describes it more eloquently than anything I can say.

When we stopped, the waters of the two Niles washed my horse's hoofs; the Bahr-el-Abiad, or White Nile, and the Bahr-el-Azrek, or Blue Nile, which here united into one mighty river. The banks on either side were barren and sterile, save for a few trees dotting them here and there; a little island with one solitary palm upon it, under the shade of which some cattle were browsing, divided the current before me; and in the distance a line of mountains rose above the sandy plain. The two rivers, though united, still preserved their respective colours, the western side of the stream being a pale opaque azure, the colour of the White Nile; and the eastern side dyed deep red with the earth that the Blue Nile was bringing down from the highlands of Ethiopia. According to the Arabs, the water of the Blue Nile is better than that of the White Nile, as the latter is highly impregnated with vegetable matter, but they declare that the mixture of the waters of the two Niles is the most wholesome to drink.

It was strange to think that the very water now hurrying past me might have washed the feet of Livingstone,[*] patiently trying to unravel the secret of the great river, the secret that Father Nile has guarded so well for thousands of years, though even when his-

[*] I did not know then that Livingstone was dead.

tory was young men were seeking to discover it. The source of the Blue Nile has been found buried in the heart of the mountains of Ethiopia. Scientific men no longer hazard wild theories to account for the annual floods that fertilise Egypt. The veil has been rent, and one by one the secrets of the mysterious stream have been revealed to the light of modern science, but as yet no profane eye has looked on the birth-place of the White Nile, and many a brave life may be sacrificed before this last vestige of mystery is torn away. Time was when a young virgin was yearly sacrificed as the Nile's betrothed bride: now a clay image is all that is thrown into the flood; time will be, perhaps, when Father Nile will have to be content with no bride at all, and steamers will ply on the Victoria Nyanza, and circular tickets to the source of the Nile and back, *viâ* Thebes and Memphis, will be advertised by Cook for the long vacation.

I saw a fisherman dragging behind him a Nile fish; it was a party-coloured monster, two yards long, and wide in proportion. Afterwards, when I reached Cairo, I was shown a fish from the Nile of a kind that had hitherto been supposed to be antediluvian, but which yet existed in the old river.

Riding back along the banks of the Bahr-el-Azrek, I came to the new dockyard of Khartum. Here the scene was very different; steam engines, lathes, steam hammers and punches, in short, all the apparatus necessary for repairing and fitting up steamboats filled the workshops; and the Pacha's steam yacht, with its elegant saloon, furnished with blue satin, lay alongside the jetty.

Quitting this noisy spot, I returned to the White Nile, and rode far up its banks, for I felt as if I could never tire of watching this great stream, flowing smoothly down from its unknown source beyond the equator, changeless and inscrutable, through wet and dry season, ever bringing to the main trunk of the Nile that unfailing supply of water which enables it to traverse a thousand miles of sand without receiving the influx of a single tributary. On the farther side of the river a few mud huts denoted a village; beyond this nothing but barren sand met the eye, except where, here and there, little green islands of tangled vegetation impeded the current, and afforded a home for innumerable water-birds.

The hot rays of the sun presently warned me to regain the town, for my head was only protected by a Glengarry cap, so turning my horse, who seemed to wish for nothing better than permission to gallop unchecked, from sunrise till sunset, I rode towards the town, passed low flat-roofed houses of dark Nile mud, round which goats and fowls were running, and apparently picking up a sustenance from the sand; passed brown Arab girls with bare arms and feet, adorned with great silver anklets, and draped in long blue skirts that but half concealed their lithe figures as they moved gracefully about with enormous water jars on their heads, their already dark eyes looking still more lustrous from the black *bórqua*, or veil, that hid the lower part of their faces; passed fat merchants, grown rich with dealing in human flesh, who jogged by, in spotless white robes and turbans on sturdy donkeys from Arabia the Holy; passed half-naked peasants returning from the *soog*, or market, balancing newly-purchased melons on their heads with the skill of practised jugglers; passed the little Christian cemetery, with its four plain walls, and a cross over the door; passed the Moorish burial-ground, with its white turbaned head-stones gleaming in the sunshine, and contrasting with the red minaret of the mosque hard by; till at last we again reached the Bahr-el-Azrek, and saw a group of naked negresses, hideous creatures from the Silouk country, with half-a-dozen rings in their noses and ears, sitting half in the water and half out of it, like hippopotami; and so, wending our way among the palm trees and water-wheels by the river side, reached home.

The gift of a red *tarboush* satisfied the demands for *backsheesh* of the *saïs*, who had run after me like a greyhound the whole morning, and came up in time to hold my stirrup as I dismounted. At Cairo I have known one of these men run for five miles before a carriage going at a brisk trot, and I believe the next day the fellow complained to his master that he did not get exercise enough, and was afraid of growing fat!

I went to an old silversmith to look for a silver-mounted Nubian sword; he showed me a very handsome one, but I could not induce him to part with it for love or money, as it was warranted to cut iron, and such a sword is valued by the Arabs of this country even more than a gun. I therefore commissioned him to mount in silver the Sheik of Gondar's sword, which he promised to do, *inshallâh*, in two days, though he complained bitterly of the short time I allowed him. While we were discussing the matter over the inevitable *finjal* of coffee, two veiled ladies came to have their ornaments weighed; the fair daughters of the Prophet wished to know the value of the presents they had received from their lords and masters.

The rooms the Pacha had assigned me opened on a cool verandah, overlooking the Blue Nile, where I sat all the afternoon receiving numbers of long-nosed Arab visitors. As I had sent Mustafa marketing, the conversation was rather broken; however, my monkey helped me to do the honours to his countrymen, and seemed to entertain them greatly. I think they took as much pleasure in looking at him as a lady does in seeing her features reflected in a mirror.

I was never quite alone, for a young Egyptian, who was supposed to attend to the telegraph, occupied one of my rooms. His only *real* occupation was lying on his back in the shade and killing flies, which indeed appeared to be the principal employment of the people of Khartum.

At sunset I joined the Pacha on the banks of the river, where he always sat in the cool of the evening. He had invited me to dine with him, and had three guests to meet me; Monsignore ——, who had come to visit the Austrian Catholic mission at Khartum, over which he held authority; the Austrian Vice-consul placed at Khartum to protect the interests of the mission; and a young Egyptian Bey, the aide-de-camp of the Pacha. A band of negro soldiers played some very well-selected airs, and dinner being announced, we were ushered into a large square room, adorned with a full-length portrait of Mahomet Ali. The Pacha pointed to the portrait, and said that all the Pachas of Khartum had religiously preserved this room in the same state as when the famous old warrior had held his divan in it, after braving the fatigues of the journey across the Nubian deserts when more than fourscore years of age.

At Cairo I had been told that forks and spoons were unknown luxuries at Khartum, but the brilliantly lighted table round which we now sat was shining with cut glass and silver, while the *meu* soup, Nile fish, meat, game, &c., might have done credit to a French cook; in fact, everything was as much *en règle* as if we had been in Europe. The conversation was carried on in French; the Pacha made a charming host; Monsignore was well informed, and had brought out a stock of the latest *on dits* current in society; the Austrian consul had travelled extensively with Munzinger; and the young Egyptian colonel had a new and original theory to propound—viz., that the physical superiority of the British race was owing to our due regard to the proportion of things, as he had heard that the tall men in England always married short wives, and the short men tall ones, thereby preserving a just equilibrium.

After the healths of Her Majesty and the Viceroy had been duly drunk in excellent Bordeaux, we repaired to the river side for coffee and cigarettes. It was more like being on the banks of the Blue Danube than on those of the Blue Nile. The Pacha said, with a smile, that he had intended the dinner should be followed by a dance of *Ráwázi*, or dancing girls, but he did not know what Monsignore might think of such an entertainment. Monsignore at once pulled off his broad brimmed hat, and politely disclaimed any desire to interfere with our amusement, only he would beg leave to withdraw when the *Ráwázi* came, as the presence of a dignitary of the Church would be hardly consistent. The Pacha, of course, would not consent to this, and proposed to change the entertainment to a war-dance by a regiment of soldiers entirely recruited from the Silouks, the first really savage race on the banks of the White Nile.

The night was a bright moonlight one. Presently fearful yells—

> " And sounds that mingled laugh and shout and scream
> To freeze the blood, in one discordant jar—"

came borne down on the wind, and we saw a dark crowd rushing towards us. It was the Silouks hurrying to the war-dance. They were all jet-black negroes of enormous stature, and seemed to take a fierce delight in leaping and yelling like fiends. They divided into two parties, and carried on a mimic battle, which was occasionally suspended for a dance of triumph, and a song of victory, as one party or the other gained some supposed advantage. Now a dusky warrior rolled on the ground, professing to be dead; now the flying enemy wheeled round, and delivered an imaginary flight of arrows among the ranks of their pursuers. Like all African music, their songs had a plaintive chord running through them, even when they sang loudest of victory, and throughout their wildest movements they kept perfect time to the music which they chanted.

They presented a weird effect, these savage-looking negroes, most of whom were over six feet high, bounding and yelling in the moonlight beside the tranquil river, probably forgetting for the moment that they were no longer free. Here they were dressed in the white cotton uniform of the Egyptian infantry, but in their native forests, higher up the White Nile, they had been wont to walk naked as Adam through the thickest jungle, their only arms the bow, the shield, and the spear.

"When an Arab Sheik will not pay me his tribute," said the Pacha, "I dispatch a company of Silouks to his village, and they very soon frighten him into sending it. The Arabs have a horror of my Silouk regiment." "Do you find the Silouks give *you* no trouble?" I enquired. "Not much," he said; "give them a few sweet dates and plenty of common tobacco, and they are happy as the day is long. They want nothing more, and are no more difficult to manage than children." "And how do you make the roving Arabs of the desert pay you tribute?" I asked. "Why," said he, "we wait till the dry season is well advanced, and then send troops to the few wells that still contain water. The Arabs must drive their flocks to these wells or see them perish, and we take this opportunity of collecting our tithes in kind." Truly the Egyptian government knows well how to tax other people, if not how to pay its own debts!

CHAPTER XXIX.

KHARTUM CONTINUED—DEPARTURE FOR BERBER.

June 5th.—The Arab merchants of Khartum, knowing that I must part with my camels before sailing down the Nile, would only offer a few dollars for them; but the Pacha, hearing of this, immediately ordered one of the Sheiks to buy them for sixty dollars. The Sheik dared not disobey, and this morning astonished me by offering sixty dollars for the camels, and at the same time asking me to let him have them for less. When I made out the reason of this rather Irish proceeding I gave him the three camels for fifty dollars (£10).

Mustafa had seen a boat which could be hired for twenty-five Turkish dollars to go to Berber, a town on the Nile more than two hundred miles below Khartum. The Pacha sent for the owner—a gorgeously-attired Armenian—to ratify the bargain, but as soon as he saw that it was a European who wanted his boat, he declared that it was impossible his *reïs*, or skipper, could have agreed to go to Berber for twenty-five dollars, and asked that he might be sent for. The *reïs* came, and was confronted with Mustafa. He stole a glance at his master, and then, regarding Mustafa with well-feigned surprise, lifted up his hands and eyes to heaven, and exclaimed: "I swear by my beard"—he had not got any—"by Allah above! by the Prophet, and by my eyes!"—a solemn oath with Mahometans—"that I never saw this man Mustafa before. How, then, could I have agreed to let him the *dahabeah* for twenty-five Turkish dollars?" Though I believed Mustafa, there was no going against such a solemn asseveration, and I agreed to pay a higher price. No sooner, however, had we left the divan than the *reïs* went up to Mustafa, who was looking quite bewildered, and, bursting into a hearty fit of laughter, asked him what he thought of his powers of lying. Such is the character of these people!

More than two thousand years ago a deformed Greek slave wittily said, that the only advantage gained by liars in the end is, that they are not believed even when they speak the *truth*. The wise sayings of Æsop travelled into Arabia, but though nearly twenty centuries have passed, the Arabs have not yet begun to profit by his wisdom, and are never so happy as when they have told a successful lie; nay, more, it is a common belief in Egypt that to tell a lie in the morning ensures luck for the rest of the twenty-four hours, so that it has become a favourite way of beginning the day. The only disgrace that attaches itself to a liar is the disgrace of not having lied cleverly enough, should his lie fail. If, on the contrary, it succeed, he feels quite proud and happy, like a man who has achieved a good and great action.

Even honest Mustafa, when we first engaged him, gave as a reason for requiring rather high wages, that he had a wife to support, and when we objected that we could not take a married man, as we were going into the interior of Africa, and should not feel justified in separating him from his family, he at once repudiated all matrimonial obligations, alleging that he had made a slight mistake, and meant he had a mother dependent on him. Afterwards I discovered that the only real foundation for this story was that he had a grandmother on whom he was dependent, the old lady being rich in goats and date palms, which Mustafa hoped to inherit. Yet Mustafa was one of the most truthful Arabs I ever met! One day he told me his grandmother was ninety years old, and never seemed going to die. " Why, Mustafa," I said, "you surely do not wish her to die; that would be very wrong." " Well, no sar"—with hesitation—" I not *wish* her to die, but I think she *ought* not to live any longer. What good she now, sar ?" There was something horribly practical about this, savouring of the principles of the West Africans, who, when a relation gets past work, eat him. I believe they do not think this shows a want of respect. What more touching tribute could the most exacting of parents desire than that his children should make a family vault of their own bodies?

Mustafa had once been put in prison for saying in a public place at Cairo that he did not think the Christians could be all accursed, since Allah made them so prosperous, and an old Fakeer was sent to explain to him the comfortable doctrine that the Franks were only permitted by Allah to be prosperous in *this* world, because they were certain of being damned in the *next*.

"Well, Mustafa," I said, "the lot the Franks allow to you is even harder; for not only are you, as you admit, to be poorer in this world, but they believe you will be damned in the next as well."

I breakfasted with the Pacha, who this time ate with his fingers, the meal being served in the Eastern fashion; but as I did not feel capable of performing this exercise with the same grace that he did, I begged permission to use a knife and fork. His Excellency pointed out to me one of the stews before us as having been the favourite dish of the Prophet. It did considerable credit to the Prophet's taste. "There are two things in this world that delight me," said Mahomet: "women and perfumes;" and he might have added, this stew.

While we were breakfasting, people were continually coming to the Pacha with papers requiring the impression of his seal, and cases that they wanted him to judge. One of these latter was curious, as illustrating the state of the country:—The wife of a Silouk soldier had been stolen; some time afterwards the soldier heard that she was a slave in the house of a woman at Khartum, and went to the Pacha to beg him to have the house searched for his wife. Though the search proved unsuccessful, the wife subsequently managed to effect her escape and join her husband, who was in raptures at getting back his ebony Venus. But now the woman whose slave the wife had been, claimed to have her back again, on the plea that she had been assigned to her by another Silouk in payment of a debt of fifty dollars.

Ismael Pacha, however, did not approve of this convenient way of paying a debt by handing over another man's wife, and dismissed the case.

We saw a little Arab boy making his *salaam* at a respectful distance. The Pacha called to him to ask what he wanted. "I want to enter your Excellency's service," replied he, as glibly as possible. "Well," said the Pacha, "you had rather a good idea there; will you go to school?" There was a long pause, during which a thoughtful expression stole over the youthful countenance, for the child was not prepared for this proposition. At last he replied: "Effendi, I *cannot* go to school," as if it was an undertaking quite beyond his strength. We laughed, and in obedience to a sign from the Pacha a *Kerwas* stepped up, and led the boy away to the college, where he would be taught to read and write, and fitted for a calling.

Hospitable Ismael Pacha wished me to delay my departure for a couple of weeks, and take a trip with him up the White Nile in his steam-yacht. He was enthusiastic about Khartum, and believed it was destined to have a great future. Gold, skins, bees'-wax, coffee, cotton, &c., were to flow down to it in profusion by the Blue Nile from Abyssinia and the Galla countries, while the White Nile was to open up the vast unexplored regions of Equatorial Africa; and Khartum, being at the junction of the two great rivers, was to be the store-house of boundless riches, and the mighty emporium of the produce of the African continent, which was to be transported by a railway across the desert to the shores of the Red Sea, from whence deep-laden Argosies, full of precious woods, metals, ivory, fragrant gums, and spices, would bear their valuable cargoes to European ports. In anticipation of these palmy days, he was building a palace on the banks of the Blue Nile, which he invited me to visit. It was really a very handsome construction, built of brick and faced with stone. On the first floor were the chambers designed for the hareem, and below the state rooms for men. On each floor a long corridor ran the whole length of the building for the attendants, and behind the palace was a large garden full of palms, pomegranates, and grape-vines; while to the North, the side facing the town, a park of artillery was stationed behind fortifications, in case of an insurrection. Of the dockyard I have already made mention, and the active Pacha also contemplated building a new bazaar, and opening a public garden, which would really make Khartum quite a habitable place. At present it is said to be frightfully unhealthy, and certainly some of the inhabitants looked more like sickly ghosts than human beings. But, standing as it does on a sandy plain, at some considerable elevation above the sea-level, with a great river flowing on either side of it, and bringing down each evening what little fresh air is to be obtained in this scorching climate, it ought to be fairly salubrious, and I am not sure that it is not more the crowding, dirt, and vices of the slave-trading population that have so long inhabited it, than any fault in its natural situation, that makes Khartum a hotbed of fever and disease. It is only fair to add that, as far as my personal experience went, I saw and heard of very little sickness while I was there. Nor was there anything wild in the Pacha's dreams of what Khartum might become, only the reality is very different from the theory in this land of mismanagement. Each palm-tree, from which the Arab gains a scanty sustenance, is taxed; the very water-wheels necessary to cultivation, and which, therefore, *ought* to be encouraged, are taxed; the new countries that Egypt annexes in the interior she only values because she gains new subjects to tax; she never really thinks of encouraging their cultivation —has she not enormous tracts of uncultivated country nearer home? For one good Governor like Ismael Pacha, a dozen who rule the Soudan only seek to make all they can while they are in power. Ismael Pacha told me himself that every improvement he sought to make was misrepresented at Cairo, and any day he might be replaced. Everything is mismanaged, rotten, and bad; money is spent like water on fêtes and palaces, but the country remains a desert; and even the dead do not escape taxation, for I was told that some of the taxes had been levied five years in advance.

Near the new palace I saw the fragment of a kind of Sphinx, with a bird's head, a bull's feet, and a scaly body. It had been brought from a village up the Blue Nile, where still remained a few ruins of some city which, like lost Meröe, had once flourished, but was now—save for these odd fragments of stone—as if it had never been.

Perhaps this Sphinx made a sculptor's fame, perhaps it gained him the prize for which he had toiled patiently for many years—the wife whose hand was to be the reward of his efforts to achieve fame. Perhaps thousands of palpitating human beings bowed round it in adoration; and the fame of the sculptor, the passions of the multitude, where are they now? A traveller, passing through Khartum, turns aside for a minute to gaze with a vague curiosity at the work of hands that have lain in the grave for thousands of years—that is all. The hopes, the fears, the affections and feelings that twined themselves round that stone are unknown to him; yet even now there is a chord in his heart that faintly responds to them, for does he not know that Nature ever repeats herself, and the feelings that stir men in the present are but the reflex of the same feelings that have stirred them in the past?

While I am digressing, let me mention a curious phenomenon—the wonderful rapidity with which we accustom ourselves to a strange country. We visit a place we have never seen or heard described before, and yet we are rarely taken quite by surprise. No scene, however new, appears entirely unfamiliar to us: we seem to have imagined it already, to know intuitively it would be as it appears. I believe there are few travellers that have not felt something of this sensation.

I had dined with the Pacha in the open air, and we were sitting by the moonlit river, when a party of veiled women glided noiselessly towards us. After they had each in turn kissed our hands, and pressed them to their foreheads, they threw off the long white draperies in which they were enveloped, and prepared to dance. They were dressed in the tight silk jackets and loose rose-coloured trousers usually worn by the *Ráwâzi*, and had a profusion of little gold coins strung on their foreheads· and in their hair. One of them was an Abyssinian, but the others were much fairer, being of that pale moonlit complexion one sometimes sees among the daughters of Arabia. Their feet were bare, and in their hands they held brass castanets, which made a gay ringing sound as they moved. The dance was like that of the Spanish *gitanas*, but rather more animated and idealised in character, the peculiar undulating movement they imparted to their bodies being of course the chief feature. The movement of the arms was also exceedingly graceful.

They were accompanied by an old Arab, in a white gown and turban, who played on an extraordinary kind of violin, made of a gourd, with a skin and strings stretched across it. There were also some women who beat hand-drums and tambourines, while a chorus of girls sang a pretty, plaintive, Arab air. On a table hard by two gigantic Turkish lanterns of red and yellow glass threw a variegated light over the scene.

It was a fairy-like sight, to see these graceful creatures in their light fluttering draperies—

"Chase one another, in the varying dance
Of mirth and languor, coyness and advance
Too eloquently like love's warm pursuit"—

on the margin of the broad Blue Nile, flowing by like a sheet of silver beneath the starry sky.

Suddenly the twinkling feet stopped, and the castanets were silent, while a new party of dancers approached. These were Arab girls of the Soudan, dark, lithe, snake-like creatures, with long black hair plaited after the manner of the ancient Egyptian dancers. They were utterly innocent of clothing, save for a narrow belt round the waist, to which hung a long fringe, adorned with beads and cowery shells; while round the neck of each was a cord supporting a number of amulets. They came forwards with a slow undulating step, to a low, sad chorus, sung, or rather chanted, by the other dancers, who struck their tambourines at regular intervals. The old Arab, with the primitive violin, got quite excited as he played, and looked as if he would like to dance himself. There was no figure in the dance; only the slow, mysterious undulating of the body as the girls passed before us, their breasts heaving like the waves of the ocean, every muscle apparently endowed with separate motion, their lustrous eyes turned upwards, their arms thrown back over their heads, and their feet beating the ground with a measured cadence.

After this three buffoons appeared on the scene. These men belonged to the lowest class of the rabble, and were privileged jesters, who said anything that came into their heads, even to the Pacha, sung impromptu songs, and improvised dialogues, frequently hitting each other sounding blows on the head to amuse the spectators. Their dress was a round white cap and loose blue shirt, tied round the waist with a cord : both very dirty. They had a look about them of the ancient Roman ragamuffin, and, like him, were witty, but coarse.

After an interlude by these buffoons, the *Almehs* danced again, three Arab women, who were looking on, being made to throw off their clothes and join, which they did without much hesitation. I noticed a young girl, almost a child, in a pink *Razieh* costume, who stood apart. Her companions said she was, as yet, only a student; but when, at the Pacha's command, she executed a little *pas seul* with fear and trembling, it struck me that she was perhaps more graceful than her companions, for she had not acquired, as they had, the art of undulating the hips, in a manner so extraordinary as almost to verge on the horrible. The poor child seemed quite overcome with delight when we rewarded her with a handful of dollars.

Before leaving, the *Ráwázi* again approached, and, bending low before us, pressed our hands to their lips and foreheads; for, in the East, however beautiful a woman may be, she is taught never to forget that she is a slave. The magnificent Pacha may smile on his favourite to-day, but there is a sack and a bowstring for the morrow should she displease him; and the eunuch who walks in the corridor carries a whip in his hand.

June 6th.—I was unwell and lying idly in my verandah, overlooking the Blue Nile, when a workman from the dockyard brought me a much thumbed copy of

Byron's poems—Don Juan, and Childe Harold, in Upper Nubia! I could not discover who the traveller was who had brought them here; but, after being so long without literature, it was pleasant to read again how

> "Juan and Haidee gazed upon each other
> With swimming looks of speechless tenderness,"

and to wander in imagination with Childe Harold through the old cities of Europe. The man who gave me this book had been sent to Khartum as a convict for three years; but, when his term of punishment was over, he still found himself a prisoner; for the governor of the dockyard had no notion of depriving himself of the services of a man who had learned his work, required no wages, and had become inured to the climate by the fiery ordeal of many fevers, so he kept him, giving him from time to time enough spirit to get drunk on, and then telling him that he must work off the fines he had incurred. The poor fellow was now come to beg that I would intercede for him with the Pacha, as otherwise he saw no hope of his captivity ever ending. Mustafa told me he had known him at Alexandria, and that, when he was a young man, he had inherited considerable wealth from his father, who was a merchant; but, it seems, a fatal predilection for the forbidden juice of the grape, and the songs of the 'Awâlim, had dissipated all the old man's savings in less than two years; and, to complete his misfortunes, one day a party of Arabs, travelling on the line from Cairo to Alexandria, complained that they had been robbed while under the influence of some narcotic drug. This man was in the carriage with them, and the evil character of his associates being known, he was suspected, and finally condemned to three years' penal servitude at Khartum, notwithstanding his assertion that, like his fellow travellers, he was also under the influence of the narcotic, and knew nothing of what had passed. He told me that he had already been through, I think, eleven attacks of fever, and he thought another year or two at Khartum would kill him, which was not improbable considering his love for drink. Indeed he looked more like a ghost than a man.

Giving the poor fellow a trifle—he was quite destitute—I bid him make his petition in the evening when I was sitting with the Pacha after dinner; for, without going quite so far as Moseilma, the rival of Mahomet, who averred that the soul of man is situated in his abdomen, I felt pretty sure that the post-prandial half hour was the best moment to make an appeal to the Pacha's philanthropy.

My next visitor was the old merchant who had introduced himself to me as the American Vice-Consul; he brought me a horn from the White Nile, as a present. It was made of an entire tusk of the finest ivory, beautifully hollowed, with a hole at the side like the mouthpiece of a flute. It was not, however, intended to produce any musical sound, the Silouks merely using these instruments like speaking trumpets to augment the frightful yells that delight their savage ears.

After the merchant, came the silversmith with the

handle of my sword mounted in curiously-wrought silver, and after him the Pacha; so, as it was no use attempting to lie quiet any longer, I rose and strolled with His Excellency along the bank of the Bahr-el-Azrek to enjoy the evening air.

The scene was profoundly calm and peaceful, and the sun was sinking through a cloudless sky. Just as, when the sun rises, all nature seems to rejoice; so—except in large cities—there is always a sort of awed stillness, at the moment when it sheds its farewell rays on our side of the earth, which is very impressive; and now—

> " Hark! from the mosque the mighty solemn sound,
> The Muzzin's call, doth shake the minaret.
> There is no God but God, to prayer, lo! God is great!
> And there is silence while the faithful pray."

But the Pacha did not pray, on the contrary, he clapped his hands, and a succulent dinner was brought us on a large brass tray, with plenty of Medoc and pale ale to wash it down.

Presently the negro band appeared and played some plaintive Arab airs, one called "The Rose," another "The Maiden's Black Eyes." I now thought it a good opportunity to obtain for my *protégé* his liberty. He had been hovering round us some time, not daring to approach, and I had to beckon to him frantically before he could summon up sufficient courage to come forward and make his request. At last, however, the petition was stammered forth, and the Pacha turning to me with a smile asked if I really took an interest in the case. "It gives me great pleasure to be able to please you so easily," continued he courteously, and then he told the man he was free. I do not know whether he made a good use of his freedom, but it was pleasant to see the poor fellow's delight at the prospect of quitting Khartum, a place which everybody except the Pacha seemed to regard as a sort of purgatory. Perhaps being a Pacha makes people see things from a different point of view!

I copy from my journal—

"*June 7th.*—Ready for departure. Ismael Pacha has given me a letter to the *Mudir*, or governor, of Berber. Have been to make my *salaam*. The Pacha walked with me to the shore, where he bid me a cordial farewell before I embarked on my *dahabeah*,* as Mustafa proudly terms the boat. Such a dahabeah! A little raised cabin at the stern, with two narrow shelves to lie on, may entitle it to the name; but I fancy it bears a closer resemblance to that primitive vessel we are told was constructed by the hundred-eyed son of Aristor, what time Jason sought the golden fleece, so I christen it the 'Argo.' In the bows are a couple of live sheep and a large basket of bread which the hospitable Pacha has sent me for the journey, the enormous crocodile skin from the White Nile is stowed smiling pleasantly on the top of the cabin, by knocking out half the sides of which, I have established a little ventilation; and at last we are under way, and, passing some flat sandy islands, bid adieu to the Bahr-el-Azrek, and Bahr-el-Abiad, and move slowly down the great main trunk of the Nile.

* The luxurious boats that can be hired at Cairo for the ordinary winter trip up the Nile, are called *dahabeahs*.

"I am constantly discovering new and interesting entomological specimens in my bark; cockroaches, hairy spiders, with eyes in their backs, green and black mosquitos, and in particular a race of fat soft white worms that *will* keep dropping on my head and into my cup and plate, share my cabin with me. If there is one thing I object to it is to have a large white worm in my hair.

" 9 P.M.—All day long we have glided past low monotonous mud-banks, the deposit of centuries. Now that the moon is risen, and it is bearably cool, I am sitting on the roof of the cabin making a footstool of the crocodile, and listening to the boatmen, who are singing as they row, a chorus that sounds like *Yas Allah ley, hi ah hey*, to a low hymn-like tune.

" *June 8th.*—We anchored in the night, having approached some rapids, on the rocks of which the *Reïs* of course managed to bump the unfortunate Argo; however, with daylight we got off again, and continued our voyage. Here and there villages dot the banks of the great river, and sometimes a solitary Arab may be seen riding his camel down to drink, or a quaint boat with graceful lateen sails glides up the stream—for the wind is against us—and hails us with guttural greetings as she passes.

"Towards noon the scenery becomes more picturesque; grey rocks rise on all sides from the water, which eddying round them forms into sudden whirlpools, with a loud rushing sound, and then glides smoothly on as before. The banks are no longer barren like yesterday, but clothed with bright green bamboo-grass, and crowned with palms and other graceful trees. Before us a rocky island divides the river, its bushes brushing the glistening surface of the water, and a dark cluster of palms growing in the centre. In the distance the red mountains of Royan, and Agaba, rise like islands from the vast plain extending on either side. As we row along, flocks of pelicans float gently by, as undisturbed by our presence as ducks on a farm pond. The wind is now so strong against us that both sail and mast have to come down, and the poor Argo is thus bereft of the very little beauty she ever possessed.

"As the day gets old, we pass the foot of Jebel Royan, a great square flat-topped mass of rock sloping down to the water's edge. It is the first of the range of the mountains of Agaba, a great chain of rocks through the centre of which the Nile forces its way; though why it should have taken this course, instead of following the plain that extends right round them, is a mystery I cannot solve.

"The river is thickly dotted with emerald knobs of tropical vegetation, growing on the projecting rocks, which form an asylum for innumerable beautiful white water-birds. Gigantic storks, as big as a child five years old, strut gravely along the shore; and on a little island of silver sand three juvenile crocodiles, no longer than my arm, are disporting themselves blithely in the broiling sunshine, while their more cautious mother swims round and round them with only her nose out of the water. So even crocodiles, the most phlegmatic of animals, obey the universal law of nature, that makes all young things joyous and playful! Why do they lose this gaiety when they grow older? Surely a crocodile, between the cataracts where steamers venture not, should lead a happy life, and even if it *does* shed tears when it devours some incautious Nubian, it must be with a softened, almost a pleasing, sadness.

"If I had as few cares as a crocodile, I think I could be as blithe all the year round as the painted butterfly, that lives but a day, and has no time to grow old and careworn. At present a vision *will* haunt me of some hundreds of miles that must be marched across the desert under a June sun. But 'sufficient unto the day is the evil thereof.'

"As the sun sinks in a cloudless sky, we enter the passage through the Agaba mountains; they are of red rock, and wondrously picturesque in shape. Indeed, were it not for the deep blue of the heavens and the brilliant tints and warm glow that pervade everything, I could fancy that we were gliding up some beautiful Scottish lock or Norwegian *fiord;* so broad and tranquil is the river, so grand the sloping mountains on either side, now breaking into miniature bays and valleys, and again rising abruptly from the water, in which their rugged outlines are reflected as in a mirror.

"Moonlight succeeds the day, and a flight of bats, emblematic of the night, skim overhead. The cool breath of the evening fans our foreheads, and enables us to enjoy the full beauty of the fairy-like scene; but my men—savages who prefer sleep to moonlight effects—

want to moor for the night, declaring that the passage between the mountains is full of hidden rocks and very dangerous. The *Reïs* testifies to this with so many solemn oaths, that I decide it *must* be false; and, telling him I will recompense him for the Argo if I sink her, take the tiller in my own hands and guide her on her moon-lit way through the windings of the hills for nearly three hours, when the roar of the sixth cataract of the Nile warns us with hoarse voice that it is time to stop.

"*June 9th.*—At sunrise we shoot the cataract. The current is impetuous, and some jagged rocks show their heads like teeth on the left; but there is plenty of water, and we sweep down without difficulty into the less troubled stream beyond. The Nile is here divided by charming islands, covered with trees and bushes, from the branches of which depend long tropical creepers in snake-like folds, that trail in the current, swaying grace-fully to and fro with the movement of the waves. There is one tree, with a delicate silvery-green leaf, the twisted roots of which, being cleansed from earth by the annual floods of the Nile, rise high above the water in the most fanciful gothic tracery that can possibly be imagined. Dark clusters of date-palms, feathery mi-mosas, and emerald bamboo-grass, fringe the shore, washed by the red waves that swirl rapidly onward, reflecting in every alternate ripple the bright blue of the summer sky:—a brilliant and beautiful foreground; while, in the distance, rise the rose-coloured mountains we have left behind us, looking like the gateway to those still undefined regions of the Upper Nile that have preserved a halo of mystery for so many thousand years.

"About 3 P.M. we pass some low ridges of sandy rock, and, save mimosas, there are now few trees. Occasionally we see a village of little extinguisher-shaped huts, and frequently mighty herds of goats, camels, and cows come to drink at the river side ; while sometimes a party of dusky maidens walk down the bank with graceful swaying gait, balancing on their heads enormous earthen water-jars, and beautifying and brightening up the barren scene as woman always does by her gentle presence. The heat is intense, and there are numbers of crocodiles basking on the sand-banks. Mustafa is very anxious I should shoot a juvenile one for him to eat, as the Arabs consider the flesh of the young a great delicacy. I believe the crocodiles reciprocate this feeling.

"My monkey, Jacko, has developed a decided taste for cockroaches : whenever he sees one crawling up the side of the cabin, he trembles all over with excitement, and pouncing on it, tears it limb from limb and devours it with the utmost relish ; fortunately for him, the supply of cockroaches on the Argo seems inexhaustible. When I show him his reflection in a looking glass it is amusing to see him stretch out his paw behind it to feel for the *other* monkey. This little glass is a luxury I got at Khartum ; in Abyssinia, the case of my watch was my only mirror for many months.

"Jacko is the torment of Mustafa's life ; and truly it is astonishing to see the spirit of mischief that dwells in his tiny body—a dozen ordinary Pixes, Elves, Pucks, Bogies, Brownies, and Wood-sprites, would not come up to him for cunning and perseverance in the art of wanton aggravation. When I am watching him, he sits demurely on his haunches, looking as grave and virtuous as a candidate for canonization; but if I close my eyes for a moment, my rifle, cartridges, water-bottle, clothes, watch, in short everything that is moveable, are immediately pulled down and dragged about the cabin floor, till the crash of falling things awakens me, and he springs back to his old place and gazes at me as innocently as a medium, when the lights are turned up, and he informs his audience that it is the spirits, and not he, that sent the furniture flying about the room. I have tried punishing him, but nothing will cure him of this unconquerable desire to 'make hay' of everything he can get hold of. He knows it is wrong, or, what to his mind is the same thing, that he will be punished; and sometimes I do believe he tries to struggle against temptation;—at least, watching him furtively, I have seen him drawing near to the leather water-bottle with the laudable intention of emptying it over my boots, and then suddenly withdraw his paw and turn his head away from the tantalising prospect, as if determined to shut it out of sight; but the flesh is weak, gradually the temptation becomes too strong, and at last he can resist no longer—out goes the little paw, down comes the bottle, splash goes the water, and he dances about with wild delight, till suddenly, perceiving my eyes on him, he relapses into a fit of such preternatural gravity that it sets me laughing and procures him a pardon for his offence.

"9 *p.m.*—The moon is shining brightly, and I have ordered some of the crew to row alternately till morning.

"*June* 11*th.*—I wake to find the boat gliding under the shadow of a long forest of palms.

"Like the mimosa, these trees are both beautiful and useful, and the traveller in Africa cannot look on them without a mingled feeling of admiration and gratitude. They are beautiful from the graceful shapes and clusters in which they grow, while the cool shade they afford, the sweet and nourishing nature of their fruit, the toughness of their leaves, from which the natives make many articles, and the pleasant qualities of the milk or wine that may be extracted from them, render them one of the most precious of the many gifts that Nature has bestowed on Africa. Indeed, a single palm combines in itself, as it were, the three necessaries of life in this climate—shade, food, and drink; and, according to Munzinger, the natives of the salt plains know no other home and no other harvest than that afforded by their palm-trees, which supply all their wants, and the wine of which is so sweet to their taste that the mere recollection of it will make them leave more civilized regions to return to their simple life beneath the palm-tree's shade.

"We can now sometimes hear the murmur of the *sageer*, or water-wheel, indicating some attempt at irrigation, though the vast plains on either side of the river still seem to be wonderfully little cultivated.

When every *sageer* is taxed, how can it be otherwise? Well may you—

> 'Ask the squalid peasant how
> His gains repay his broiling brow!'

while such a monstrous system exists.

" In Lower Egypt the peasant in charge of a *sageer* squats on the ground, merely goading the oxen as they pass him, and it is needless to say those intelligent animals relapse into a snail's pace the moment they are out of his reach. The Nubian peasant is more clever, *he* sits on the bar to which his buffaloes are harnessed, and follows them all the way round.

" We pass a canoe scooped out of the trunk of a single tree, like Robinson Crusoe's boat. Further on, a group of swarthy Arabs are laying a net, and presently we see Jebel Omalie, some low sandy hills to the right, on the top of one of which, the *Reïs* says, still stand the brick walls of an ancient house or temple. And now, oh science! the posts and wires of the telegraph come in view. When I was a boy telegraphy was hardly understood, and now in these upper regions of the Nile, cut off from the rest of the world by rocks, mountains, and waterless deserts, there are telegraphs and steam boats!

" Five days ago, at Khartum, I saw a party of black Silouk soldiers—men who a few years past were savages roaming naked through their virgin forests—being dispatched up the Blue Nile in a steam-boat, for the charitable purpose of frightening an Arab village into paying its taxes. And now all that I can write here may be learned in a few hours by 'wiring' to Upper Nubia. Truly I may close my journal! And yet the journey is not nearly ended. There are twelve hundred miles between this and the Mediterranean, and there are nearly three hundred miles of desert to be crossed before the Red Sea can be reached, which will certainly entail some suffering and danger to health, perhaps even to life; but science outstrips everything, and a message flies along a thousand miles of telegraph wire while the tired wanderer has not plodded as many yards through the burning sand!

"*June 11th.*—Another hot and tranquil day, rowing down the river to the merry song of the boatmen. These fellows * know how to sing well in parts, and some of their songs are very pretty, resembling more the Negro melodies sung by the Christy Minstrels than the ordinary Arab music. The Nile here is very wide, and looks almost like an estuary of the sea. The shore is fringed with trees, among which I notice the dome palm (*Hyphœne Thebaica*). The leaves are lighter in colour than those of the date palm, and the stem does not, as a rule, grow to such a height, generally dividing into two or three heads. The dome is a true child of the tropics, and does not grow in Lower Egypt.

"4 P.M.—We have reached the junction of the Atbara with the Nile, the spot where Baker began those wonderful hunting adventures so graphically described in his 'Nile tributaries.' The Atbara, the *Astaboras* of the

* They were nearly all natives of Dongola.

ancients, is here a fine river over 400 yards wide, and the limpid blue of its waters contrasts strongly with the deep earthy red of the swollen Nile. When I saw the Atbara near its head in Abyssinia, not a month ago, it was very muddy, but I suppose its long journey across the desert sands has cleared the water. A flock of pelicans are paddling lazily at the junction of the two rivers, and the farther bank of the Atbara is covered with long fresh-looking grass, and quite a little plantation of dome palms. Some way up the stream a tiny island is tenanted by a number of long-legged white birds, who are busily engaged catching the passing fish. I send a rifle shot among the pelicans, but they only fly a few yards and then float lazily on again, with 'that peculiar smiling expression which their enormous beak gives to them.

"The Atbara is the last tributary of the Nile: from this point the grand old river, 'The Father of Waters '— as Dr. Johnson calls it—' whose bounty pours down the streams of plenty, and scatters over half the world the harvest of Egypt,' flows serenely on through 12,000 miles of sand, without receiving the waters of any other stream to feed it on its way to the Mediterranean Sea.

" At night the moon rises through a thin mist, shedding a green grey light over the landscape, like that the Dutch painters loved to depict. The *Reïs* is very ill with fever, and I cannot give the poor fellow much help, as I have none of the necessary medicines.

" No sooner do I fall asleep than the Arabs leave off rowing and fall asleep too, they never can be depended on unless someone is looking after them. Luckily I awake, and we get under way again, and about 10 P.M. we reach Berber, where we moor alongside some other boats till morning.

"To-morrow I shall bid farewell to the Nile."

CHAPTER XXX.

BERBER.—DEPARTURE FOR SUAKIN.

June 12*th.*—Journal continued.—" The sun is rising through a golden mist, against which the mosque and palm trees of Berber stand out quite black. The town is some distance from the shore, as when the Nile rises it overflows its banks. The *Reïs* still suffers: poor Jacko, my monkey, is dead. He fell ill at the same time as the *Reïs*, and like him, I believe, of fever;[*] it was piteous to see him yesterday; all his love of mischief seemed to have gone. When I caressed him he looked in my face and brightened up for a moment, but the heavy eyes closed again, and the little head drooped lower and lower till it rested on my hand, as the lethargy crept over him, and this morning Mustafa found him lying quite dead beside my couch. He had often declared that Jacko was the torment of his life, but now, as the honest fellow carried the frail little body in

---

[*] I remember being told by a learned Russian doctor, who had studied the habits of monkeys, that he believed they are subject to the same epidemic diseases as human beings, and that when rheumatic fever is prevalent in a West African village, it often happens that the monkeys in the surrounding woods become so stiff in the joints, that they cannot run away if you try to catch them.

his arms, I thought I saw a tear glistening on his dark cheek, and he laid Jacko very gently in the grave we had dug under a sweet-scented mimosa on shore. Poor Jacko!

"I have been to the divan, where I found the *Mudir's* chief clerk trying some prisoners; he has promised to get me camels on the morrow for my desert journey. Presently the *Mudir* arrived in person, and of course gave me spiced coffee; it was served in rhinoceros horn *jinjals*, which gave to the hot coffee a mingled flavour of rhinoceros and burnt horn that was anything but an improvement. As the *Mudir* has not a house to lend me, he has established me in an unoccupied wing of the hareem, with a bath attached to it, and has sent me a sheep, some bread, and a number of large juicy melons, which are a great luxury. The jalousies of the hareem look on a pretty garden, where I can see an unfortunate prisoner, with two enormous iron shackles on his ancles, linked together by a heavy chain, picking away at the earth with a short hoe in the burning sunshine, and looking like the traditional picture of an Algerine captive in the good old piratical days. It is no joke to be a prisoner here.

"In the East you are either a slave yourself, or surrounded by slaves, and it is wonderful with what rapidity a divan will form itself about you if you have anything to do. I sent for my boatmen to pay them, and immediately my room was filled with scribes, whip-bearers, soldiers, attendants, &c., who seemed to come from nowhere in particular, and, as soon as the men

Departure for Suakin.

were dismissed, disappeared again as silently and mysteriously as they had appeared.

"And still the wretched prisoner outside is pick, pick, picking away at the hard earth. How different are the fortunes of men!"

Next morning, June 13th, I made preparations to continue my journey, and as we should not be able to procure food on the way, purchased two dozen small boxes of sardines which a Greek merchant happened to have in his store; with these, and two small bags of coffee and flour, I calculated I should be able to reach the shores of the Red Sea.

Berber is an important Nubian town, and has direct camel communication across the desert with Korosko on the Nile, and Suakin on the Red Sea. I decided to follow the latter route, in the hope of catching at Suakin an Egyptian steamer, that was expected to touch there on its way up the Red Sea to Jiddah and Suez. I was told that we might be a fortnight on the desert, and that the wells were nearly dry. So I sent Mustafa to buy water skins. In the telegraph office of Berber I found a Coptic clerk, who could speak a little English; he was a ghastly sight, wasted almost to a skeleton, having been "caught by the fever," as he expressed it. Full often does the black camel kneel before the threshold at Berber, and sooner or later the fever seems to "catch" all who stay there. If they do not take refuge in flight, it ends by carrying them off.

The *Mudir* came and presented me with a rhinoceros horn cup, expressing with Arab courtesy an elaborate hope that he might thus dwell in the habitation of my thoughts whenever I quenched my thirst. Rhinoceros horn appears to be held in great estimation here.

It was some hours after noon when five camels knelt at my door, one for myself, one for Mustafa, and the other three for the crocodile skin, the baggage, and last, not least, the water skins. I sent for a sixth camel, insisting that my Arab guide should also be mounted. If I remember right I paid three dollars (twelve shillings) apiece for these camels, which were to convey me nearly three hundred miles.

No sooner had we left the town than we entered on the desert, an arid reddish plain of corrugated sand and grit. At sunset, as at sunrise, there was a golden haze over Berber, and—a rare phenomenon in this climate— the sun looked quite opaque, as when seen through a London fog. Though Berber was enveloped in these vapours, we were now past the limit of the tropical rains, and the only supply of water we could look forward to in the future was that which might have filtered its way below the surface of the ground. At nightfall we reached the first well, where we filled the water skins, and made a fire of camels' dung, the only fuel on the desert. When the moon rose we continued the journey, and marched all night.

June 14th.—We were still plodding slowly along when the sun peeped over the horizon, casting a bright roseate glow upon the sky and plain. Not a vestige of vegetation was to be seen, my six camels looked like a

Departure for Suakin.

fleet of ships sailing over a glassy sea.* The crocodile skin was a great nuisance, being so long that one end or the other was always slipping down and tracing our path along the sand; what with stoppages to re-adjust baggage, and the slow pace of our heavy-baggage camels, our average rate of marching was little more than two miles an hour. When the sun got high, the water, as usual, visibly evaporated through the skins, which being new had imparted to it a most odious colour and flavour. But that thirst is the least bearable of all agonies here, we should have found it perfectly undrinkable.

Horace says that care sits behind the horseman's back, and heavily does she ride behind the hump of a camel. If I had not been hardened by a previous desert journey, the slow monotonous swaying backwards and forwards in the intense heat would have been insupportable: as it was, after this day's march the whole of my back, where exposed to the sun, rose up nearly half an inch in one enormous blister; but the human frame adapts itself to all situations with wonderful rapidity, and soon I began to feel quite at home on my camel, and in fact to rather pride myself on my riding; though I think I never experienced a nightmare more weird or fantastic than the *reality* of one of these beasts when restive. A refractory camel usually begins by turning round and round, roaring horribly, like a gigantic humming top; the enormous length of its legs—it seems

* "The camel has been termed the ship of the desert," says Washington Irving; "the caravan may be termed its fleet."

all legs—unpleasantly magnifying every uncouth movement, and the contest usually ending by its dropping suddenly down on its knees, and thus placing its rider at an angle of 45°; a manœuvre as alarming as it is generally successful. Whyte-Melville somewhere relates how a Frenchman said to him, apropos of fox hunting, "*Monsieur, nous ne cherchons pas nos émotions, nous autres Français, à nous casser le cou;*" but a camel gives you your emotions whether you seek them or not. In justice to my beasts, however, I must say that they rarely performed these antics unless their girths were badly adjusted and hurting them.

We saw in the distance some isolated mountains to the right and left, at the foot of one of which (Jebel Duquaiah) the guide said there was a well built of stone, so ancient that not even Arab tradition could point to its origin. The ordinary Arab wells are merely round holes dug in the hard sand, and innocent of masonry.

At 11 A.M. we came to some tufts of dry grass and a few dead bushes, white and colourless as the sand, under the meagre shelter of which we halted, having marched continuously for more than twelve hours. It was what a Spanish sailor would have called *una calma furiosa*, and the heat was tremendous, but as I had now no instruments I could not measure it.

About 3 P.M. we re-mounted our camels. The desert was again barren sand without a trace of vegetation, but the mirage spread its wonderful illusions about us, and from our lofty situation we seemed to see green trees and fresh lagoons on all sides. Curiously enough, the phenomenon was not visible when we stood on the ground, but this only increased the delusion, as it appeared quite natural that a lake which could be seen on the horizon from the back of a tall camel, should be out of view to a man on the plain.

At dark we halted for four hours, after which we continued our way by Cynthia's friendly light.

June 15th.—(Sunday).

"The Sabbath comes, a day of blessed rest,"

to those at home, but it brought not rest to us, for there was still no water. We met three caravans. At first they appeared on the horizon like little black ants, then they gradually grew bigger and passed us, only to disappear again over the sky line behind, leaving the desert seemingly more lonely than before. I noticed many women accompanying these caravans, walking on foot, while their lords and masters rode on the camels with their long swords and giraffe-hide shields slung beside them. So inveterate a habit is it with the Nubian women to carry something on their heads, that one girl was trudging stoutly along with a big round stone balanced on hers, which certainly appeared a work of supererogation.

We did not halt till it was nearly noon. There was not the least shade anywhere. I took up some of the sand in my hand, and it was so hot it nearly burnt me, yet, to my astonishment, I found it alive with insects. Without apparently a particle of nourishment or moisture, for here there is no rain, thousands of these wonderful little creatures, perfect in a delicate and complicated organisation, were existing in the desert sand, and apparently enjoying life too! Why they should be there, what their use was, or how they could possibly exist, were some of those mysteries of Nature that make man feel how painfully small is the boasted knowledge by which he thinks he can rule and measure the order of the Universe.

In the thriving city, the hive of his own creation, where the very heavens are obscured by the smoke of his factories, and every object that meets the eye is a triumph of his own ingenuity, Man sometimes almost forgets that he *has* a Creator. But when he crawls like some tiny insect over these vast plains, only bounded by the blue of the sky above him, his eyes are opened by the Majesty of Nature. He sees the least of God's works far surpassing the highest effort of his human skill, a sense of his feebleness comes upon him, and his heart is humbled . . . . No longer does he strive "to gauge the heavens with a two-foot rule"; his conceptions expand, and looking reverently and with wonder at the might and beauty of his Maker's works, he seems to be drawn nearer to that Maker's presence, and to behold afar off the lowest step of the Eternal throne.

In years to come, perhaps, a railway will traverse the African desert; and the traveller, no longer the tiny insect crawling across the plain, will feel like some winged geni flying over it at forty miles an hour. If then his heart should become elated with pride, and in the contemplation of his own power, he should turn ungratefully from the Power that made him—as Eastern stories tell us the genii did of old—let him take up a handful of sand, and looking on the perfect formation of its myriads of denizens, read his lesson there. When night approaches, thousands of brilliant stars will shine in the sky, and as he raises his gaze towards the heavens, perhaps his thoughts will turn with awe and gratitude to that Creator who, though this world of ours be but one of the smaller planets, has watched with such tender care over the creation of the smallest insect of the desert sand, and whose love, like His power, is infinite!

At 3 P.M. we continued the march. We had now entered a vast region of loose yellow sand, mottled by the action of the wind, like sand on the seashore where the waves have been. Into this shifting surface our camels sank so deep at each step, that our progress became even slower than before. Presently we approached a line of low sand hills, as soft as drifted snow, which, however, are dignified by the name of "Jebel Bab." * Crossing these, we entered a plain terminated on the farther side by a range of black mountains, and found a great concourse of merchants, with their camels, waiting to get water at some dozen small round wells dug in the sand, the hum of voices and the roar of camels contrasting strangely with the silence of the desert, to which we had become accustomed. I sent Mustafa to

* *Jebel*, in Arabic, means a hill or mountain.

mount guard with my rifle over two of the wells, as there was so little water that we were told it would be five hours before enough would collect in them for us to replenish the skins. In the meanwhile a merchant from Stamboul came and smoked his long *chibuk* beside me, addressing me from time to time in Turkish, which I do not understand. However, he seemed quite satisfied with an occasional *tāïb* (it is well), accompanied with a long puff of smoke, which I threw in sententiously as my share of the conversation; and I have no doubt, that if he judged me by the Oriental axiom, "Speech is silver, but silence is gold," he thought me a very wise man.

When the camels had drunk and the moon was risen, we proceeded on our way.

June 16*th*.—The rising sun found us winding our course through the chain of low mountains we had seen in the distance at sunset. They rose abruptly from the plain, which was still quite level, and were composed of a coarse black slaty rock that had split into innumerable small fragments, and gave to them the appearance of vast cinder heaps. Sometimes the level ground between the mountains was strewn with these fragments, and, save the sky above, everything that met the eye was black, making the landscape look inexpressibly desolate and dreary. Here and there, however, the yellow sand was still visible; and wherever this was the case, we found large tufts of coarse desert grass, which, though perfectly bleached and dead, was eagerly devoured by the camels. I also remarked some ridges of white quartz projecting above the plain, in dazzling contrast to the dark peaks all around, expressively named by the Arabs, "The Crow-feet Mountains."

During the midday halt, I opened one of the skins we had filled at the wells on the previous evening. To my horror, I found it contained salt water! For three days and nights we had been marching across a waterless desert, building our hopes on those wells, and now the water we had got from them was literally as salt as if it had come from the sea. This was dreadfully disheartening. So intense was the heat that we could not exist without drinking, and yet the more we drank of this water the more horribly thirsty we became. If we did not come to another well within twenty-four hours, I felt I must expect someone to become delirious; and as we were only three, it was not a pleasant prospect.

Byron, though I believe not much addicted to water himself, has very truly said or sung—

> " Till taught by pain,
> Men really know not what good water's worth ;
> If you had been in Turkey or in Spain,
> Or with a famished boat's crew had your berth,
> Or in the desert heard the camel's bell,
> You'd wish yourself where Truth is—in a well."

I cannot tell why the wells at Jebel Bab, which are on an elevated plain more than a hundred miles from the sea, should have been salt; but not unfrequently the water found below the surface of the desert has a somewhat saline and bitter taste, and I suppose the fact of there being scarcely any water in these wells accounted for the salt being so concentrated.

In the course of the afternoon march we met a party of Arabs mounted on trotting *hygeens*, or dromedaries. Our first care was naturally to inquire the distance to the next well. They said they had left it on the previous day, at noon.

The sunset over the black desert, as I called this tract of country, was very striking. The sky was blue, green, and gold; while, for the first time, some feathery orange clouds floated over head.

When darkness enveloped the scene, we stretched ourselves on the ground, each beside his camel, to snatch a few hours' sleep. But soon we were aroused by the sound of voices singing afar off, and presently we could see a great caravan, of nearly seventy women and about twenty men, gliding past us in the starlight, as ghost-like and shadowy as

"Fancy forms of midnight cloud."

These people were going to the holy shrines of Mecca, not to pray, but to beg: their plan being to camp near each village or town, and send out all their children and old people to ask for food, money, &c., which are liberally bestowed by pious Mahomedans. The whole party was walking on foot, and they had only seven young camels with them to carry their supply of water and grain; for this reason they travelled at night to avoid the heat.

Two hours before dawn we continued our march.

June 17th.—We were still travelling through a labyrinth of low mountains, which the guide said extended in successive ranges almost to the shores of the Red Sea. The plain between them was level, as before; and we occasionally entered vast amphitheatres of sand, some twenty or thirty miles in circumference, round which the hills formed a nearly perfect circle. Here and there grew tufts of the desert grass, or a few stunted thorn-bushes might be seen, but all leafless and dead.

The vertical rays of the June sun overhead were hardly more powerful than the fierce heat that was reflected up in our faces from the white sandy plain. However, all living things are fitted for the countries they inhabit, and Nature has given to the camel, giraffe, gazelle, and even the Arabs of the desert, long thick under eyelashes, especially calculated to screen the eye from this upward glare; while the natives of colder climes are rarely so protected.

Ever since leaving Berber, our path had been strewn with the carcases of innumerable dead camels, whose remains alone would have been a sufficient guide to the caravan route across the desert. They presented a ghastly sight, for here were no hyenas to devour them, and the skin had shrivelled up in the sun like parchment, with occasionally a large bleached bone protruding through it. Nor were there wanting still sadder traces of mortality. We had passed many a little oval ring of stones, with a fragment of rock standing upright at one end, which marked the resting-place of those nameless travellers who had perished on the way from fatigue or thirst; and such deaths are not uncommon among the poorer Arabs.

It was sad to look on the scene of these lonely deaths in the desert, to see the dead camels half buried in the sand, and to think of the weary traveller lying down never to rise again, perhaps utterly alone in the midst of this silent waste, or perhaps with some companion nearly as exhausted as himself, who yet paused to scrape with pious care a shallow hole in the sand for his friend, and to place a stone at the head of his grave, before continuing that journey which for him too may have ended in death.

Has not the poet said—

> "If from society we learn to live,
> 'Tis solitude should teach us how to die !"

At night, when our camels swerved aside from one of these isolated gravestones, revealed by the pale light of the stars, it was easy to imagine that the ghost which, according to Eastern tradition, sits at the head of each tomb, was for a moment visible to mortal gaze.*

All through the day's march we saw no signs of a well, and were forced to drink the salt water, into which I put quantities of citric acid, thus in some degree counteracting its bad effects. Nor was it till many hours after nightfall that the welcome gleam of a fire and the barking of dogs announced our approach to some human habitation.

* There is a belief in the East that the ghosts of the departed sit at the heads of their graves, invisible to man.

Before a line of low Arab tents we found a half-naked girl, grinding corn between two rough stones; and hard by was a well containing the first *fresh* water we had met with for five days. Here we slept till daybreak, as the guide said the road beyond was too rough for night travelling.

June 18*th.*—Mountains to the right, mountains to the left, mountains in front; relieved, however, by a few trees. We crossed the dry bed of the Arayab, a river which only starts into life for a brief space when the tropical rains are falling up the country, but nevertheless lives sometimes to reach the sea. Our path still traversed the level plain, the guide's assertion about its roughness having been, as usual, false. To punish him, and make up for lost time, I marched till past noon, when the heat became so intense that he, though a native of the desert, implored me to halt, which I did beside some great blocks of composite rock, piled one on the top of the other in the midst of a sandy plain, as if placed there by some race of Titans. In the crevices of these stones were many colonies of bats.

Since leaving Berber I had made a rule of only halting twice in every twenty-four hours, the first halt being during the hottest part of the day—from 11 A.M. to 3 P.M., and the second from 8 P.M. to midnight. At each halt I ate a small box of sardines, drank a cup of coffee, smoked a pipe, and enjoyed three hours' sleep. The remaining sixteen hours of the day were devoted to steady marching.

" *Is maith 'n cocair an t-ocras* "—Hunger is a good

cook—said the Earl of Mar, when he made crowdie in the heel of his shoe. But a limited ration of sardines, and *toujours* sardines and nothing else, had become somewhat monotonous, and I have never been able to look at these delicate fish since without a shudder.

I found that if I limited myself to two pipes a-day, the tobacco served as an excellent soporific, to counteract the exciting tendencies of the coffee, and enabled me to fall asleep at once. By drinking, when possible, plenty of water, I kept myself fresh and cool, and was able to support the heat as well, or better, than the Arabs; and, though I sometimes drank as much as two gallons of water in the day, it never did me the slightest harm. This I attribute to the fact that my Abyssinian water-bottle was of greased leather, and kept the water at the normal temperature of the outer air, so that it produced no chill on the stomach. The Arab *zemzemirs* of porous leather, which render the water delightfully cool by evaporation, are most dangerous; for nothing is so certain to bring on disease in this climate as the practice of imbibing cold fluids when the body is hot.

At 3 P.M. we continued the march across a wide tract of arid sand, bounded by a range of mountains of more majestic dimensions than any we had as yet seen. Three white gazelles scampered across the plain, far out of range.

As the Norwegian hare turns white when the winter snow is on the *field*, so in Africa the gazelles, birds, lizards, and even insects that are found on the desert, take the same light colour as the sand; while, among the flowering trees and long yellow grass of the jungle, their tints are rich and varied.

It was not till we were close under the chain of mountains before us that any way through them was visible; then we discovered a pass full of luxuriant vegetation—a truly refreshing sight. We crossed the dry beds of three streams, children of the thunderstorm, the secret of whose birth and death was known only to the mountain peaks and the thirsty sands, for the guide could tell nothing of where they came from, or whither they went, save that they never reached the sea.

We met a wild-looking Shoho Arab, a friend of the guide, who wished us to halt that he might stay with us, and watch through the night, lest any of his fellow mountaineers, "intercepters of the way," as he termed them, should approach on a predatory expedition. It, however, struck me that the spot he proposed for an encampment would be very *unfavourable* in case of an attack, and I, therefore, determined to push on to the next well on the main caravan route. Presently a party of merchants passed us, who gave us the not very cheering intelligence that they had already been nine days coming from Suakin; and at last we reached a well, where we halted till the moon rose.

June 19*th*.—The moon, "sweet regent of the sky," as an old balladist calls her, was waning fast, and lighted the path but dimly. We passed several Arab burial grounds, " villages of the silent," laid close beside the caravan route, for the Mussulman does not like to sleep far from the haunts of man, and has his grave placed where there shall be many passers-by. We also came to a desert mosque of the simplest possible form, *i. e.*, a little quadrilateral traced on the ground with four rows of pebbles, which, on the eastern side, formed a neck leading to three bigger stones set upright, so as to face the direction of Mecca. This was the holy of holies, and the passing merchant, deliberately kicking off his slippers, steps within the line of pebbles, and, turning towards the three stones, prostates himself in prayer; and certainly the followers of the Prophet do say their prayers with exemplary regularity; but why the Arabs should employ *three* stones to indicate the holy places of these primitive mosques is a point I cannot explain.

Following for some hours the dry bed of a river called Ou-Carrin, which must sometimes attain considerable dimensions, we crossed the shoulder of a hill before us, and entered another great plain, bounded in the distance by fresh ranges of mountains. My entrance into this sandy waste was more abrupt than dignified, for my camel, finding the girths were galling him, dropped suddenly down and shot me into it head foremost.

We were all day crossing the plain, and met with no incident worth mention. Sometimes a solitary Arab would pass and pause for a moment to look at our little caravan. The Nubian Arab is a fine type of "the child of Nature," untamed by civilisation; and, as he strides across the plain, his graceful sinewy figure erect and unconfined, save by the kilt of home-spun cotton twisted round his loins, his leather buckler at his back, his spear in his hand, and his long black ringlets flowing behind him, he looks every inch the free-born son of the desert, and has a dignity about him that he seems to derive from the majestic grandeur of the scenes among which his life is passed. He is courteous too, and rarely fails to greet with friendly *salaam* the stranger whom he may chance to meet.

Nothing can be more pure or delightful than the air on these great plains; and, barren and waterless though they often are, there is a freedom about the rolling waste of sand, and a wild beauty in the mountains which rise like islands above it, changing their tints with every hour of the day, that lends a peculiar charm to the desert, and makes one soon begin to love it as a sailor loves the ocean. All through the year the blue sky remains unclouded, and yet the desert is not monotonous. As a hundred shades of expression chase each other across the face of a dreamer, the aspect of the desert is ever varying for those who know it well, and it is always beautiful. Beautiful in the early morning, when the newly-risen sun glances over the horizon, and the blush of Aurora is reflected by rocky peaks and glistening sand. Beautiful at noon, when the whole atmosphere quivers with heat, and the distant mountains look as if they were floating in the air, and the witchery of the mirage turns the arid desert into a charming park. Beautiful at eve, when the violet shadows of night creep softly over the plain which but a moment before was turned to gold by the setting sun. Beautiful at night, when thousands of stars are shining on it, bright as the regard of angels watching over the sleeping earth. And beautifully grand, as the tempest sweeps across it, and the heavens are dark with

> " ——That crimson haze,
> By which the prostrate caravan is aw'd
> In the red desert, when the wind's abroad."

I cannot understand how men who have lost fame and fortune, can remain at home sinking lower and lower till they become a disgrace to their families, and a burden to their friends. Were I in such an unfortunate position, I think I would beg, borrow, or steal a rifle, and come to these plains of the Soudan, to join the Arabs in their wild hunter-life on the banks of the Atbara. I would seek the friendship of some chief, and, while helping his people in the chase, strive to promote their happiness at home, and rejoice that, though weak and erring myself, I was still able to do some good among these rude tribes, while enjoying all the pleasures of a sportsman's life.

CHAPTER XXXI.

DESERT JOURNEY CONTINUED.—THE STORY OF LEILA.

June 20th.—We had halted at dark near the foot of the mountains, and I continued the march before the moon rose, much to the disgust of the guide. The night was lovely, and the stars—

"Which are the poetry of heaven—"

were shining with a wonderful brilliancy.

" There is an hour when angels keep
Familiar watch o'er men ; "

and I have always associated this beautiful thought with that period between midnight and dawn, when the current of our life is feeblest, and millions of human beings are lying helpless in sleep. Presently, over the farthest range of mountains there appeared a bright gleam of light, as from a watch fire; a few moments later the thin crescent of the moon rose through the clear ether like a silver boat, and the stars veiled their lustre before their queen.

The guide descended from his camel to prostrate himself to the risen moon, and then rode on again, chanting in a low tone some wild Arab song or invocation to it. I wish I could convey even a faint idea of the beauty of these nights on the desert; alas, my pen is too feeble to do so, and I can only say, like Childe Harold:

"And this is night, *most glorious* is night!"

Those who have been long with Nature for their sole companion, alone know what intense pleasure it is to watch every change in her varying face.

And now a few faint purple clouds floated in the sky, which was of the purest azure, and the morning star ascended slowly in all its beauty, like a single diamond in a field of blue enamel. Then came the sun, flooding the landscape with its warm yellow rays, and infusing new life into all our veins.

We were riding through a narrow gorge in the mountains, along the bed of a torrent. The sand was apparently quite dry, but by digging with a spear to a depth of two feet we came to water, which, when the sand settled, was clear and good. I discovered that I had only one box of sardines remaining, and as dinner depended on our procuring some game, it was with much pleasure that I espied a fine buck gazelle, on the side of a neighbouring mountain, and I stalked him with great care. I had sighted behind the shoulder, but I suppose my anxiety to secure a dinner made my hand less steady than usual, for the bullet struck the middle of the haunch; however the gazelle dropped at once, and I ran forward to secure my prize. The conical rifle-bullet had gone right through, for there was blood spurting from the wound on the reverse side, but strange to say, the gazelle was not even crippled, and when I was close upon him he rose and bounded up the mountain, as if nothing had happened. Forgetting the heat of the sun, and only remembering dinner, I gave chase, sometimes catching sight of him, sometimes following the blood trail; but, after climbing over half the mountain, I had the disappointment of finding that my dinner had "gone away," and, like the King of France, had to march sadly down again. Fortunately we met, shortly afterwards, some Hadarba Arabs tending a flock of sheep, one of which I bought for three quarters of a dollar; the owner having no change, cheerfully offered to accompany me five miles to get it at his camp, an offer I did not think worth accepting. The round shields of these Arabs were made from the hide of the camel-leopard, which is quite white and very tough. With some difficulty I persuaded one of them to part with his shield, spear, and knife, which formed his complete armament. For these and the sheep I paid five dollars (£1).

At noon we emerged from the mountains on a great plain of sand. The sun was so powerful that I could hardly bear to touch the butt of my rifle, and I had to loosen with my hunting knife all the screws of the lock, as the metal had expanded to such a degree that the springs would no longer work.

While we were travelling across this plain in the afternoon, I saw for the first time those pillars of sand of which Bruce gives so dreadful an account. They were certainly an imposing sight. A sort of whirlwind caught up the loose sand, and raised it in great spiral columns over two hundred feet high, which sped across the plain with amazing velocity, now breaking and disappearing in a shower of dust, only to rise up again in some other spot to a greater height than before; and, when three or four of these gigantic pillars advanced in line, casting their shadows before them, the effect was very striking. I do not wonder at the simple Arabs' believing that the powerful pre-Adamite race of genii traverse the deserts on the wings of the *zo-ba'ha* or whirlwind, enveloped in these flying columns of sand, and it is natural they should regard them with some awe; but there is really little danger of a caravan, or even a single traveller, being overwhelmed by them beyond the possibility of escape.

I remember once on a stormy day in the North Sea, about a day's sail from Christiansand, on the Norwegian coast, seeing nine waterspouts come sweeping across the ocean towards us at the same time, like a line of black soldiers. The phenomenon was exactly the same, the water being whirled up in a spiral form by the wind to a prodigious height, with only this difference, that as the watery columns rose the dark thunder-clouds overhead bent down to meet them, while, in the desert, the sand was dissipated in the clear air.

To give some idea of the size of these waterspouts I may mention that one of them breaking a mile to windward drenched our decks with water.

It is very difficult on the desert to realise that one is making any progress. When on a perfectly open plain,

I often tried to counteract this feeling by watching some distant stone or camel's skeleton, until we reached it, and then riding towards some object beyond, and so on. But we now had mountains behind us, and mountains in front, and it naturally appeared that with every step the mountains behind should look further off, and the mountains in front nearer; yet the clear, rarified air made distant objects appear so distinct, that five or six hours' hard marching did not produce any perceptible effect, and we seemed to have approached no nearer to the mountain range before us, while that behind looked but little further away. It was not till after nightfall that we at last gained the foot of a red mountain—rich in iron ore—which we had seen before us all day, and I felt that we had earned a few hours' repose.

June 21st.—We started before dawn, and rode through a labyrinth of rocky hills along the dry course of a river, in which we could see the slot marks of many gazelles, whose instinct had taught them to scrape holes at various places, to get the water which lay two feet below the surface of the sand.

At noon we came to a charming verdant spot, hidden away in the heart of the mountains, the steep rocky sides of which formed an inaccessible wall around it. A level lawn of the softest grass spread like a green carpet under foot, while a variety of beautiful trees afforded a pleasing shade from the powerful rays of the sun. One of these trees, named by the Arabs the *Hebe*, had a light-green oval leaf, and bore clusters of transparent red berries, like currants, which they also resembled in taste, though with the addition of a slight pungent flavour, such as would be produced by eating red currants with young mustard leaves. When this fruit of the desert was dried in the sun, however, its pungency quite disappeared, and the sweet flavour alone remained. There was a tree of the acacia kind, called the "sun tree," round which a number of goats were kneeling, while a naked Arab shook down the seed-pods, which were eagerly devoured by them. There were also sweet-scented mimosas, and numbers of graceful creepers interlacing themselves with the boughs of the trees, and forming natural arbours. Indeed, it was quite a little garden, such as Young tells us Nature delights to create in the wilderness.

> " In distant wilds, by human eye unseen,
> She rears her flowers, spreads her velvet green;
> Pure gurgling rills the lonely desert trace,
> And waste their sweetness on a savage race."

Lying down on the soft grass to rest, we listened lazily to the hum of insects and the tapping of the woodpeckers among the trees.

There is a curious Turkish superstition about the woodpecker, which I once accidentally overheard an old man relating, and I will try to sketch the story here in as few words as I can.

The Story of Leila.

It is related, but Allah is all knowing! that in a lonely tower on the shores of the Bahr-el-Ahmar, or

The Story of Leila.

Red Sea, there once dwelt a beautiful maiden, the daughter of an old Pacha, a fierce and skilful warrior, who had built this fortress as a habitation for his child when he was engaged in distant wars.

The maiden was fairer than the moon of Ramadan in its fourteenth lustre, her figure was more graceful than the oriental willow, her hair was of the darkest hue of night, her eyes were like two bright stars, and she was named Leila. Leila's mother, a beautiful Georgian, had died in giving life to her daughter, and from that day the world had become black before the eyes of the Pacha. At his frown his attendants felt the bowstring tightening around their necks, and the glance of his eye was like the edge of a keen sword, making men's heads loose on their shoulders. But as Leila grew in loveliness and intelligence, she wound herself like a vine around the fiery old Moslem's heart; and, though he still remained a persecution to his enemies, and a terror to all men, he was gentle to her, and she became as a precious jewel in his sight. So he built the lonely fortress on a rock beside the Bahr-el-Ahmar, and made in it a pleasant garden, and placed his daughter there, with women and black slaves to tend and guard her, and when he went away to fight the battles of El Islam, he fastened the gate with seven great locks, that no one might enter or go forth until he returned.

Now it happened one night that Leila stood by her window singing, and her voice was so melodious that the roses in the garden thought it was their lover the

Bul-bul, and opened their fairest blossoms, and filled the air with their sweetest fragrance, and the poor nightingale broke his heart in despair, and the stars were jealous of the west wind that stole through the casement to kiss her cheek, and then whispered of the marvel of her beauty to the waves, which repeated it to one another, and murmured the praise of Leila even on the shores of the most distant countries of the earth.

And as Leila stood by the window there approached a youth full of comeliness and strength, and he rode a horse as white as camphor, and he was a chief among the Bedawees. He had been parted from his companions hunting; and it came to pass that, as he neared the tower, he heard Leila's song; and when he saw her looking out upon the night, as if the rising sun beamed from her face, he no longer beheld the constellations of heaven, and stood as one entranced. And when his eyes met hers, it pleased Allah, whose name be exalted! to infuse love into both their hearts, and the Bedawee warrior became as a slave at the feet of the Turkish maiden.

So they ceased not to converse until the day began to gleam, and the sun rose in splendour, when she bid him leave her, and he rode away to a solitary place mourning over his fate, for there was war between the Pacha and the Bedawees, and he knew that the implacable General would never consent to give him his daughter.

Now, as he sat and meditated upon these things, lo! an old man came past, and his robe was of green, and his beard white, and his back bent as with the burden of many years. So the youth rose and invited him to rest, and spread what food he had before him; but he eat not himself, his heart being heavy with love. And when the old man saw this, he lifted his head, and said: "My son, tell me thy sorrow, and it may be that I can give thee comfort, for wisdom is the recompense of the aged, and I have lived many years; aye, even since the days of Abraham the son of Terah."

Now, when the Bedawee heard these words, his spirit was troubled with fear, and he kissed the ground before the old man, for he knew that he could be none other than El-Khider, the comforter of the afflicted: he who had drunk of the fountain of life, and had lived ever since the days of Zu-l Karmeyn the Conqueror, and whose knowledge was the history of the world. So when he had related his story he stood silent, with his head hung in bashfulness; but El-Khider touched him on the breast, and said unto him: "My son, be of good cheer, for it is written that a woman shall leave the father that reared her, to cleave to the husband she loves, and thou mayest obtain Leila for thy wife, if thou wilt give heed to my counsel, and put thy trust in God Therefore, when the sun is at its highest, ride thou towards it for the space of seven hours, when thou wilt come to a river overshadowed by green trees, in the trunk of one of which a woodpecker has built her nest. And when the bird leaves the nest take heed to plug up the hole, for know that Allah, from whom nothing is concealed! has given to the woodpecker the knowledge of a wonderful balsam, before which all obstacles give way; and when she discovers that the entrance to her nest is closed, she will depart in search of this, and return bearing a drop of it in her bill, and thou must abide under the tree for her coming, and when she is near wave thy red scarf at her, and she will be frightened and drop the balsam ; and thou must collect it, and take it to the tower where thy love dwelleth, and the gates will open before thee, and the chains fall asunder; but forget not before thou leavest to withdraw the plug from the woodpecker's nest, that she may be rewarded." So saying, the old man gathered up his robes, and departed on his way.

And the Bedawee rode across the plain in the direction of the sun for the space of seven hours, when he came to a valley abounding with trees, and fruits, and birds, and running streams; and, lo! in the hollow trunk of one of the trees a woodpecker had built her nest; and the Bedawee closed up the entrance as he had been directed, and the bird flew round and round, uttering a plaintive cry, but the ring-doves cooed " *Kereem! Towwab!* " which those learned in the language of birds, say means " bountiful! propitious !" So the youth hardened his heart, and at length the woodpecker shot away like an arrow in the direction of the setting sun, and was lost to view. And it was the hour of *asr* on the following day when she returned, and her wings beat the air slowly and feebly, as though she came from a weary journey.

Now when the Bedowee perceived her, he unwound his sash and waved it over his head, crying out in a loud voice, and the bird was terrified, and opened her bill, and let fall a drop of clear gum on the sash, and he wrapped this up; whereupon the bird alighted on the tree and mourned, for she knew that her young ones would die before she could bring another drop of balsam. But the youth forgot not the injunction of El-Khider, and withdrew the plug from the nest ere he departed, and left the bird rejoicing.

And in the third quarter of the night he reached Leila's tower, and saw her sitting by her window singing of his absence, and her voice was more soft than zephyr passing over the flowers of a garden. Then he touched the seven locks of the gate with the balsam, and they opened before him, and he entered the tower, and all there were wrapped in slumber; so he ascended to Leila's chamber, and took her by the hand, and led her forth, and placed her on his steed; and God let down the veil of his protection upon them, and they departed and rode towards the country of his people.

But on the following day the father of Leila returned, and, when he called out for his child, lo! there was no answer, for the female slaves had hidden themselves in their fear of him. And when he found that Leila was gone, the vein of anger swelled between his eyes, and he put on the crimson apparel of wrath, and, summoning his horsemen about him, commanded them to go forth, and return not until they had found her; and they said: "We hear and obey."

And on the third day they overtook Leila and her husband at a spring where they were reposing, and they encompassed them round about, and bound them, and brought them before the Pacha, who, when he beheld Leila's husband, looked very fiercely upon him, and said : "Thy father, O Bedawee! slew my brother; wherefore should I not slay thee?" Then the Bedawee lifted up his head, and replied : "Oh, Pacha! thy brother had a sword in his hand when my father slew him : is it not thus that a warrior should die?" And Leila threw herself at her father's feet, and cried: "O my father! if thou killest my husband thou wilt assuredly kill me, for without him I cannot live ; but if thou sparest him, not only wilt thou save the life of thy child, but thou wilt gain a son." And when the Pacha heard these words, and looked upon her, and saw how beautiful she was, God changed his spirit into mildness, and his heart was moved with a great compassion ; and he bid them loose the bonds from Leila's husband, and embraced him, and there was peace.

Such is the story of "Leila and the Woodpecker."

We continued our march at 3 P.M., the way becoming gradually more uneven, and after dark we descended a mountain path, so precipitous that we had to dismount and lead the camels, whose large soft feet were much hurt by the broken fragments of rock. At eight we lighted a fire, and made our last bivouack; for we calculated that we should gain Suakin on the morrow. Our beds were of sharp stones, but camel riding is conducive to slumber; and what speaks well for the air of the desert is, that in only four meals I had finished an entire sheep to my own knife and fork.

June 22nd (*Sunday*).—An hour before sunrise I roused my men, and rode forwards. Presently the day dawned, pale and pure as a young girl before she bursts into the first bloom of womanhood, and night fled silently to the other half of the globe. There is something almost touching in these changes of nature. The sun rises and reaches its meridian, anon the shadows of evening lengthen, and the newly-born stars are all that remain of the radiance that was before. Another day, which dawned bright and glorious, has passed away irretrievably for ever, adding a page that cannot be cancelled to the history of the world.—But these are idle fancies, born of lonely days and nights on the desert, and I will return to my journey.

At 9 A.M. we crossed the last range of mountains, and saw a broad and verdant plain stretching below us, bounded by the bright blue sea. To people who had been so long traversing sand and rocks, this was a delightful sight; large herds of gazelles were grazing among the park-like scenery, the birds were singing blithely, and the sea-breeze was whispering among the trees with that soft harmony Zorilla has so prettily described in "Don Juan Tenorio":

> "Esa armonia que el viento
> Recoge entre esos millares
> De floridos olivares,
> Que agita con manso aliento."

At 11 A.M. we reached a well, and lay down under some mimosas for a few hours' rest. The spot was teeming with animal life: an enterprising company of ants established a mountain route across my blanket ; a great black salamander with a big head dropped down with a flop on my pillow, and looked quite astonished at his own temerity. Then two legal-looking lizards approached, and made raids on the company of ants; then a hawk, who appeared to be young and inexperienced, came and eyed me critically ; while an old vulture, who was suffering from heat and corpulence, took the whole shade of a tree to himself, and panted there in ease and luxury. An adventurous stag beetle reconnoitred my pillow, with a view to crawling over my neck, and on my disputing the right of way, waxed wroth ; another beetle, black and many-jointed, made a voyage of discovery up my leg as far as my knee, where the difficulties of the road became too much for him. I have a fellow-feeling with travellers, and expelled him gently, mindful of my uncle Toby's address to the blue-bottle fly : " Go, go, poor devil !—get thee gone : why should I hurt thee ? This world is surely wide enough to hold both thee and me." But I fear he did not appreciate my kindness, and curled up his tail in a deeply-injured manner.

Again we were riding along under the blinding sun, and at last the flat-roofed houses of Suakin appeared in sight. The waves were dashing merrily against the coral-reefs as we approached the little town, and rode through the straggling street, stared at by the whole population, who marvelled much at the crocodile skin and my strange dress, which, having been made in Abyssinia of a *kuarie*, had a broad crimson stripe meandering over it in a rather startling manner. When we reached the market-place, the weary camels, thinking their journey over, lay down; but we urged them to the water's-edge, and, embarking in a canoe, were paddled to the governor's residence. There was a new governor now—in Egypt they change fast—and the son of a great man's favourite Circassian slave had been raised to the office. He had his mother's beautiful eyes, but was not otherwise handsome; however, he received me courteously, and appointed me an empty house to live in till the steamer should arrive. The difficulties of the journey were now over, and I therefore this day closed my journal.

On the 27th June, after four idle days passed in the baking atmosphere of Suakin, I embarked, with my servant Mustafa, on board an Egyptian steamer which had come up from Massowah, and was bound for Jiddah, a port situated a very short distance from Mecca, on the coast of Arabia el Hidjaz. I had thought the Red Sea unbearably hot the last time I sailed upon it, but now it was hotter than ever. The sultry wind brought no freshness, the seething waters appeared to be steaming and simmering in the sunshine, and only at night, when the sea mirrored the stars in every ripple, like a lover extolling his mistress in countless similes, did we get a few brief hours of relief.

Nothing could be prettier than the view of Jiddah as I first saw it, in the glow of an Eastern sunrise. The white houses with their latticed windows, the delicate minarets of the mosques, the glistening coral-reefs stretching far out to sea, intersected by channels of bright green water, so clear that we could watch the party-coloured sea-weed waving fathoms below; the quaint coasting-vessels in the harbour, with their high sterns and lateen sails, and the long tawny line of the Arabian mountains in the background, all combined to produce a most picturesque effect, very different from the desert scenes we had left behind. As I walked forwards to enjoy the view, a gaily-painted boat, with a party of musicians, and some veiled ladies in the stern, rowed rapidly past our bows, and the sound of the music lingered upon the water, long after the boat had disappeared among the other vessels, awakening a hundred memories of the Arabian Nights.

The steamer was to remain some days at Jiddah before proceeding to Suez, and the captain lent me his boat to go on shore. Landing at the mole of the Custom-house, and passing under an arched gateway, Mustafa and I soon found ourselves in the principal street of the town. It was roofed over with loose planks to keep out the sun, and the merchants were sitting cross-legged in little open shops at either side, wherein were displayed all the varied merchandise of an Eastern port. Jewelled knives and pistols, carpets, embroidered slippers, costly stuffs, and strings of beads of the black coral for which Jiddah is famous, were to be bought of many a merchant whose shop was no bigger than a cobbler's stall; while the unpaved street was thronged with picturesque groups of Arabs, Turks, Armenians, and negroes, clad in every variety of national dress, and mostly armed to the teeth.

The doorways and windows of the houses, with their projecting jalousies of carved wood, presented several beautiful specimens of Arabian design and workmanship, well worthy the study of an artist. Opening from one of the streets, was a narrow passage leading to the slave market, but an old merchant at the entrance warned me not to go there unless I wished to create a riot, and I noticed that many of the Arabs scowled at my European dress as I passed, and some even uttered a curse; for the inhabitants of Jiddah, being so close to Mecca, are very fanatical, and the governor of the town does not profess to be responsible for Christians who venture beyond the walls. Indeed not very many years ago there was a general massacre, in which the English and French consols lost their lives, together with most of the Copts and Greeks who were in the town. They say an English frigate was in the port at the time, and a Greek managed to swim out to her and give tidings of what was going on. If *then* the frigate had fired a broadside into Jiddah, the fanatics might perhaps have been cowed; but instead of doing this, she fired one *over* the town, which only made matters worse, for the people cried out that a miracle had taken place, and the shot of the unbelievers had been turned aside by the hand of Allah; so they continued the massacre, while the frigate sailed away for *instructions*, for British officers have learned by bitter experience the danger of acting on their own responsibility, even when the lives of hundreds of their fellow-creatures are imperilled, and a brave man is left the choice of breaking his heart, or being broken himself. I believe that weeks *after* the massacre, the frigate returned with full instructions to demand the punishment of the ringleaders, and at last tired out with the governor's delays, her commander fired a broadside, this time *at* the governor's house, and knocked it about his ears, which so frightened the old Turk that there was hardly time to fire another broadside before the ringleaders of the massacre had been all strangled, and harmony was restored.

The ruins of the government buildings knocked down by this broadside still remain a monument of British vengeance, but I cannot help thinking that the broadside came a little late, and it would have been more satisfactory to have saved a dozen of the innocent people who were massacred, than to punish whole scores of the murderers. However, I only tell the story as it was related to me at Jiddah, and will not be responsible for the details.

There is a handsome carved window in the house where the French consul was killed. The poor fellow was sitting with his daughter when the fanatical crowd burst in upon him, and snatching down his diplomatic sword from the wall, he defended himself with that frail tailor's weapon till he was overpowered and hacked to pieces. His daughter was placed in a hareem, but afterwards, with much difficulty, released.

A short distance beyond the walls of Jiddah is the tomb of Eve, and naturally my first care was to seek the spot where tradition places the remains of our great ancestress.

When Adam and Eve were cast out from Paradise they fell in different parts of the earth, Adam alighting on a mountain—probably Adam's Peak—in the island of Ceylon, and Eve on the coast of the Red Sea, near Jiddah. When "the grand old gardener and his wife" met again, it was on Mount Arafat, near Mecca, and when Eve died she was buried close to the spot where Jiddah now stands. Such is the Arabian tradition.*

Passing through a gate in the walls of the town, I came to a sandy plain, and a short walk brought me to a Moslem cemetery, in the centre of which was the tomb of Eve. It is said that Adam's height was thirty cubits, and this tomb tallied with the colossal proportions assigned to our first parents. Two low walls, about thirty paces long, enclosed it on either side, and the earth between them, which was slightly convex, was covered with flowers. A little shrine had been erected above a flat stone, placed directly over the spot supposed to be the centre of Eve's body, and this stone was regarded with great reverence by the Arabs.†

From times long antecedent to the birth of Mahomet, the Arabs have preserved a tradition, that Abraham built into the Caaba at Mecca a stone which fell from Paradise on the expulsion of our first parents, but I do not know that their belief in the tomb of Eve can be

---

* See Washington Irving's "Life of Mahomet."
† I regret I cannot describe this monument more accurately, for the day after my visit to it I was attacked with a fever which prevented me making notes at the time, and has ever since left me rather a confused recollection of my sojourn at Jiddah.

traced so far back. However this may be, the greatest sceptic could hardly look unimpressed upon a spot which tradition has consecrated as the last resting-place of the Mother of mankind.

Gathered around were the graves of many generations of her children, a weak and puny race, but have not the very beasts dwindled down since the days of the Mammoths? As I stood on the verge of the arid waste that surrounds Jiddah, and watched the loose sand whirled about by the wind, I could not help reflecting, like Longfellow :

> " How many weary centuries has it been
> About these deserts blown !
> How many strange vicissitudes has seen
> How many histories known ?"

On returning to the town, I made my way to the British consulate. I found that the only representative of England at Jiddah was a Mahometan Indian, who could not even speak English, and whose sympathies, some merchants who had sought his assistance assured me, were entirely with his co-religionists. Leaving this valuable official, I called on an Englishman whom I had heard was acting as vice-consul for the Dutch. I need not say my fellow-countryman received me kindly, and he asked me to make his house my home during my stay. I decided to avail myself of his hospitality for that night, and the next morning I had no choice in the matter, for I was down with the African fever. It is said that if you escape fever in the interior of Africa, you will get it when you leave the country.

For months past my bed had been upon the ground, and constant exposure to the noonday heat and night air had gradually done their work; I had felt this at times, but the fine air of the plains, and the perpetual necessity for action during the desert marches, had enabled me to fight against the malady which, now that my task was ended, came upon me.

"O, blessed health!" exclaims Walter Shandy, "thou art above all gold and treasure. . . . . He that has thee, has little more to wish for; and he that is so wretched as to want thee, wants everything with thee." I do not remember how long the fever lasted, but I had ample time to realise this. Every muscle in my body ached excruciatingly, my head felt as if the top had been taken off, and some one was tickling my brain with a feather, violent burning and shivering fits followed each other in fantastic succession, and the slightest noise or movement made me shrink as if I had been struck with a sledge-hammer. Fortunately I still possessed a little muriatic acid and quinine, and with these, and some tartarised antimony which Mustafa procured from a Greek, I proceeded to doctor myself during the intervals of the attack. A good constitution did the rest. The day the steamer started for Suez I was able to rise, and, thanking my host for his kindness, tottered down to the shore, feeling as weak as a child. The cabin of the steamer was unbearable, so a mattrass was placed for me on the deck; each day I took five minutes' walk, and then had to lie down again quite exhausted; but a strong head wind kept us seven or eight days at sea, and before we reached Suez the voyage had placed me on the road to convalescence.

We were nearing the island of Shadawan when a steamer approached. Shrieks proceeded from the forecastle, and I saw that a sailor was being flogged before the captain, who sat calmly smoking his *chibuk* the while. As the vessel passed, I discovered that she was the Kosseir, the steamer on which C. and I had sailed down the Red Sea, and the fat Turkish captain was at his old amusement of rope-ending his crew.

Three days later I was installed in Shepherd's Hotel at Cairo, the only other occupant of which was poor Winwood Read, so soon destined to fall a victim to the climate of the West African coast.

APPENDIX.

Note A.

THE Khedive professes to have abolished slavery in his dominions, but I found a slave market flourishing at Galabat, when the town was garrisoned by Egyptian troops,* and I will now relate an instance of the way slaves are treated at Massowah; my authority being M. de Sarzec, late vice-consul for France at that port, and present French consul at Bussorah.

1st case.—A slave applied at the consulate for protection: M. de Sarzec accordingly demanded his card of emancipation from the governor of Massowah, but was informed—1st, that the freedom of no slave would be recognised unless he could prove in a court of inquiry that he had been *cruelly* treated by his master; 2ndly, that such court must be composed *exclusively* of Mahometans; and 3rdly, that if the slave *were* granted his freedom, he must enter the Khedive's army, *i.e.*, exchange one servitude for another.

2nd case.—A woman begged for protection, stating that she had been made a slave, although she was the wife of a soldier in the Khedive's army. M. de Sarzec demanded her freedom of the local government, which, as usual, refused his application; he therefore gave the woman a card, stating her to be under the protection of the French con-

* See Vol. II, p. 168.

sulate, but shortly afterwards her husband complained that, notwithstanding this, his wife had been forcibly seized by her master, and again placed in captivity. M. de Sarzec thereon made a second application for her freedom, which was again refused, while the unfortunate soldier was placed in irons and imprisoned for upwards of two months, as a punishment for having dared to protest against the enslavement of his wife. It was only when a French frigate entered the port of Massowah, and, at the consul's request, refused to salute the governor's flag, that the Egyptian officials became alarmed, and set the woman free, just four months after M. de Sarzec's first application. It may be imagined, therefore, how many slaves are released in a year.

The following anecdote will also give some idea of Egyptian justice. After the Magdala campaign, an Abyssinian, named Wolkaïti Beru, who had been educated at Malta, and enjoyed both English and French protection, was commissioned to accompany the gifts sent by the British government to Prince Kassa. He performed this duty, and returned to Massowah, where he had not been long before he was summoned into the presence of M. Munzinger, the governor, who ordered him to relate what was the purport of the letters addressed by England to Prince Kassa, and also what the prince had said in reply. On Beru's refusing to commit this breach of trust, he was immediately given 200 blows with the bastinado, and cast into prison, where he was kept without the knowledge of the French consul, although M. Munzinger knew perfectly well that he was under French protection, as he himself had formerly been French consul at Massowah, and signed Wolkaïti Beru's papers in that capacity. Beru could not communicate with his consul, but the king of Abyssinia learned his position, and expressed to M. de Sarzec his surprise that an agent who had been sent to him by England, should receive such treatment. The French consul thereon, of course, took immediate measures to procure Bern's release, which, however, he only obtained by threatening to take down his flag, and after the poor fellow had been six weeks in the common gaol of Massowah, suffering the greatest hardships.

I will not discuss whether the Khedive himself is sincere in wishing to suppress the slave trade. The Scotch engineer of one of his highness's own steamers assured me that the vessel had been employed to transport slaves from the Soudan to Arabia; but even if the Khedive's private sentiments are everything that can be desired, it makes little difference so long as he suffers his officials not only to permit the slave trade, but to encourage and profit by it, in those parts of the Soudan where it is supposed that there is nobody to reveal what goes on. Egypt, with no little ostentation, sent an expedition to suppress the slave trade of Central Africa, by which means she also secured a claim to what may prove a very valuable tract of country; but, while Sir Samuel Baker was risking his life to put down slavery in the interior, slaves were being bought and sold in the Soudan behind him, and the very agents whose machinations he was trying to defeat were receiving high protection much nearer Cairo. No one knows this better than the gallant traveller himself, and I doubt if he was much pleased at the discovery. Of course, after so many promises, Egypt has been forced to stop the direct transit of negroes down the White Nile, and occasionally a *dow* is captured, but it would be interesting to know how the slaves thus professedly released are disposed of. A German at Cairo, who had been in the Egyptian telegraph service, told me a very ugly story, to the effect that while he was stationed at Khartum, some slave *dows* were taken, and the slaves, several hundred in number, temporarily enclosed in a large building near the Blue Nile. The capture was telegraphed to Cairo, and made the most of; but it was nobody's business in the meantime to look after the slaves, and they were left shut up in their enclosure, many of them still chained together as they had been taken from the *dows*. When, after a week or two, instructions about them arrived from Cairo, the enclosure was visited, but it was then found that the slaves, who had been so generously set free by the Egyptian government, had saved that government all further trouble, for the poor creatures, unable to get out of the enclosure, had died of thirst and starvation where they lay. I trust for the sake of humanity that this was an exceptional case; there seems, however, little doubt that the so-called liberty accorded to slaves means, that, if they are women, they are given to the soldiers, while, if they are men, they merely change masters, and have to serve in the army which is thus economically recruited.

Colonel Chaillé Long, of the Egyptian staff, tells us in his book,* that at every Egyptian camp and garrison a fugitive slave may seek protection and freedom by simply declaring that he wants protection of the government. No doubt the author of "Naked Truths about Naked People" is correct in saying he may *seek* it, but the facts mentioned at the commencement of this note, on the authority of the French consul at Massowah, and my own experience at Galabat, do not uphold the theory that he will get it. However, it seems that Colonel Chaillé Long is gifted with peculiar fortitude when called upon to behold the sufferings of other people, for according to his own account (p. 107), he allowed King M'Tse to have thirty unresisting victims slaughtered in *his* honour, without entering a single protest, because, forsooth, to do so would, "if nothing more serious, have subjected me to ridicule and loss of prestige." I believe Livingstone would have told a different story, and considering that not to protest at such a massacre was to lead M'Tse to infer that it was agreeable

* "Central Africa ; or Naked Truths about Naked People."

to his white guest, and that Africans naturally judge of a whole country by the one representative of it whom they see, it appears probable that the character for justice and humanity which white travellers have hitherto maintained in Africa, may be much benefited should all who follow in the footsteps of Colonel Long display the same laudable phlegm.

Most of the slaves shipped from the Soudan are sold at the markets on the Arabian coast, and I will give a précis of a letter I received, in 1875, from an English merchant, who was residing at Jiddah when I visited that port. He writes—"It will hardly be credited when I assert that the Khedive's steamers continually bring slaves, especially the pale and expensive ones, from Suakin and Massowah, and *dows* arrive daily which import each month several thousand poor creatures to Jiddah alone, the dealers paying a poll-tax to the Turkish government on each slave. The Turkish government recognises the respective positions of master and slave, and the Pacha or governor of a town publicly adjudicates in council on the slave trade disputes which arise daily between the slave brokers and their clients. The governor, chief of police, or port officers, will inflict corporal punishment, or imprisonment, on a slave, at his master's request. If a slave absents himself, or absconds, the police will apprehend him, his escape is notified by the public crier, and a reward offered for his recapture. The wages earned by a slave are paid to his *master*, and even Europeans are compelled to comply with this rule if they hire the services of slaves; yet if a slave cannot procure work, his master need not feed or shelter him, and he may die of want, as the law does not make his owner liable. A poor Arab has generally one or more slaves whom he has bought on credit, or received as a gift; in the majority of cases the Arab has not enough to feed himself, and if the slave cannot provide for both, dreadful hardship is the result; not unfrequently the slave has to work day and night for a bare sufficiency of food. It is common to see old men and women, unfit for work, begging at large, as also young negroes who have incurable injuries of the body; these are allowed to perish like brutes in the roads and streets, and I have even seen dogs given bread and water when no notice was taken of a destitute negro. Boat owners equip their vessels almost entirely with slaves, thus saving all expense for labour beyond the miserable food they give them. Perhaps the most curious fact of all is, that many ships which sail under the British flag, belong to Arab owners, and have the greater part of their crews composed of slaves; these slaves visit foreign ports, but rarely avail themselves of the freedom they might thus obtain, as their owners make them believe that the form of signing articles before consuls is another form of securing their bondage."

Talking of Sir Bartle Frere's expedition, my correspondent says,—"The slave traders on the coasts of the Red Sea were stricken with terror when they heard that England had sent an expedition to Zanzibar, which, with oriental exaggeration, was represented as visiting all Eastern ports, and dealing out condign punishment to towns and people engaged in the slave trade; this seemed confirmed when an English gun-boat actually chased some slavers near Aden; but the panic died away when the Zanzibar expedition returned without visiting the Red Sea ports, which have now become the great emporiums for slaves; though the mere presence of an armed cruiser in the Red Sea, seconded by the honest efforts of consular officers, would produce an effect as permanent as it would be humane and desirable." He also remarks that from January, 1870, to the end of 1874, the British consulate at Jiddah was left in charge of a dragoman. Certainly, when I was at Jiddah, in 1873, the only representative of Eng-

Appendix. 309

land was an Indian Mahometan, who could not even speak English.

The horrors of the slave trade have been so often ably described, that I need not dwell on them here. There is also a *practical* side to the question; so long as the African slave trade exists, so long must it be the interest of the slave traders to close the country to the traveller, and to stir up strife between the native tribes. The colonist is the true pioneer of civilization, but the traveller is the pioneer of the colonist, and so long as he is exposed to the constant difficulties and dangers that it is the interest of the slave traders to place in his way, so long will the civilization of Africa be retarded. It is well that England has compelled the Sultan of Zanzibar to put down the slave trade, but it is not well that she should permit Egypt and Turkey to carry on a traffic in slaves across the Red Sea, so much nearer home. To stop this traffic would be no difficult task; I have shown that the King of Abyssinia is willing to prevent the export of slaves from his country, and if we entered into an understanding with him, and placed a cruiser in the Red Sea, the markets of the Soudan would receive a double blow: first, because they could no longer procure their supply of expensive slaves from Ethiopia; and secondly, because there would be no means of exporting them to the markets of Arabia. With these difficulties in its way, the East African slave trade would soon disappear, and one of the principal obstacles to the development and civilization of the Continent would disappear with it.

NOTE B.

The necrology of Abyssinian travellers certainly presents a somewhat gloomy subject for contemplation. Of the five *savants* forming the French expedition sent out by Louis

Philippe, Dillon died of fever caught in the vale of the Mareb; Petit was devoured by a crocodile, whilst crossing the Abaï, or Blue Nile; Sheffner died of dysentery at Antichon; Vigneau at Jiddah, of a fever caught at Massowah or Souakin; whilst Lieutenant Lefebre alone lived to return to France, but, again tempting fate, returned to Abyssinia, where he went mad, was put in chains by Consul Cameron, and died shortly afterwards at Jiddah, on his way home.

Ferret and Galinier, also sent by the French government to examine the resources of Abyssinia, lost their companion, M. Jules Rouget, of dysentery, at Antichon.

Plowden, Cameron's predecessor, was speared on his way to Adowa, whilst his friend and companion, Bell, was first half killed at Korata, for the sake of a few dollars which he had unluckily shown whilst buying mules at the market of Ifag, and some years later killed outright in a fight between King Theodorus and his foster brother Garrad.

Powell, his wife and child, and an Alsatian servant, were murdered in the Shangalla country.

General Kirkham, whom I have so often mentioned in this book, died recently at Massowah, and Count Vilmos Zichy was killed near Gundet.

Add to this formidable list the names of those who have been made captive in Abyssinia, and it will be found that a very small percentage of European travellers have escaped losing either life or liberty in this ill-fated country.

The death of Bell was related to my brother by Likamanguas Warki, formerly private secretary to King Theodorus, in the following manner:—

Dedjatch Kounfu, half-brother to Theodorus, made war upon him at Metemma. Kounfu was older than Theodorus. Theodorus defeated and killed Kounfu and all his men. Kounfu's son, Dedjatch Garrad, then joined a rebel named

Appendix. 311

Dedjach Negoussié, who rose against Theodorus, while he was on an expedition to Shoa.

Father Jacobus, the Roman Catholic bishop, had agreed with Negoussié to convert Abyssinia. Likamangnas Warki, who was then at Adowa, heard of this, and wrote in secret to Theodorus to expose the plans of Negoussié and Jacobus, and to say that they had written to France for assistance and cannon. Theodorus, on receiving this news, was so enraged, that he flung down on the ground a pistol he held in his hand. Soon afterwards he met Garrad, at Waldubba, on his way back from Shoa. A battle ensued, but the soldiers of Theodorus fled, leaving him alone with Bell, or Likamanquos Yohannes, as he was called in Abyssinia.

On the other side, Garrad's soldiers had moved away, leaving him and his brother also alone on the field—four only of all the combatants. They fought. Bell slew Garrad's brother; Garrad slew Bell; Theodorus shot Garrad. Theodorus remained the victor.

His followers now rallied, and 3000 of Garrad's men were made prisoners. Theodorus took them to his camp at Debarek. He ordered all his troops to form a circle, and then placed the prisoners in the centre. Advancing towards them, he addressed them thus: "You fought against me with the Galla Ras Ali, and I pardoned you. Again you fought against me, under Menin; and again I forgave you. A third time you fought against me, with Dedjatch Gushu (the grandfather of Ras Desta); and a third time you were pardoned. Again you fought against me, with Alegas Beru; and for the fourth time I pardoned you. With Dedjatch Oubi you attacked me again, and again I showed you my clemency. Again, when I conquered Dedjatch Beru, I found you among my enemies. I have often released you, but you are incorrigible. Night and day you wish for my death. Each day I have done my utmost for your good. Now you have killed this stranger, who was with me. Nothing remains but to slaughter you like cattle." Before the sun set, the 3000 prisoners had ceased to live.

NOTE C.

According to one of the native traditions, the custom of eating raw meat was introduced into Abyssinia at the time when the Portuguese were assisting the Abyssinians to repel the invasion of Mahomet Graign, the gigantic governor of Zeila. The Abyssinians and their Portuguese allies had been defeated, and forced to take refuge among some wooded hills. The Portuguese leader advised that they should remain concealed therefor two or three days; "for," said he, "the Moslems will feast and carouse after their victory, and we shall then have an opportunity of falling upon them unawares and putting them to the sword. But that they may not discover where we are, you must light no fires." "Your council is good," said the Abyssinians; "but how shall we cook our meat?" The Portuguese then ordered some cows to be killed, and showed them that they could eat the meat raw. Soon afterwards Graign was defeated; and the Abyssinians attributed their victory to the strength given them by the raw meat, wherefore they have continued to eat it ever since.

NOTE D.

There are four great families in Abyssinia. The first is of Tigre, province of Enderta; and Ras Michael, Ras Weldo Selassy, Dedjatch Wagardis, and the present king, Yohannes, who before his coronation bore the name of Kassa Michael, are its latest representatives.

The second family is of Sokota, and claims descent from Menilek. Its latest representatives are Dedjatch Garamadin and his son, Takala Georgis.

Appendix. 313

The third family is of Galla origin, and is represented by Ras Guksa, Ras Ali, Ali Faris, and the present Ali Beru.

The fourth family is of Godjam, and descended from Queen Muntuav. Its latest representatives are Beru Gushu and the present Dedjatch Desta.

NOTE E.

The Abyssinians give the following reason for their only wearing crimson and white. Our Lord, being innocent of all sin, was clothed in white until the day of his crucifixion, when blood flowed from his wounds and stained his garments red. In remembrance of this, the crimson stripe of the *kuarie* is worn over the left breast, that being the side where the lance pierced the body of our Lord.

NOTE F.

In illustration of the king's decision of character, I will relate an episode which occurred during the late war between Egypt and Abyssinia, and which I have on the authority of an eye-witness.

At the moment that King Yohannes was leaving Adowa at the head of his army to fight the Egyptians, a great earthquake occurred, and part of a mountain came crashing down in front of the king's horse, so close that the king narrowly escaped being crushed by it. The Abyssinian soldiers are naturally superstitious, and stood petrified with terror at this unlucky accident; but the king, who knows the character of his people, without a moment of hesitation leaped from the saddle, and, flinging himself on his knees, lifted up his hands and gave thanks aloud to Heaven before the whole army : " God," he cried, " has sent this in his mercy as a sign that the power of the Moslems shall fall before me as this mountain has rolled down at my feet!" Had Yohannes been frightened, or wavered for a moment, a panic would probably have been the result; but his prompt and courageous conduct kindled the enthusiasm of his troops, who now rent the air with their shouts, and pushed eagerly forward, certain that they were marching to predestined victory. By his presence of mind, the soldier king had half gained a victory before he had fought a battle; but, nevertheless, like a good general, he was careful to take the Egyptians by surprise, and his *naphteñas* did the rest, for they threw themselves upon the enemy with an impetuosity that nothing could check. An Egyptian officer, speaking afterwards of the battle, said:—" What can you do against people who come boldly up to the muzzles of your guns, and stab at the men who are serving them with their spears?"

NOTE G.

It appears that from time immemorial three days have been the prescribed term for rendering hospitality to a guest throughout the East. The Prophet said: " Whosoever believeth in God and the day of resurrection, must respect his guest; and the time for being kind to him is one day and one night; and the period of entertaining him is three days: and after that, if he does it longer, he benefits him more; but it is not right for a guest to stay in the house of the host so long as to incommode him."

That the reader may form some idea of the hospitality which an Abyssinian village is supposed to render to the king's guests, I copy from my brother's diary the *menu* of the dinner furnished by one village for two Europeans and six native servants: 100 cakes of white bread, 200 cakes of black ditto, 10 *gumbos* of beer, containing three gallons each;

Appendix. 315

1 *gumbo* of *tedge* ditto, 1 *gumbo* of white honey, 1 cow, 100 eggs, 10 fowls, 3 small *gumbos* of butter for cooking, 1 ditto of fresh butter, 2 ditto of curry, 1 ditto of milk, and 1 *madega* of corn. This repast required thirty-five men to carry it. The same morning the same village had furnished for breakfast 200 cakes of bread, 1 goat, 60 eggs, 15 fowls, and 2 *gumbos* of beer. Total, for eight people in one day: 500 cakes of bread, each a foot and a half in diameter; 1 cow, 1 goat, 25 fowls, 160 eggs, 36 gallons of beer, 3 gallons of *tedge*, 3 gallons of honey, besides butter, curry, corn, &c. Certainly the supply was sufficient for people of moderate appetite, and the value of such a repast will have been about twenty dollars. On the other hand, all the *shoums* of the villages were not so well disposed; and it sometimes happened that we were nearly starving. It is, therefore, always a wise maxim in Abyssinia to eat while you can.

NOTE H.

The name of this adventurous German was Hugo Alfary. In a letter addressed to my brother, in 1874, he draws the following picture of the Egyptian camp at Keren in Bogos, one of the provinces which have been taken from Abyssinia by Egypt:—

"The pay of the troops has not been forthcoming for four months, and, owing to this, the discipline has fallen off considerably. Desertion does not take place at the rate of one man, but always eight or ten at a time, with arms and accoutrements, who roam about as robbers, and make the country much more unsafe than it was under the Abyssinian rule. The clanking of the chains of captured soldiers, and native Sheiks and chiefs who have expressed discontent at the Egyptian supremacy, and have to work in chains on a ship's biscuit a day, is dreadful to hear in the camp at Keren.

"With regard to the promotion of trade, the Egyptian Government does just the reverse of what it parades in newspaper reports as the main object of its policy of conquest—viz., the promotion of security on the trade routes. In the space of two months, no less than three caravans were seized and plundered. I myself was a witness of it; but the commander excused himself by saying he was in need of the cargo of the camels. The trade route from Kassala to Massowah can only be used by avoiding all Egyptian posts and camps, and the merchants go out of their way, through Hamasen, in order not to fall in with the troops in occupation; for the result of such a meeting would be maltreatment and the total loss of their goods."

This sad picture supports what I have before asserted—namely, that Egypt is doing more harm than good by her ambitious policy of annexation. The vast plains of the Soudan, through which the Nile flows down to Lower Egypt, are the real field to which the Khedive should turn his attention. It is lamentable to think that the Egyptian peasants are still forced to irrigate the land by means of hand wells and *sageers* turned by buffaloes, when such a mighty water power is at their command. A little engineering skill would make the Nile lift its own waters, and irrigate hundreds of miles of the fertile plains that border it on either side—I say fertile, for so productive is the sand of these plains, that when they are subjected to the action of water, vegetation appears on them spontaneously, and grows with the most marvellous rapidity. One half the ingenuity which the Egyptian Government has exercised in acquiring new provinces, would, if properly applied, have converted hundreds of thousands of acres of the Soudan into fruitful fields for the growth of cotton, coffee, &c.; while the money, time, and labour which have been wasted on the invasion of Abyssinia, would have sufficed to make a railway to Khartum.

Egypt is blessed with a mine of wealth in the Nile; let her cultivate its banks, and ameliorate the condition of her *own* peasantry; but until she enjoys the benefits of civilization at home, it is useless for her to pretend that she is doing good by extending her conquests abroad.

THE END.

BRADBURY, AGNEW, & CO., PRINTERS, WHITEFRIARS.

50A, ALBEMARLE STREET, LONDON,
September, 1877.

MR. MURRAY'S
GENERAL LIST OF WORKS.

ABINGER'S (LORD Chief Baron of the Exchequer) Life. By the Hon. P. CAMPBELL SCARLETT. Portrait. 8vo. 15s.

ALBERT MEMORIAL. A Descriptive and Illustrated Account of the National Monument erected to the PRINCE CONSORT at Kensington. Illustrated by Engravings of its Architecture, Decorations, Sculptured Groups, Statues, Mosaics, Metalwork, &c. With Descriptive Text. By DOYNE C. BELL. With 24 Plates. Folio. 12l. 12s.

——— HANDBOOK TO, 1s.; or Illustrated Edition, 2s. 6d.

——— (PRINCE) SPEECHES AND ADDRESSES, with an Introduction, giving some outline of his Character. With Portrait. 8vo. 10s. 6d.; or *Popular Edition*, fcap. 8vo. 1s.

ALBERT DÜRER; his Life, with a History of his Art. By DR. THAUSING, Keeper of Archduke Albert's Art Collection at Vienna. Translated from the German. With Portrait and Illustrations 2 vols. 8vo. [*In the Press.*

ABBOTT'S (REV. J.) Memoirs of a Church of England Missionary in the North American Colonies. Post 8vo. 2s.

ABERCROMBIE (JOHN). Enquiries concerning the Intellectual Powers and the Investigation of Truth. Fcap. 8vo. 3s. 6d.

——— Philosophy of the Moral Feelings. Fcap. 8vo. 2s. 6d.

ACLAND (REV. CHARLES). Popular Account of the Manners and Customs of India. Post 8vo. 2s.

ÆSOP'S FABLES. A New Version. With Historical Preface. By Rev. THOMAS JAMES. With 100 Woodcuts, by TENNIEL and WOLF. Post 8vo. 2s. 6d.

AGRICULTURAL (ROYAL) JOURNAL. (*Published half-yearly.*)

AIDS TO FAITH: a Series of Theological Essays. By various Authors. 8vo. 9s.
Contents:—Miracles; Evidences of Christianity; Prophecy & Mosaic Record of Creation; Ideology and Subscription; The Pentateuch; Inspiration; Death of Christ; Scripture and its Interpretation.

AMBER-WITCH (THE). A most interesting Trial for Witchcraft. Translated by LADY DUFF GORDON. Post 8vo. 2s.

ARMY LIST (THE). *Published Monthly by Authority.*

ARTHUR'S (LITTLE) History of England. By LADY CALLCOTT. *New Edition, continued to* 1872. With 36 Woodcuts. Fcap. 8vo. 1s. 6d.

AUSTIN (JOHN). LECTURES ON GENERAL JURISPRUDENCE; or, the Philosophy of Positive Law. Edited by ROBERT CAMPBELL. 2 Vols. 8vo. 32s.

——— STUDENT'S EDITION, by ROBERT CAMPBELL, compiled from the above work. Post 8vo. 12s.

——— Analysis of. By GORDON CAMPBELL, M.A. Post 8vo. 6s.

ARNOLD (THOS.). Ecclesiastical and Secular Architecture of Scotland: The Abbeys, Churches, Castles, and Mansions. With Illustrations. Medium 8vo. [*In Preparation.*

B

LIST OF WORKS

ATKINSON (Dr. R.) Vie de Seint Auban. A Poem in Norman-French. Ascribed to MATTHEW PARIS. With Concordance, Glossary, and Notes. Small 4to, 10s. 6d.

ADMIRALTY PUBLICATIONS; Issued by direction of the Lords Commissioners of the Admiralty:—

A MANUAL OF SCIENTIFIC ENQUIRY, for the Use of Travellers. *Fourth Edition.* Edited by ROBERT MAIN, M.A. Woodcuts. Post 8vo. 3s. 6d.

GREENWICH ASTRONOMICAL OBSERVATIONS 1841 to 1846, and 1847 to 1871. Royal 4to. 20s. each.

MAGNETICAL AND METEOROLOGICAL OBSERVATIONS. 1840 to 1847. Royal 4to. 20s. each.

APPENDICES TO OBSERVATIONS.
- 1837. Logarithms of Sines and Cosines in Time. 3s.
- 1842. Catalogue of 1439 Stars, from Observations made in 1836 to 1811. 4s.
- 1845. Longitude of Valentia (Chronometrical). 3s.
- 1847. Description of Altazimuth. 3s.
  - Twelve Years' Catalogue of Stars, from Observations made in 1836 to 1847. 4s.
  - Description of Photographic Apparatus. 2s.
- 1851. Maskelyne's Ledger of Stars. 3s.
- 1852. I. Description of the Transit Circle. 3s.
- 1853. Refraction Tables. 3s.
- 1854. Description of the Zenith Tube. 3s.
  - Six Years' Catalogue of Stars, from Observations. 1848 to 1853. 4s.
- 1862. Seven Years' Catalogue of Stars, from Observations. 1854 to 1860. 10s.
  - Plan of Ground Buildings. 3s.
  - Longitude of Valentia (Galvanic). 2s.
- 1864. Moon's Semid. from Occultations. 2s.
  - Planetary Observations, 1831 to 1835. 2s.
- 1868. Corrections of Elements of Jupiter and Saturn. 2s.
  - Second Seven Years' Catalogue of 2760 Stars for 1861 to 1867. 4s.
  - Description of the Great Equatorial. 3s.
- 1856. Descriptive Chronograph. 3s.
- 1860. Reduction of Deep Thermometer Observations. 2s.
- 1871. History and Description of Water Telescope. 3s.

Cape of Good Hope Observations (Star Ledgers). 1856 to 1863. 2s.
— — ——— 1856. 5s.
——————— Astronomical Results. 1857 to 1858. 5s.
Report on Teneriffe Astronomical Experiment. 1856. 5s.
Paramatta Catalogue of 7385 Stars. 1822 to 1826. 4s.

ASTRONOMICAL RESULTS. 1847 to 1871. 4to. 3s. each.

MAGNETICAL AND METEOROLOGICAL RESULTS. 1847 to 1871. 4to. 3s. each.

REDUCTION OF THE OBSERVATIONS OF PLANETS. 1750 to 1830. Royal 4to. 20s. each.
——————— LUNAR OBSERVATIONS. 1750 to 1830. 2 Vols. Royal 4to. 20s. each.
——————— 1831 to 1851. 4to. 10s. each.

BERNOULLI'S SEXCENTENARY TABLE. 1778. 4to. 5s.

BESSEL'S AUXILIARY TABLES FOR HIS METHOD OF CLEARING LUNAR DISTANCES. 8vo. 2s.

ENCKE'S BERLINER JAHRBUCH, for 1830. *Berlin*, 1828. 8vo. 9s.

HANSEN'S TABLES DE LA LUNE. 4to. 20s.

LAX'S TABLES FOR FINDING THE LATITUDE AND LONGITUDE. 1821. 8vo. 10s.

LUNAR OBSERVATIONS at GREENWICH. 1783 to 1819. Compared with the Tables, 1821. 4to. 7s. 6d.

MACLEAR ON LACAILLE'S ARC OF MERIDIAN. 2 Vols. 20s. each.

ADMIRALTY PUBLICATIONS—continued.
MAYER'S DISTANCES of the MOON'S CENTRE from the PLANETS. 1822, 3s.; 1823, 4s. 6d. 1824 to 1835. 8vo. 4s. each.
———— TABULÆ MOTUUM SOLIS ET LUNÆ. 1770. 5s.
———— ASTRONOMICAL OBSERVATIONS MADE AT GOTTINGEN, from 1756 to 1761. 1826. Folio. 7s. 6d.
NAUTICAL ALMANACS, from 1767 to 1877, 80s. 2s. 6d. each.
———————— SELECTIONS FROM, up to 1812. 8vo. 5s. 1834-54. 5s.
———————— SUPPLEMENTS, 1828 to 1833, 1837 and 1838. 2s. each.
———————— TABLE requisite to be used with the N.A. 1781. 8vo. 5s.
SABINE'S PENDULUM EXPERIMENTS to DETERMINE THE FIGURE OF THE EARTH. 1825. 4to. 40s.
SHEPHERD'S TABLES for CORRECTING LUNAR DISTANCES. 1772. Royal 4to. 21s.
———————— TABLES, GENERAL, of the MOON'S DISTANCE from the SUN, and 10 STARS. 1787. Follo. 5s. 6d.
TAYLOR'S SEXAGESIMAL TABLE. 1780. 4to. 15s.
———————— TABLES OF LOGARITHMS. 4to. 60s.
TIARK'S ASTRONOMICAL OBSERVATIONS for the LONGITUDE of MADEIRA. 1822. 4to. 5s.
———————— CHRONOMETRICAL OBSERVATIONS for DIFFERENCES of LONGITUDE between DOVER, PORTSMOUTH, and FALMOUTH. 1823. 4to. 5s.
VENUS and JUPITER: OBSERVATIONS of, compared with the TABLES. London, 1822. 4to. 2s.
WALES' AND BAYLY'S ASTRONOMICAL OBSERVATIONS. 1777. 4to. 21s.
———————— REDUCTION OF ASTRONOMICAL OBSERVATIONS MADE IN THE SOUTHERN HEMISPHERE. 1764-1771. 1788. 4to. 10s. 6d.

BARBAULD (MRS.). Hymns in Prose for Children. With Illustrations. Crown 8vo.

BARCLAY (JOSEPH, LL.D.). The Talmud: being Selected Extracts, chiefly illustrating the Teaching of the Bible. With an Introduction describing the General Character of the Talmud. 8vo.

BARKLEY (H. C.). Five Years among the Bulgarians and Turks between the Danube and the Black Sea. Post 8vo. 10s. 6d.

———————— My Boyhood: a True Story. With Illustrations. Post 8vo. A Christmas Book for Schoolboys and others.

BARROW (SIR JOHN). Autobiographical Memoir, from Early Life to Advanced Age. Portrait. 8vo. 16s.

———————— (JOHN) Life, Exploits, and Voyages of Sir Francis Drake. Post 8vo. 2s.

BARRY (SIR CHARLES). Life and Works. By CANON BARRY. With Portrait and Illustrations. Medium 8vo. 15s.

BATES' (H. W.) Records of a Naturalist on the River Amazon during eleven years of Adventure and Travel. Illustrations. Post 8vo. 7s. 6d.

BAX (CAPT. R.N.). Russian Tartary, Eastern Siberia, China, Japan, and Formosa. A Narrative of a Cruise in the Eastern Seas. With Map and Illustrations. Crown 8vo. 12s.

BELCHER (LADY). Account of the Mutineers of the 'Bounty,' and their Descendants; with their Settlements in Pitcairn and Norfolk Islands. With Illustrations. Post 8vo. 12s.

BELL'S (SIR CHAS.) Familiar Letters. Portrait. Post 8vo. 12s.

BELL (DOYNE C.). Notices of the Historic Interments in the Church of St. Peter ad Vincula, in the Tower of London, with an account of the discovery of the remains of Queen Anne Boleyn. With Illustrations. Crown 8vo. 14s.

BELT (THOS.). Naturalist in Nicaragua, including a Residence at the Gold Mines of Chontales; with Journeys in the Savannahs and Forests; and Observations on Animals and Plants. Illustrations. Post 8vo. 12s.

BERTRAM (JAS. G.). Harvest of the Sea: an Account of British Food Fishes, including sketches of Fisheries and Fisher Folk. With 50 Illustrations. 8vo. 9s.

BIBLE COMMENTARY. EXPLANATORY and CRITICAL. With a REVISION of the TRANSLATION. By BISHOPS and CLERGY of the ANGLICAN CHURCH. Edited by F. C. COOK, M.A., Canon of Exeter. VOLS. I. to VI. (The Old Testament). Medium 8vo. 6l. 15s.

Vol. I. 30s.	GENESIS. EXODUS. LEVITICUS. NUMBERS. DEUTERONOMY.	
Vols. II. and III. 36s.	JOSHUA, JUDGES, RUTH, SAMUEL, KINGS, CHRONICLES, EZRA, NEHEMIAH, ESTHER.	
Vol. IV. 24s.	JOB. PSALMS. PROVERBS. ECCLESIASTES. SONG OF SOLOMON.	
Vol. V. 20s.	ISAIAH. JEREMIAH.	
Vol. VI. 25s.	EZEKIEL. DANIEL. MINOR PROPHETS.	

BIGG-WITHER (T. P.). Pioneering in S. Brazil; three years of forest and prairie life in the province of Parana. Map and Illustrations. 8vo. [*In the Press.*

BIRCH (SAMUEL). History of Ancient Pottery and Porcelain: Egyptian, Assyrian, Greek, Roman, and Etruscan. With Coloured Plates and 200 Illustrations. Medium 8vo. 42s.

BIRD (ISABELLA). Hawaiian Archipelago; or Six Months among the Palm Groves, Coral Reefs, and Volcanoes of the Sandwich Islands. With Illustrations. Crown 8vo. 7s. 6d.

BISSET (GENERAL). Sport and War in South Africa from 1834 to 1867, with a Narrative of the Duke of Edinburgh's Visit. With Map and Illustrations. Crown 8vo. 14s.

BLACKSTONE'S COMMENTARIES; adapted to the Present State of the Law. By R. MALCOLM KERR, LL.D. *Revised Edition,* incorporating all the Recent Changes in the Law. 4 vols. 8vo. 60s.

BLUNT (REV. J. J.). Undesigned Coincidences in the Writings of the Old and New Testaments, an Argument of their Veracity: containing the Books of Moses, Historical and Prophetical Scriptures, and the Gospels and Acts. Post 8vo. 6s.

———— History of the Church in the First Three Centuries. Post 8vo. 6s.

———— Parish Priest; His Duties, Acquirements and Obligations. Post 8vo. 6s.

———— Lectures on the Right Use of the Early Fathers. 8vo. 9s.

———— University Sermons. Post 8vo. 6s.

———— Plain Sermons. 2 vols. Post 8vo. 12s.

BLOMFIELD'S (BISHOP) Memoir, with Selections from his Correspondence. By his Son. Portrait, post 8vo. 12s.

BOSWELL'S (James) Life of Samuel Johnson, LL.D. Including the Tour to the Hebrides. Edited by Mr. Croker. *Seventh Edition.* Portraits. 1 vol. Medium 8vo. 12s.

BRACE (C. L.) Manual of Ethnology; or the Races of the Old World. Post 8vo. 6s.

BOOK OF COMMON PRAYER. Illustrated with Coloured Borders, Initial Letters, and Woodcuts. 8vo. 18s.

BORROW (George) Bible in Spain; or the Journeys, Adventures, and Imprisonments of an Englishman in an Attempt to circulate the Scriptures in the Peninsula. Post 8vo. 5s.

—— Gypsies of Spain; their Manners, Customs, Religion, and Language. With Portrait. Post 8vo. 5s.

—— Lavengro; The Scholar—The Gypsy—and the Priest. Post 8vo. 5s.

—— Romany Rye—a Sequel to "Lavengro." Post 8vo. 5s.

—— Wild Wales: its People, Language, and Scenery. Post 8vo. 5s.

—— Romano Lavo-Lil; Word-Book of the Romany, or English Gvp-y Language; with Specimens of their Poetry, and an account of certain Gypsyries. Post 8vo. 10s. 6d.

BRAY (Mrs.) Life of Thomas Stothard, R.A. With Portrait and 60 Woodcuts. 4to. 21s.

BRITISH ASSOCIATION REPORTS. 8vo.

York and Oxford, 1831-32, 13s. 6d.
Cambridge, 1833, 12s.
Edinburgh, 1834, 15s.
Dublin, 1835, 13s. 6d.
Bristol, 1836, 12s.
Liverpool, 1837, 16s. 6d.
Newcastle, 1838, 15s.
Birmingham, 1839, 13s. 6d.
Glasgow, 1840, 15s.
Plymouth, 1841, 13s. 6d.
Manchester, 1842, 10s. 6d.
Cork, 1843, 12s.
York, 1844, 20s.
Cambridge, 1845, 12s.
Southampton, 1846, 15s.
Oxford, 1847, 18s.
Swansea, 1848, 9s.
Birmingham, 1849, 10s.
Edinburgh, 1850, 15s.
Ipswich, 1851, 16s. 6d.
Belfast, 1852, 15s.
Hull, 1853, 10s. 6d.
Liverpool, 1854, 18s.
Glasgow, 1855, 15s.
Cheltenham, 1856, 18s.
Dublin, 1857, 15s.
Leeds, 1858, 20s.
Aberdeen, 1859, 15s.
Oxford, 1860, 25s.
Manchester, 1861, 15s.
Cambridge, 1862, 20s.
Newcastle, 1863, 25s.
Bath, 1864, 18s.
Birmingham, 1865, 25s
Nottingham, 1866, 24s.
Dundee, 1867, 26s.
Norwich, 1868, 25s.
Exeter, 1869, 22s.
Liverpool, 1870, 18s.
Edinburgh, 1871, 16s.
Brighton, 1872, 24s.
Bradford, 1873, 25s.
Belfast, 1874, 2)s.
Bristol, 1875, 25s.
Glasgow, 1876, 25s.

BROUGHTON (Lord) Journey through Albania, Turkey in Europe and Asia, to Constantinople. Illustrations. 2 Vols. 8vo. 30s.

—— - Visits to Italy. 2 Vols. Post 8vo. 18s.

BRUGSCH (Professor) History of Egypt, from the earliest period. Derived from Monuments and Inscriptions. *New Edition.* Translated by H. Danby Seymour. 2 vols. 8vo. [*In Preparation.*

BUCKLEY (Arabella B.) Short History of Natural Science, and the Progress of Discovery from the time of the Greeks to the present day, for Schools and young Persons. Illustrations. Post 8vo. 9s.

BURGON (Rev. J. W.). Christian Gentleman; or, Memoir of Patrick Fraser Tytler. Post 8vo. 9s.

—— Letters from Rome. Post 8vo. 12s.

BURN (Col.). Dictionary of Naval and Military Technical Terms, English and French—French and English. Crown 8vo. 15s.

BUXTON'S (Charles) Memoirs of Sir Thomas Fowell Buxton, Bart. With Selections from his Correspondence. Portrait. 8vo. 16s. *Popular Edition.* Fcap. 8vo. 5s.

————— Ideas of the Day. 8vo. 5s.

BURCKHARDT'S (Dr. Jacob) Cicerone ; or Art Guide to Painting in Italy. Edited by Rev. Dr. A. Von Zahn, and Translated from the German by Mrs. A. Clough. Post 8vo. 6s.

BYLES' (Sir John) Foundations of Religion in the Mind and Heart of Man. Post 8vo. 6s.

BYRON'S (Lord) Life, Letters, and Journals. By Thomas Moore. *Cabinet Edition.* Plates. 6 Vols. Fcap. 8vo. 18s.; or One Volume, Portraits. Royal 8vo., 7s. 6d.

————— and Poetical Works. *Popular Edition.* Portraits. 2 vols. Royal 8vo. 15s.

————— Poetical Works. *Library Edition.* Portrait. 6 Vols. 8vo. 45s.

————— *Cabinet Edition.* Plates. 10 Vols. 12mo. 30s.

————— *Pocket Edition.* 8 Vols. 24mo. 21s. *In a case.*

————— *Popular Edition.* Plates. Royal 8vo. 7s. 6d.

————— *Pearl Edition.* Crown 8vo. 2s. 6d.

————— Childe Harold. With 80 Engravings. Crown 8vo. 12s.

————————————— 16mo. 2s. 6d.

————————————— Vignettes. 16mo. 1s.

————————————— Portrait. 16mo. 6d.

————— Tales and Poems. 24mo. 2s. 6d.

————— Miscellaneous. 2 Vols. 24mo. 5s.

————— Dramas and Plays. 2 Vols. 24mo. 5s.

————— Don Juan and Beppo. 2 Vols. 24mo. 5s.

————— Beauties. Poetry and Prose. Portrait. Fcap. 8vo. 3s. 6d.

BUTTMAN'S Lexilogus ; a Critical Examination of the Meaning of numerous Greek Words, chiefly in Homer and Hesiod. By Rev. J. R. Fishlake. 8vo. 12s.

————— Irregular Greek Verbs. With all the Tenses extant—their Formation, Meaning, and Usage, with Notes, by Rev. J. R. Fishlake. Post 8vo. 6s.

CALLCOTT (Lady). Little Arthur's History of England. *New Edition,* brought down to 1872. With Woodcuts. Fcap. 8vo. 1s. 6d.

CARNARVON (Lord). Portugal, Gallicia, and the Basque Provinces. Post 8vo. 3s. 6d.

CARTWRIGHT (W. C.). The Jesuits : their Constitution and Teaching. An Historical Sketch. 8vo. 9s.

CASTLEREAGH (The) Despatches, from the commencement of the official career of Viscount Castlereagh to the close of his life. 12 Vols. 8vo. 14s. each.

CAMPBELL (Lord). Lord Chancellors and Keepers of the Great Seal of England. From the Earliest Times to the Death of Lord Eldon in 1838. 10 Vols. Crown 8vo. 6s. each.

————— Chief Justices of England. From the Norman Conquest to the Death of Lord Tenterden. 4 Vols. Crown 8vo. 6s. each.

CAMPBELL (Lord). Lives of Lyndhurst and Brougham. 8vo. 16s.
——— Shakspeare's Legal Acquirements. 8vo. 5s. 6d.
——— Lord Bacon. Fcap. 8vo. 2s. 6d.
——— (Sir George) India as it may be: an Outline of a proposed Government and Policy. 8vo. 12s.
——— Handy-Book on the Eastern Question; being a Very Recent View of Turkey. With Map. Post 8vo. 9s.
——— (Thos.) Essay on English Poetry. With Short Lives of the British Poets. Post 8vo. 3s. 6d.
CAVALCASELLE and CROWE'S History of Painting in North Italy, from the 14th to the 16th Century. With Illustrations. 2 Vols. 8vo. 42s.
——— Early Flemish Painters, their Lives and Works. Illustrations. Post 8vo. 10s. 6d.; or Large Paper, 8vo. 15s.
——— Life and Times of Titian, with some Account of his Family. With Portrait and Illustrations. 2 vols. 8vo. 42s.
CESNOLA (Gen. L. P. di). Cyprus; its Ancient Cities, Tombs, and Temples. A Narrative of Researches and Excavations during Ten Years' Residence in that Island. With numerous Illustrations. Medium 8vo. [In Preparation.
CHILD (G. Chaplin, M.D.). Benedicite; or, Song of the Three Children; being Illustrations of the Power, Beneficence, and Design manifested by the Creator in his works. Post 8vo. 6s.
CHISHOLM (Mrs.).. Perils of the Polar Seas; True Stories of Arctic Discovery and Adventure. Illustrations. Post 8vo. 6s.
CHURTON (Archdeacon). Poetical Remains, Translations and Imitations. Portrait. Post 8vo. 7s. 6d.
——— New Testament. Edited with a Plain Practical Commentary for Families and General Readers. With 100 Panoramic and other Views, from Sketches made on the Spot. 2 vols. 8vo. 21s.
CICERO'S Life and Times. His Character as a Statesman, Orator, and Friend, with a Selection from his Correspondence and Orations. By William Forsyth. With Illustrations. 8vo. 10s. 6d.
CLARK (Sir James). Memoir of Dr. John Conolly. Comprising a Sketch of the Treatment of the Insane in Europe and America. With Portrait. Post 8vo. 10s. 6d.
CLIVE'S (Lord) Life. By Rev. G. R. Gleig. Post 8vo. 3s. 6d.
CLODE (C. M.). Military Forces of the Crown; their Administration and Government. 2 Vols. 8vo. 21s. each.
——— Administration of Justice under Military and Martial Law, as applicable to the Army, Navy, Marine, and Auxiliary Forces. 8vo. 12s.
CHURCH (The) & THE AGE. Essays on the Principles and Present Position of the Anglican Church. By various Authors. 2 vols. 8vo. 26s.
COLCHESTER (The) Papers. The Diary and Correspondence of Charles Abbott, Lord Colchester, Speaker of the House of Commons, 1802-1817. Portrait. 3 Vols. 8vo. 42s.
COLERIDGE'S (Samuel Taylor) Table-Talk. Portrait. 12mo. 3s. 6d.
COLLINGWOOD (Cuthbert). Rambles of a Naturalist on the Shores and Waters of the China Sea. With Illustrations. 8vo. 16s.
COLONIAL LIBRARY. [See Home and Colonial Library.]

8 LIST OF WORKS

COMPANIONS FOR THE DEVOUT LIFE. Lectures delivered in St. James's Church. 1st Series, 1875. 2nd Series, 1876. New Edition in 1 vol., post 8vo. [*In the Press.*
COOK (Canon). Sermons Preached at Lincoln's Inn. 8vo. 9s.
COOKE (E. W.). Leaves from my Sketch-Book. Being a selection from sketches made during many tours. 25 Plates. Small folio. 31s. 6d.
——— A Second Series of Leaves from my Sketch Book. Consisting chiefly of Views in Egypt and the East. With Descriptive Text. Small folio. [*In the Press.*
COOKERY (MODERN DOMESTIC). Founded on Principles of Economy and Practical Knowledge. By a Lady. Woodcuts. Fcap. 8vo. 5s.
COOPER (T. T.). Travels of a Pioneer of Commerce on an Overland Journey from China towards India. Illustrations. 8vo. 16s.
CORNWALLIS (THE) Papers and Correspondence during the American War,—Administrations in India,—Union with Ireland, and Peace of Amiens. 3 Vols. 8vo. 63s.
COWPER'S (COUNTESS) Diary while Lady of the Bedchamber to Caroline, Princess of Wales, 1714—20. Portrait. 8vo. 10s. 6d.
CRABBE (REV. GEORGE). Life and Poetical Works. With Illustrations. Royal 8vo. 7s.
CRAWFORD & BALCARRES (Earl of). Etruscan Inscriptions. Analyzed, Translated, and Commented upon. 8vo. 12s.
——— ——— Argo ; or the Quest of the Golden Fleece. A Metrical Tale, in Ten Books. 8vo. 10s. 6d.
CROKER (J. W.). Progressive Geography for Children. 18mo. 1s. 6d.
——— Stories for Children, Selected from the History of England. Woodcuts. 16mo. 2s. 6d.
——— Boswell's Life of Johnson. Including the Tour to the Hebrides. *Seventh Edition.* Portraits. 8vo. 12s.
——— Early Period of the French Revolution. 8vo. 15s.
——— Historical Essay on the Guillotine. Fcap. 8vo. 1s.
CROWE AND CAVALCASELLE. Lives of the Early Flemish Painters. Woodcuts. Post 8vo, 10s. 6d.; or Large Paper, 8vo, 15s.
——— History of Painting in North Italy, from 14th to 16th Century. Derived from Researches into the Works of Art in that Country. With Illustrations. 2 Vols. 8vo. 42s.
——— Life and Times of Titian, with some Account of his Family, chiefly from new and unpublished records. With Portrait and Illustrations. 2 vols. 8vo. 42s.
CUMMING (R. GORDON). Five Years of a Hunter's Life in the Far Interior of South Africa. Woodcuts. Post 8vo. 6s.
CUNYNGHAME (SIR ARTHUR). Travels in the Eastern Caucasus, on the Caspian and Black Seas, in Daghestan and the Frontiers of Persia and Turkey. With Map and Illustrations. 8vo. 18s.
CURTIUS' (PROFESSOR) Student's Greek Grammar, for the Upper Forms. Edited by DR. WM. SMITH. Post 8vo. 6s.
——— Elucidations of the above Grammar. Translated by EVELYN ABBOT. Post 8vo. 7s. 6d.
——— Smaller Greek Grammar for the Middle and Lower Forms. Abridged from the larger work. 12mo. 3s. 6d.
——— Accidence of the Greek Language. Extracted from the above work. 12mo. 2s. 6d.
——— Principles of Greek Etymology. Translated by A. S. WILKINS, M.A., and E. B. ENGLAND, B.A. 2 vols. 8vo. 15s. each.

PUBLISHED BY MR. MURRAY. 9

CURZON (Hon. Robert). Visits to the Monasteries of the Levant.
Illustrations. Post 8vo. 7s. 6d.

CUST (General). Warriors of the 17th Century—The Thirty Years'
War. 2 Vols. 16s. Civil Wars of France and England. 2 Vols. 16s.
Commanders of Fleets and Armies. 2 Vols. 18s.

―――― Annals of the Wars—18th & 19th Century, 1700—1815.
With Maps. 9 Vols. Post 8vo. 5s. each.

DAVIS (Nathan). Ruined Cities of Numidia and Carthaginia.
Illustrations. 8vo. 16s.

DAVY (Sir Humphry). Consolations in Travel; or, Last Days
of a Philosopher. Woodcuts. Fcap. 8vo. 3s. 6d.

―――― Salmonia; or, Days of Fly Fishing. Woodcuts.
Fcap. 8vo. 3s. 6d.

DARWIN (Charles). Journal of a Naturalist during a Voyage
round the World. Crown 8vo. 9s.

―――― Origin of Species by Means of Natural Selection;
or, the Preservation of Favoured Races in the Struggle for Life.
Crown 8vo. 7s. 6d.

―――― Variation of Animals and Plants under Domestication.
With Illustrations. 2 Vols. Crown 8vo. 18s.

―――― Descent of Man, and Selection in Relation to Sex.
With Illustrations. Crown 8vo. 9s.

―――― Expressions of the Emotions in Man and Animals.
With Illustrations. Crown 8vo. 12s.

―――― Various Contrivances by which Orchids are Fertilized
by Insects. Woodcuts. Crown 8vo. 9s.

―――― Movements and Habits of Climbing Plants. Woodcuts. Crown 8vo. 6s.

―――― Insectivorous Plants. Woodcuts. Crown 8vo. 14s.

―――― Effects of Cross and Self-Fertilization in the Vegetable Kingdom. Crown 8vo. 12s.

―――― Facts and Argument for Darwin. By Fritz Muller.
Translated by W. S. Dallas. Woodcuts. Post 8vo. 6s.

―――― Different Forms of Flowers on Plants of the same
Species. Crown 8vo. 10s. 6d.

DE COSSON (E. A.). The Cradle of the Blue Nile; a Journey
through Abyssinia and Soudan, and a residence at the Court of King
John of Ethiopia. Map and Illustrations. 2 vols. Post 8vo. 21s.

DELEPIERRE (Octave). History of Flemish Literature. 8vo. 9s.

DENNIS (George). The Cities and Cemeteries of Etruria. An
entirely new Edition, with a new Chapter on Etrurian Bologna.
Numerous Illustrations. 2 vols. 8vo. [In the Press.

DENT (Emma). Annals of Winchcombe and Sudeley. With 120
Portraits, Plates and Woodcuts. 4to. 42s.

DERBY (Earl of). Iliad of Homer rendered into English
Blank Verse. 10th Edition. With Portrait. 2 Vols. Post 8vo. 10s.

DERRY (Bishop of). Witness of the Psalms to Christ and Christianity. The Bampton Lectures for 1876. 8vo. 10s. 6d.

DEUTSCH (Emanuel). Talmud, Islam, The Targums and other
Literary Remains. 8vo. 12s.

DILKE (Sir C. W.). Papers of a Critic. Selected from the
Writings of the late Chas. Wentworth Dilke. With a Biographical Sketch. 2 Vols. 8vo. 24s.

DOG-BREAKING, with Odds and Ends for those who love the Dog and Gun. By GEN. HUTCHINSON. With 40 Illustrations. Crown 8vo. 7s. 6d.

DOMESTIC MODERN COOKERY. Founded on Principles of Economy and Practical Knowledge, and adapted for Private Families. Woodcuts. Fcap. 8vo. 5s.

DOUGLAS'S (SIR HOWARD) Life and Adventures. Portrait. 8vo. 15s.

————— Theory and Practice of Gunnery. Plates. 8vo. 21s.

————— Construction of Bridges and the Passage of Rivers, in Military Operations. Plates. 8vo. 21s.

————— (WM.) Horse-Shoeing; As it Is, and As it Should be. Illustrations. Post 8vo. 7s. 6d.

DRAKE'S (SIR FRANCIS) Life, Voyages, and Exploits, by Sea and Land. By JOHN BARROW. Post 8vo. 2s.

DRINKWATER (JOHN). History of the Siege of Gibraltar, 1779-1783. With a Description and Account of that Garrison from the Earliest Periods. Post 8vo. 2s.

DUCANGE'S MEDIÆVAL LATIN-ENGLISH DICTIONARY. Translated and Edited by Rev. E. A. DAYMAN and J. H. HESSELS. Small 4to. [In preparation.

DU CHAILLU (PAUL B.). EQUATORIAL AFRICA, with Accounts of the Gorilla, the Nest-building Ape, Chimpanzee, Crocodile, &c. Illustrations. 8vo. 21s.

————— Journey to Ashango Land; and Further Penetration into Equatorial Africa. Illustrations. 8vo. 21s.

DUFFERIN (LORD). Letters from High Latitudes; a Yacht Voyage to Iceland, Jan Mayen, and Spitzbergen. Woodcuts. Post 8vo. 7s. 6d.

DUNCAN (MAJOR). History of the Royal Artillery. Compiled from the Original Records. With Portraits. 2 Vols. 8vo. 30s.

————— The English in Spain; or, The Story of the Civil War between Christinos and Carlists in 1834 and 1840. Compiled from the Letters, Journals, and Reports of the British Commissioners with Queen Isabella's Armies. With Plates. 8vo.

EASTLAKE (SIR CHARLES). Contributions to the Literature of the Fine Arts. With Memoir of the Author, and Selections from his Correspondence. By LADY EASTLAKE. 2 Vols. 8vo. 24s.

EDWARDS' (W. H.) Voyage up the River Amazons, including a Visit to Para. Post 8vo. 2s.

EIGHT MONTHS AT ROME, during the Vatican Council, with a Daily Account of the Proceedings. By POMPONIO LETO. Translated from the Original. 8vo. 12s.

ELDON'S (LORD) Public and Private Life, with Selections from his Correspondence and Diaries. By HORACE TWISS. Portrait. 2 Vols. Post 8vo. 21s.

ELGIN'S (LORD) Letters and Journals. Edited by THEODORE WALROND. With Preface by Dean Stanley. 8vo. 14s.

ELLESMERE (LORD). Two Sieges of Vienna by the Turks. Translated from the German. Post 8vo. 2s.

ELLIS (W.). Madagascar Revisited. Setting forth the Persecutions and Heroic Sufferings of the Native Christians. Illustrations. 8vo. 16s.

————— Memoir. By HIS SON. With his Character and Work. By REV. HENRY ALLON, D.D. Portrait. 8vo. 10s. 6d.

————— (ROBINSON) Poems and Fragments of Catullus. 16mo. 5s.

ELPHINSTONE (Hon. Mountstuart). History of India—the Hindoo and Mahomedau Periods. Edited by Professor Cowell. Map. 8vo. 18s.

——— ——(H. W.) Patterns for Turning; Comprising Elliptical and other Figures cut on the Lathe without the use of any Ornamental Chuck. With 70 Illustrations. Small 4to. 15s.

ENGLAND. See Callcott, Croker, Hume, Markham, Smith, and Stanhope.

ESSAYS ON CATHEDRALS. With an Introduction. By Dean Howson. 8vo. 12s.

ELZE (Karl). Life of Lord Byron. With a Critical Essay on his Place in Literature. Translated from the German. With Portrait. 8vo. 16s.

FERGUSSON (James). History of Architecture in all Countries from the Earliest Times. With 1,600 Illustrations. 4 Vols. Medium 8vo.
Vol. I. & II. Ancient and Mediæval. 63s.
Vol. III. Indian and Eastern. 42s.
Vol. IV. Modern. 31s. 6d.

——————— Rude Stone Monuments in all Countries; their Age and Uses. With 230 Illustrations. Medium 8vo. 24s.

——————— Holy Sepulchre and the Temple at Jerusalem. Woodcuts. 8vo. 7s. 6d.

FLEMING (Professor). Student's Manual of Moral Philosophy. With Quotations and References. Post 8vo. 7s. 6d.

FLOWER GARDEN. By Rev. Thos. James. Fcap. 8vo. 1s.

FORD (Richard). Gatherings from Spain. Post 8vo. 3s. 6d.

FORSYTH (William). Life and Times of Cicero. With Selections from his Correspondence and Orations. Illustratious. 8vo. 10s. 6d.

——————— Hortensius; an Historical Essay on the Office and Duties of an Advocate. Illustrations. 8vo. 12s.

——————— History of Ancient Manuscripts. Post 8vo. 2s. 6d.

——————— Novels and Novelists of the 18th Century, in Illustration of the Manners and Morals of the Age. Post 8vo. 10s. 6d.

——————— The Slavonic Provinces South of the Danube; a Sketch of their History and Present State. Map. Post 8vo. 5s.

FORTUNE (Robert). Narrative of Two Visits to the Tea Countries of China, 1843-52. Woodcuts. 2 Vols. Post 8vo. 18s.

FORSTER (John). The Early Life of Jonathan Swift. 1667-1711. With Portrait. 8vo. 15s.

FOSS (Edward). Biographia Juridica, or Biographical Dictionary of the Judges of England, from the Conquest to the Present Time, 1066-1870. Medium 8vo. 21s.

FRANCE (History of). See Markham—Smith—Student's.

FRENCH (The) in Algiers; The Soldier of the Foreign Legion— and the Prisoners of Abd-el-Kadir. Translated by Lady Duff Gordon. Post 8vo. 2s.

FRERE (Sir Bartle). Indian Missions. Small 8vo. 2s. 6d.

——————— Eastern Africa as a field for Missionary Labour. With Map. Crown 8vo. 5s.

——————— Bengal Famine. How it will be Met and How to Prevent Future Famines in India. With Maps. Crown 8vo. 5s.

GALTON (FRANCIS). Art of Travel; or, Hints on the Shifts and
Contrivances available in Wild Countries. Woodcuts. Post 8vo.
7s. 6d.

GEOGRAPHICAL SOCIETY'S JOURNAL. (*Published Yearly.*)

GEORGE (ERNEST). The Mosel; a Series of Twenty Etchings, with
Descriptive Letterpress. Imperial 4to. 42s.

——— Loire and South of France; a Series of Twenty
Etchings, with Descriptive Text. Folio. 42s.

GERMANY (HISTORY OF). See MARKHAM.

GIBBON (EDWARD). History of the Decline and Fall of the
Roman Empire. Edited by MILMAN and GUIZOT. Edited, with Notes,
by Dr. WM. SMITH. Maps. 8 Vols. 8vo. 60s.

——— (The Student's Gibbon); Being an Epitome of the
above work, incorporating the Researches of Recent Commentators. By
Dr. WM. SMITH. Woodcuts. Post 8vo. 7s. 6d.

GIFFARD (EDWARD). Deeds of Naval Daring; or, Anecdotes of
the British Navy. Fcap. 8vo. 3s. 6d.

GLADSTONE (W. E.). Financial Statements of 1853, 1860, 63-65.
8vo. 12s.

——— Rome and the Newest Fashions in Religion.
Three Tracts. 8vo. 7s. 6d.

GLEIG (G. R.). Campaigns of the British Army at Washington
and New Orleans. Post 8vo. 2s.

——— Story of the Battle of Waterloo. Post 8vo. 3s. 6d.

——— Narrative of Sale's Brigade in Affghanistan. Post 8vo. 2s.

——— Life of Lord Clive. Post 8vo. 3s. 6d.

——— Sir Thomas Munro. Post 8vo. 3s. 6d.

GLYNNE (SIR STEPHEN). Notes on the Churches of Kent.
With Illustrations. 8vo. [*In Preparation.*

GOLDSMITH'S (OLIVER) Works. Edited with Notes by PETER
CUNNINGHAM. Vignettes. 4 Vols. 8vo. 30s.

GORDON (SIR ALEX.). Sketches of German Life, and Scenes
from the War of Liberation. Post 8vo. 3s. 6d.

——— (LADY DUFF) Amber-Witch: A Trial for Witchcraft. Post 8vo. 2s.

——— French in Algiers. 1. The Soldier of the Foreign
Legion. 2. The Prisoners of Abd-el-Kadir. Post 8vo. 2s.

GRAMMARS. See CURTIUS; HALL; HUTTON; KING EDWARD;
ATTHIÆ; MAETZNER; SMITH.

GREECE (HISTORY OF). *See* GROTE—SMITH—Student.

GREY (EARL). Parliamentary Government and Reform; with
Suggestions for the Improvement of our Representative System.
Second Edition. 8vo. 9s.

GUIZOT (M.). Meditations on Christianity. 3 Vols. Post 8vo. 30s.

GROTE (GEORGE). History of Greece. From the Earliest Times
to the close of the generation contemporary with the death of Alexander
the Great. *Library Edition.* Portrait, Maps, and Plans. 10 Vols. 8vo.
120s. *Cabinet Edition.* Portrait and Plans. 12 Vols. Post 8vo. 6s. each.

——— PLATO, and other Companions of Socrates. 3 Vols. 8vo. 45s.

PUBLISHED BY MR. MURRAY. 13

GROTE (GEORGE). ARISTOTLE. 2 Vols. 8vo. 32s.
——— Minor Works. With Critical Remarks on his
Intellectual Character, Writings, and Speeches. By ALEX. BAIN, LL.D.
Portrait. 8vo. 14s.
——— Fragments on Ethical Subjects. Being a Selection from
his Posthumous Papers. With an Introduction. By ALEXANDER
BAIN, M.A. 8vo. 7s.
——— Letters on the Politics of Switzerland in 1847. 6s.
——— Personal Life. Compiled from Family Documents,
Private Memoranda, and Original Letters to and from Various
Friends. By Mrs. GROTE. Portrait. 8vo. 12s.

HALL (T. D.) AND Dr. WM. SMITH'S School Manual of English
Grammar. With Copious Exercises. 12mo. 3s. 6d.
——— Primary English Grammar for Elementary Schools.
Based on the above work. 16mo. 1s.
——— Child's First Latin Book, including a Systematic Treat-
ment of the New Pronunciation, and a full Praxis of Nouns, Adjec-
tives, and Pronouns. 16mo. 1s. 6d.

HALLAM (HENRY). Constitutional History of England, from the
Accession of Henry the Seventh to the Death of George the Second.
Library Edition. 3 Vols. 8vo. 30s. *Cabinet Edition*, 3 Vols. Post 8vo. 12s.
——— Student's Edition of the above work. Edited by
WM. SMITH, D.C.L. Post 8vo. 7s. 6d.
——— History of Europe during the Middle Ages. *Library
Edition*. 3 Vols. 8vo. 30s. *Cabinet Edition*, 3 Vols. Post 8vo. 12s.
——— Student's Edition of the above work. Edited by
WM. SMITH, D.C.L. Post 8vo. 7s. 6d.
——— Literary History of Europe, during the 15th, 16th and
17th Centuries. *Library Edition*. 3 Vols. 8vo. 86s. *Cabinet Edition*.
4 Vols. Post 8vo. 16s.
——— (ARTHUR) Literary Remains; in Verse and Prose.
Portrait. Fcap. 8vo. 3s. 6d.

HAMILTON (GEN. SIR F. W.). History of the Grenadier Guards.
From Original Documents in the Rolls' Records, War Office, Regimental
Records, &c. With Illustrations. 3 Vols. 8vo. 63s.

HART'S ARMY LIST. (*Published Quarterly and Annually*.)

HAY (SIR J. H. DRUMMOND). Western Barbary, its Wild Tribes
and Savage Animals. Post 8vo. 2s.

HEAD (SIR FRANCIS). Royal Engineer. Illustrations. 8vo. 12s.
——— Life of Sir John Burgoyne. Post 8vo. 1s.
——— Rapid Journeys across the Pampas. Post 8vo. 2s.
——— Bubbles from the Brunnen of Nassau. Illustrations.
Post 8vo. 7s. 6d.
——— Stokers and Pokers; or, the London and North Western
Railway. Post 8vo. 2s.
——— (SIR EDMUND) Shall and Will; or, Future Auxiliary
Verbs. Fcap. 8vo. 4s.

HEBER'S (BISHOP) Journals in India. 2 Vols. Post 8vo. 7s.
——— Poetical Works. Portrait. Fcap. 8vo. 3s. 6d.
——— Hymns adapted to the Church Service. 16mo. 1s. 6d.

FOREIGN HANDBOOKS.

HAND-BOOK—TRAVEL-TALK. English, French, German, and Italian. 18mo. 3s. 6d.

——— HOLLAND AND BELGIUM. Map and Plans. Post 8vo. 6s.

——— NORTH GERMANY and THE RHINE,— The Black Forest, the Hartz, Thüringerwald, Saxon Switzerland, Rügen the Giant Mountains, Taunus, Odenwald, Elsass, and Lothringen. Map and Plans. Post 8vo. 10s.

——— SOUTH GERMANY,— Wurtemburg, Bavaria, Austria, Styria, Salzburg, the Austrian and Bavarian Alps, Tyrol, Hungary, and the Danube, from Ulm to the Black Sea. Map. Post 8vo. 10s.

——— PAINTING. German, Flemish, and Dutch Schools. Illustrations. 2 Vols. Post 8vo. 24s.

——— LIVES OF EARLY FLEMISH PAINTERS. By CROWE and CAVALCASELLE. Illustrations. Post 8vo. 10s. 6d.

——— SWITZERLAND, Alps of Savoy, and Piedmont. Maps. Post 8vo. 9s.

——— FRANCE, Part I. Normandy, Brittany, the French Alps, the Loire, the Seine, the Garonne, and Pyrenees. Post 8vo. 7s. 6d.

——— Part II. Central France, Auvergne, the Cevennes, Burgundy, the Rhone and Saone, Provence, Nimes, Arles, Marseilles, the French Alps, Alsace, Lorraine, Champagne, &c. Maps. Post 8vo. 7s. 6d.

——— MEDITERRANEAN ISLANDS—Malta, Corsica, Sardinia, and Sicily. Maps. Post 8vo. [In the Press.

——— ALGERIA. Algiers, Constantine, Oran, the Atlas Range. Map. Post 8vo. 9s.

——— PARIS, and its Environs. Map. 16mo. 3s. 6d.

₊ MURRAY'S PLAN OF PARIS, mounted on canvas. 3s. 6d.

——— SPAIN, Madrid, The Castiles, The Basque Provinces, Leon, The Asturias, Galicia, Estremadura, Andalusia, Ronda, Granada, Murcia, Valencia, Catalonia, Aragon, Navarre, The Balearic Islands, &c. &c. Maps. 2 Vols. Post 8vo. 24s.

——— PORTUGAL, LISBON, Porto, Cintra, Mafra, &c. Map. Post 8vo. 12s.

——— NORTH ITALY, Turin, Milan, Cremona, the Italian Lakes, Bergamo, Brescia, Verona, Mantua, Vicenza, Padua, Ferrara, Bologna, Ravenna, Rimini, Piacenza, Genoa, the Riviera, Venice, Parma, Modena, and Romagna. Map. Post 8vo. 10s.

——— CENTRAL ITALY, Florence, Lucca, Tuscany, The Marches, Umbria, and late Patrimony of St. Peter's. Map. Post 8vo. 10s.

——— ROME AND ITS ENVIRONS. Map. Post 8vo. 10s.

——— SOUTH ITALY, Two Sicilies, Naples, Pompeii, Herculaneum, and Vesuvius. Map. Post 8vo. 10s.

——— KNAPSACK GUIDE TO ITALY. 16mo.

——— PAINTING. The Italian Schools. Illustrations. 2 Vols. Post 8vo. 30s.

——— LIVES OF ITALIAN PAINTERS, FROM CIMABUE to BASSANO. By Mrs. JAMESON. Portraits. Post 8vo. 12s.

——— NORWAY, Christiania, Bergen, Trondhjem. The Fjelds and Fjords. Map. Post 8vo. 9s.

——— SWEDEN, Stockholm, Upsala, Gothenburg, the Shores of the Baltic, &c. Post 8vo. 6s.

——— DENMARK, Sleswig, Holstein, Copenhagen, Jutland, Iceland. Map. Post 8vo. 6s.

PUBLISHED BY MR. MURRAY. 15

HAND-BOOK—RUSSIA, St. Petersburg, Moscow, Poland, and Finland. Maps. Post 8vo. 18s.

———— GREECE, the Ionian Islands, Continental Greece, Athens, the Peloponnesus, the Islands of the Ægean Sea, Albania, Thessaly, and Macedonia. Maps. Post 8vo. 15s.

———— TURKEY IN ASIA—Constantinople, the Bosphorus, Dardanelles, Broussa, Plain of Troy, Crete, Cyprus, Smyrna, Ephesus, the Seven Churches, Coasts of the Black Sea, Armenia, Mesopotamia, &c. Maps. Post 8vo. 15s.

———— EGYPT, including Descriptions of the Course of the Nile through Egypt and Nubia, Alexandria, Cairo, and Thebes, the Suez Canal, the Pyramids, the Peninsula of Sinai, the Oases, the Fyoom, &c. Map. Post 8vo. 15s.

———— HOLY LAND—Syria, Palestine, Peninsula of Sinai Edom, Syrian Deserts, Petra, Damascus, and Palmyra. Maps. Post 8vo. 20s. *₊* Travelling Map of Palestine. In a case. 12s.

———— INDIA — Bombay and Madras. Map. 2 Vols. Post 8vo. 12s. each.

ENGLISH HANDBOOKS.

HAND-BOOK—MODERN LONDON. Map. 16mo. 3s. 6d.

———— ENVIRONS OF LONDON within a circuit of 20 miles. 2 Vols. Crown 8vo. 21s.

———— EASTERN COUNTIES, Chelmsford, Harwich, Colchester, Maldon, Cambridge, Ely, Newmarket, Bury St. Edmunds, Ipswich, Woodbridge, Felixstowe, Lowestoft, Norwich, Yarmouth, Cromer, &c. Map and Plans. Post 8vo. 12s.

———— CATHEDRALS of Oxford, Peterborough, Norwich, Ely, and Lincoln. With 90 Illustrations. Crown 8vo. 18s.

———— KENT, Canterbury, Dover, Ramsgate, Sheerness, Rochester, Chatham, Woolwich. Map. Post 8vo. 7s. 6d.

———— SUSSEX, Brighton, Chichester, Worthing, Hastings, Lewes, Arundel, &c. Map. Post 8vo. 6s.

———— SURREY AND HANTS, Kingston, Croydon, Reigate, Guildford, Dorking, Boxhill, Winchester, Southampton, New Forest, Portsmouth, and Isle of Wight. Maps. Post 8vo. 10s.

———— BERKS, BUCKS, AND OXON, Windsor, Eton, Reading, Aylesbury. Uxbridge, Wycombe, Henley, the City and University of Oxford, Blenheim, and the Descent of the Thames. Map. Post 8vo. 7s. 6d.

———— WILTS, DORSET, AND SOMERSET, Salisbury, Chippenham, Weymouth. Sherborne, Wells, Bath, Bristol, Taunton, &c. Map. Post 8vo. 10s.

———— DEVON AND CORNWALL, Exeter, Ilfracombe, Linton, Sidmouth, Dawlish, Teignmouth, Plymouth, Devonport, Torquay, Launceston, Truro, Penzance, Falmouth, the Lizard, Land's End, &c. Maps. Post 8vo. 12s.

———— CATHEDRALS of Winchester, Salisbury, Exeter, Wells, Chichester, Rochester, Canterbury, and St. Albans. With 130 Illustrations. 2 Vols. Crown 8vo. 36s. St. Albans separately, crown 8vo. 6s.

———— GLOUCESTER, HEREFORD, and WORCESTER, Cirencester, Cheltenham, Stroud, Tewkesbury, Leominster, Ross, Malvern, Kidderminster, Dudley, Bromsgrove, Evesham. Map. Post 8vo. 9s.

———— CATHEDRALS of Bristol, Gloucester, Hereford, Worcester, and Lichfield. With 50 Illustrations. Crown 8vo. 16s.

HAND-BOOK—NORTH WALES, Bangor, Carnarvon, Beaumaris, Snowdon, Llanberis, Dolgelly, Cader Idris, Conway, &c. Map. Post 8vo. 7s.

———— SOUTH WALES, Monmouth, Llandaff, Merthyr, Vale of Neath, Pembroke, Carmarthen, Tenby, Swansea, The Wye, &c. Map. Post 8vo. 7s.

———— CATHEDRALS OF BANGOR, ST. ASAPH, Llandaff, and St. David's. With Illustrations. Post 8vo. 15s.

———— DERBY, NOTTS, LEICESTER, STAFFORD, Matlock, Bakewell, Chatsworth, The Peak, Buxton, Hardwick, Dove Dale, Ashborne, Southwell, Mansfield, Retford, Burton, Belvoir, Melton Mowbray, Wolverhampton, Lichfield, Walsall, Tamworth. Map. Post 8vo. 9s.

———— SHROPSHIRE, CHESHIRE AND LANCASHIRE —Shrewsbury, Ludlow, Bridgnorth, Oswestry, Chester, Crewe, Alderley, Stockport, Birkenhead, Warrington, Bury, Manchester, Liverpool, Burnley, Clitheroe, Bolton, Blackburn, Wigan, Preston, Rochdale, Lancaster, Southport, Blackpool, &c. Map. Post 8vo. 10s.

———— YORKSHIRE, Doncaster, Hull, Selby, Beverley, Scarborough, Whitby, Harrogate, Ripon, Leeds, Wakefield, Bradford, Halifax, Huddersfield, Sheffield. Map and Plans. Post 8vo. 12s.

———— CATHEDRALS of York, Ripon, Durham, Carlisle, Chester, and Manchester. With 60 Illustrations. 2 Vols. Crown 8vo. 21s.

———— DURHAM AND NORTHUMBERLAND, Newcastle, Darlington, Gateshead, Bishop Auckland, Stockton, Hartlepool, Sunderland, Shields, Berwick-on-Tweed, Morpeth, Tynemouth, Coldstream, Alnwick, &c. Map. Post 8vo. 9s.

———— WESTMORLAND AND CUMBERLAND—Lancaster, Furness Abbey, Ambleside, Kendal, Windermere, Coniston, Keswick, Grasmere, Ulswater, Carlisle, Cockermouth, Penrith, Appleby. Map Post 8vo. 6s.

*** MURRAY'S MAP OF THE LAKE DISTRICT, on canvas. 3s. 6d.

———— ENGLAND AND WALES. Alphabetically arranged and condensed into one volume. Post 8vo. [In the Press.

———— SCOTLAND, Edinburgh, Melrose, Kelso, Glasgow, Dumfries, Ayr, Stirling, Arran, The Clyde, Oban, Inverary, Loch Lomond, Loch Katrine and Trossachs, Caledonian Canal, Inverness, Perth, Dundee, Aberdeen, Braemar, Skye, Caithness, Ross, Sutherland, &c. Maps and Plans. Post 8vo. 9s.

———— IRELAND, Dublin, Belfast, Donegal, Galway, Wexford, Cork, Limerick, Waterford, Killarney, Munster, &c. Maps. Post 8vo. 12s.

HERODOTUS. A New English Version. Edited, with Notes and Essays, historical, ethnographical, and geographical, by CANON RAWLINSON, assisted by SIR HENRY RAWLINSON and SIR J. G. WILKINSON. Maps and Woodcuts. 4 Vols. 8vo. 48s.

HERSCHEL'S (CAROLINE) Memoir and Correspondence. By MRS. JOHN HERSCHEL. With Portraits. Crown 8vo 12s.

HATHERLEY (LORD). Continuity of Scripture, as Declared by the Testimony of our Lord and of the Evangelists and Apostles. 8vo. 6s. *Popular Edition.* Post 8vo. 2s. 6d.

HOLLWAY (J. G.). A Month in Norway. Fcap. 8vo. 2s.

HONEY BEE. By REV. THOMAS JAMES. Fcap. 8vo. 1s.

HOOK'S (DEAN) Church Dictionary. 8vo. 16s.

PUBLISHED BY MR. MURRAY. 17

HOME AND COLONIAL LIBRARY. A Series of Works adapted for all circles and classes of Readers, having been selected for their acknowledged interest, and ability of the Authors. Post 8vo. Published at 2s. and 3s. 6d. each, and arranged under two distinctive heads as follows:—

CLASS A.

HISTORY, BIOGRAPHY, AND HISTORIC TALES.

1. SIEGE OF GIBRALTAR. By JOHN DRINKWATER. 2s.
2. THE AMBER-WITCH. By LADY DUFF GORDON. 2s.
3. CROMWELL AND BUNYAN. By ROBERT SOUTHEY. 2s.
4. LIFE OF SIR FRANCIS DRAKE. By JOHN BARROW. 2s.
5. CAMPAIGNS AT WASHINGTON. By REV. G. R. GLEIG. 2s.
6. THE FRENCH IN ALGIERS. By LADY DUFF GORDON. 2s.
7. THE FALL OF THE JESUITS. 2s.
8. LIVONIAN TALES. 2s.
9. LIFE OF CONDÉ. By LORD MAHON. 3s. 6d.
10. SALE'S BRIGADE. By REV. G. R. GLEIG. 2s.
11. THE SIEGES OF VIENNA. By LORD ELLESMERE. 2s.
12. THE WAYSIDE CROSS. By CAPT. MILMAN. 2s.
13. SKETCHES OF GERMAN LIFE. By SIR A. GORDON. 3s. 6d.
14. THE BATTLE OF WATERLOO. By REV. G. R. GLEIG. 3s. 6d.
15. AUTOBIOGRAPHY OF STEFFENS. 2s.
16. THE BRITISH POETS. By THOMAS CAMPBELL. 3s. 6d.
17. HISTORICAL ESSAYS. By LORD MAHON. 3s. 6d.
18. LIFE OF LORD CLIVE. By REV. G. R. GLEIG. 3s. 6d.
19. NORTH - WESTERN RAILWAY. By SIR F. B. HEAD. 2s.
20. LIFE OF MUNRO. By REV. G. R. GLEIG. 3s. 6d.

CLASS B.

VOYAGES, TRAVELS, AND ADVENTURES.

1. BIBLE IN SPAIN. By GEORGE BORROW. 3s. 6d.
2. GYPSIES OF SPAIN. By GEORGE BORROW. 3s. 6d.
3 & 4. JOURNALS IN INDIA. By BISHOP HEBER. 2 Vols. 7s.
5. TRAVELS IN THE HOLY LAND. By IRBY and MANGLES. 2s.
6. MOROCCO AND THE MOORS. By J. DRUMMOND HAY. 2s.
7. LETTERS FROM THE BALTIC. By a LADY.
8. NEW SOUTH WALES. By MRS. MEREDITH. 2s.
9. THE WEST INDIES. By M. G. LEWIS. 2s.
10. SKETCHES OF PERSIA. By SIR JOHN MALCOLM. 3s. 6d.
11. MEMOIRS OF FATHER RIPA. 2s.
12 & 13. TYPEE AND OMOO. By HERMANN MELVILLE. 2 Vols. 7s.
14. MISSIONARY LIFE IN CANADA. By REV. J. ABBOTT. 2s.
15. LETTERS FROM MADRAS. By a LADY. 2s.
16. HIGHLAND SPORTS. By CHARLES ST. JOHN. 3s. 6d.
17. PAMPAS JOURNEYS. By SIR F. B. HEAD. 2s.
18. GATHERINGS FROM SPAIN. By RICHARD FORD. 3s. 6d.
19. THE RIVER AMAZON. By W. H. EDWARDS. 2s.
20. MANNERS & CUSTOMS OF INDIA. By REV. C. ACLAND. 2s.
21. ADVENTURES IN MEXICO. By G. F. RUXTON. 3s. 6d.
22. PORTUGAL AND GALICIA. By LORD CARNARVON. 3s. 6d.
23. BUSH LIFE IN AUSTRALIA. By REV. H. W. HAYGARTH. 2s.
24. THE LIBYAN DESERT. By BAYLE ST. JOHN. 2s.
25. SIERRA LEONE. By A LADY. 3s. 6d.

*** Each work may be had separately.

c

HOOK'S (THEODORE) Life. By J. G. LOCKHART. Fcap. 8vo. 1s.

HOPE (T. C.). ARCHITECTURE OF AHMEDABAD, with Historical Sketch and Architectural Notes. ' With Maps, Photographs, and Woodcuts. 4to. 5l. 5s.

―――― (A. J. BERESFORD) Worship in the Church of England. 8vo. 9s., or, *Popular Selections from*. 8vo. 2s. 6d.

HORACE; a New Edition of the Text. Edited by DEAN MILMAN. With 100 Woodcuts. Crown 8vo. 7s. 6d.

―――― Life of. By DEAN MILMAN. Illustrations. 8vo. 9s.

HOUGHTON'S (LORD) Monographs, Personal and Social. With Portraits. Crown 8vo. 10s. 6d.

―――――― POETICAL WORKS. *Collected Edition.* With Portrait. 2 Vols. Fcap. 8vo. 12s.

HUME'S (The Student's) History of England, from ˙ the Invasion of Julius Cæsar to the Revolution of 1688. Corrected and continued to 1868. Woodcuts. Post 8vo. 7s. 6d.

HUTCHINSON (GEN.) Dog Breaking, with Odds and Ends for those who love the Dog and the Gun. With 40 Illustrations. 6th edition. 7s. 6d.

HUTTON (H. E.). Principia Græca; an Introduction to the Study of Greek. Comprehending Grammar, Delectus, and Exercise-book, with Vocabularies. *Sixth Edition.* 12mo. 3s. 6d.

IRBY AND MANGLES' Travels in Egypt, Nubia, Syria, and the Holy Land. Post 8vo. 2s.

JACOBSON (BISHOP). Fragmentary Illustrations of the History of the Book of Common Prayer; from Manuscript Sources (Bishop SANDERSON and Bishop WREN). 8vo. 5s.

JAMES' (REV. THOMAS) Fables of Æsop. A New Translation, with Historical Preface. With 100 Woodcuts by TENNIEL and WOLF. Post 8vo. 2s. 6d.

JAMESON (MRS.). Lives of the Early Italian Painters— and the Progress of Painting in Italy—Cimabue to Bassano. With 50 Portraits. Post 8vo. 12s.

JENNINGS (LOUIS J.). Field Paths and Green Lanes. Being Country Walks, chiefly in Surrey and Sussex. With Illustrations. Post 8vo. [*In the Press.*

JERVIS (REV. W. H.). Gallican Church, from the Concordat of Bologna, 1516, to the Revolution. With an Introduction. Portraits. 2 Vols. 8vo. 28s.

JESSE (EDWARD). Gleanings in Natural History. Fcp. 8vo. 3s. 6d.

JEX-BLAKE (REV. T. W.). Life in Faith: Sermons Preached at Cheltenham and Rugby. Fcap. 8vo. 3s. 6d.

JOHNS' (REV. B. G.) Blind People; their Works and Ways. With Sketches of the Lives of some famous Blind Men. With Illustrations. Post 8vo. 7s. 6d.

JOHNSON'S (DR. SAMUEL) Life. By James Boswell. Including the Tour to the Hebrides. Edited by MR. CROKER. *New Edition.* Portraits. 4 Vols. 8vo. [*In Preparation.*

―――――― Lives of the most eminent English Poets, with Critical Observations on their Works. Edited with Notes, Corrective and Explanatory, by PETER CUNNINGHAM. 3 vols. 8vo. 22s. 6d.

JUNIUS' HANDWRITING Professionally investigated. By Mr. CHABOT, Expert. With Preface and Collateral Evidence, by the Hon. EDWARD TWISLETON. With Facsimiles, Woodcuts, &c. 4to. £3 3s.

KEN'S (BISHOP) Life. By a LAYMAN. Portrait. 2 Vols. 8vo. 18s.
———— Exposition of the Apostles' Creed. 16mo. 1s. 6d.
KERR (ROBERT). GENTLEMAN'S HOUSE; OR, How TO PLAN ENGLISH RESIDENCES FROM THE PARSONAGE TO THE PALACE. With Views and Plans. 8vo. 24s.
———— Small Country House. A Brief Practical Discourse on the Planning of a Residence from 2000l. to 500ol. With Supplementary Estimates to 7000l. Post 8vo. 3s.
———— Ancient Lights; a Book for Architects, Surveyors, Lawyers, and Landlords. 8vo. 5s. 6d.
———— (R. MALCOLM) Student's Blackstone. A Systematic Abridgment of the entire Commentaries, adapted to the present state of the law. Post 8vo. 7s. 6d.
KING EDWARD VITH's Latin Grammar. 12mo. 3s. 6d.
— ———————— First Latin Book. 12mo. 2s 6d.
KING GEORGE IIIRD's Correspondence with Lord North, 1769-82. Edited, with Notes and Introduction, by W. BODHAM DONNE. 2 vols. 8vo. 32s.
KING (R. J.). Archæology, Travel and Art; being Sketches and Studies, Historical and Descriptive. 8vo. 12s.
KIRK (J. FOSTER). History of Charles the Bold, Duke of Burgundy. Portrait. 3 Vols. 8vo. 45s.
KIRKES' Handbook of Physiology. Edited by W. MORRANT BAKER, F.R.C.S. 9th Edition. With 400 Illustrations. Post 8vo. 14s.
KUGLER'S Handbook of Painting.—The Italian Schools. Revised and Remodelled from the most recent Researches. By LADY EASTLAKE. With 140 Illustrations. 2 Vols. Crown 8vo. 30s.
———— Handbook of Painting.—The German, Flemish, and Dutch Schools. Revised and in part re-written. By J. A. CROWE. With 60 Illustrations. 2 Vols. Crown 8vo. 24s.
LANE (E. W.). Account of the Manners and Customs of Modern Egyptians. With Illustrations. 2 Vols. Post 8vo. 12s
LAWRENCE (SIR GEO.). Reminiscences of Forty-three Years' Service in India; including Captivities in Cabul among the Affghans and among the Sikhs, and a Narrative of the Mutiny in Rajputana. Crown 8vo. 10s. 6d.
LAYARD (A. H.). Nineveh and its Remains. Being a Narrative of Researches and Discoveries amidst the Ruins of Assyria. With an Account of the Chaldean Christians of Kurdistan; the Yezedis, or Devil-worshippers; and an Enquiry into the Manners and Arts of the Ancient Assyrians. Plates and Woodcuts. 2 Vols. 8vo. 36s.
. A POPULAR EDITION of the above work. With Illustrations. Post 8vo. 7s. 6d.
———— Nineveh and Babylon; being the Narrative of Discoveries in the Ruins, with Travels in Armenia, Kurdistan and the Desert, during a Second Expedition to Assyria. With Map and Plates. 8vo. 21s.
. A POPULAR EDITION of the above work. With Illustrations. Post 8vo. 7s. 6d.
LEATHES' (STANLEY) Practical Hebrew Grammar. With the Hebrew Text of Genesis i.—vi., and Psalms i.—vi. Grammatical Analysis and Vocabulary. Post 8vo. 7s. 6d.
LENNEP (REV. H. J. VAN). Missionary Travels in Asia Minor. With Illustrations of Biblical History and Archæology. With Map and Woodcuts. 2 Vols. Post 8vo. 24s.
———— Modern Customs and Manners of Bible Lands in Illustration of Scripture. With Coloured Maps and 300 Illustrations. 2 Vols. 8vo. 21s.

c 2

LESLIE (C. R.). Handbook for Young Painters. With Illustrations. Post 8vo. 7s. 6d.
——— Life and Works of Sir Joshua Reynolds. Portraits and Illustrations. 2 Vols. 8vo. 42s.
LETO (Pomponio). Eight Months at Rome during the Vatican Council. With a daily account of the proceedings. Translated from the original. 8vo. 12s.
LETTERS From the Baltic. By a Lady. Post 8vo. 2s.
——————— Madras. By a Lady. Post 8vo. 2s.
——————— Sierra Leone. By a Lady. Post 8vo. 3s. 6d.
LEVI (Leone). History of British Commerce; and of the Economic Progress of the Nation, from 1763 to 1870. 8vo. 16s.
LIDDELL (Dean). Student's History of Rome, from the earliest Times to the establishment of the Empire. Woodcuts. Post 8vo. 7s. 6d.
LLOYD (W. Watkiss). History of Sicily to the Athenian War; with Elucidations of the Sicilian Odes of Pindar. With Map. 8vo. 14s.
LISPINGS from LOW LATITUDES; or, the Journal of the Hon. Impulsia Gushington. Edited by Lord Dufferin. With 24 Plates. 4to. 21s.
LITTLE ARTHUR'S History of England. By Lady Callcott. New Edition, continued to 1872. With Woodcuts. Fcap. 8vo. 1s. 6d.
LIVINGSTONE (Dr.). Popular Account of his First Expedition to Africa, 1840-56. Illustrations. Post 8vo. 7s. 6d.
——————— Popular Account of his Second Expedition to Africa, 1858-64. Map and Illustrations. Post 8vo. 7s. 6d.
——————— Last Journals in Central Africa, from 1865 to his Death. Continued by a Narrative of his last moments and sufferings. By Rev Horace Waller. Maps and Illustrations. 2 Vols. 8vo. 28s.
LIVINGSTONIA. Journal of Adventures in Exploring the Lake Nyassa, and Establishing the above Settlement. By E. D. Young, R.N. Revised by Rev. Horace Waller, F.R.G.S. Maps. Post 8vo.
LIVONIAN TALES. By the Author of "Letters from the Baltic." Post 8vo. 2s.
LOCH (H. B.). Personal Narrative of Events during Lord Elgin's Second Embassy to China. With Illustrations. Post 8vo. 9s.
LOCKHART (J. G.). Ancient Spanish Ballads. Historical and Romantic. Translated, with Notes. With Portrait and Illustrations. Crown 8vo. 5s.
——————— Life of Theodore Hook. Fcap. 8vo. 1s.
LOUDON (Mrs.). Gardening for Ladies. With Directions and Calendar of Operations for Every Month. Woodcuts. Fcap. 8vo. 3s. 6d.
LYELL (Sir Charles). Principles of Geology; or, the Modern Changes of the Earth and its Inhabitants considered as illustrative of Geology. With Illustrations. 2 Vols. 8vo. 32s.
——————— Student's Elements of Geology. With Table of British Fossils and 600 Illustrations. Post 8vo. 9s.
——————— Geological Evidences of the Antiquity of Man, including an Outline of Glacial Post-Tertiary Geology, and Remarks on the Origin of Species. Illustrations. 8vo. 14s.
——————— (K. M.). Geographical Handbook of Ferns. With Tables to show their Distribution. Post 8vo. 7s. 6d.
LYTTON'S (Lord) Memoir of Julian Fane. With Portrait. Post 8vo. 5s.
McCLINTOCK (Sir L.). Narrative of the Discovery of the Fate of Sir John Franklin and his Companions in the Arctic Seas. With Illustrations. Post 8vo. 7s. 6d.
MACDOUGALL (Col.). Modern Warfare as Influenced by Modern Artillery. With Plans. Post 8vo. 12s.

MACGREGOR (J.). Rob Roy on the Jordan, Nile, Red Sea, Gennesareth, &c. A Canoe Cruise in Palestine and Egypt and the Waters of Damascus. With Map and 70 Illustrations. Crown 8vo. 7s. 6d.

MAETZNER'S ENGLISH GRAMMAR. A Methodical, Analytical, and Historical Treatise on the Orthography, Prosody, Inflections, and Syntax of the English Tongue. Translated from the German. By CLAIR J. GRECE, LL.D. 3 Vols. 8vo. 36s.

MAHON (LORD), see STANHOPE.

MAINE (SIR H. SUMNER). Ancient Law: its Connection with the Early History of Society, and its Relation to Modern Ideas. 8vo. 12s.

——— Village Communities in the East and West. With additional Essays. 8vo. 12s.

——— Early History of Institutions. 8vo. 12s.

MALCOLM (SIR JOHN). Sketches of Persia. Post 8vo. 3s. 6d.

MANSEL (DEAN). Limits of Religious Thought Examined. Post 8vo. 8s. 6d.

——— Letters, Lectures, and Papers, including the Phrontisterion, or Oxford in the XIXth Century. Edited by H. W. CHANDLER, M.A. 8vo. 12s.

——— Gnostic Heresies of the First and Second Centuries. With a sketch of his life and character. By Lord CARNARVON. Edited by Canon LIGHTFOOT. 8vo. 10s. 6d.

MANUAL OF SCIENTIFIC ENQUIRY. For the Use of Travellers. Edited by REV. R. MAIN. Post 8vo. 3s. 6d. (Published by order of the Lords of the Admiralty.)

MARCO POLO. The Book of Ser Marco Polo, the Venetian. Concerning the Kingdoms and Marvels of the East. A new English Version. Illustrated by the light of Oriental Writers and Modern Travels. By COL. HENRY YULE. Maps and Illustrations. 2 Vols. Medium 8vo. 63s.

MARKHAM'S (MRS.) History of England. From the First Invasion by the Romans to 1867. Woodcuts. 12mo. 3s. 6d.

——— History of France. From the Conquest by the Gauls to 1861. Woodcuts. 12mo. 3s. 6d.

——— History of Germany. From the Invasion by Marius to 1867. Woodcuts. 12mo. 3s. 6d.

MARLBOROUGH'S (SARAH, DUCHESS OF) Letters. Now first published from the Original MSS. at Madresfield Court. With an Introduction. 8vo. 10s. 6d.

MARRYAT (JOSEPH). History of Modern and Mediæval Pottery and Porcelain. With a Description of the Manufacture. Plates and Woodcuts. 8vo. 42s. [Post 8vo. 7s. 6d.

MARSH (G. P.). Student's Manual of the English Language.

MASTERS in English Theology. A Series of Lectures delivered at King's Coll., London, 1877. By Canon Barry, D.D., the Dean of St. Paul's; Prof. Plumptre, D.D.; Canon Westcott, D D.; Canon Farrar, D D.; and Prof. Cheetham, M.A. With an Historical Introduction. Post 8vo. [In Preparation.

MATTHIÆ'S GREEK GRAMMAR. Abridged by BLOMFIELD, Revised by E. S. CROOKE. 12mo. 4s.

MAUREL'S Character, Actions, and Writings of Wellington. Fcap. 8vo. 1s. 6d.

MAYNE (CAPT.). Four Years in British Columbia and Vancouver Island. Illustrations. 8vo. 16s.

MAYO (LORD). Sport in Abyssinia; or, the Mareb and Tackazzee. With Illustrations. Crown 8vo. 12s.

MEADE (HON. HERBERT). Ride through the Disturbed Districts of New Zealand, with a Cruise among the South Sea Islands. With Illustrations. Medium 8vo. 12s.

MELVILLE (HERMANN). Marquesas and South Sea Islands.
2 Vols. Post 8vo. 7s.

MEREDITH'S (MRS. CHARLES) Notes and Sketches of New South Wales. Post 8vo. 2s.

MESSIAH (THE): The Life, Travels, Death, Resurrection, and Ascension of our Blessed Lord. By A Layman. Map. 8vo. 18s.

MICHELANGELO - BUONARROTI, Sculptor, Painter, and Architect. His Life and Works. By C. HEATH WILSON. Illustrations. Royal 8vo. 26s.

MILLINGTON (REV. T. S.). Signs and Wonders in the Land of Ham, or the Ten Plagues of Egypt, with Ancient and Modern Illustrations. Woodcuts. Post 8vo. 7s. 6d.

MILMAN (DEAN). History of the Jews, from the earliest Period down to Modern Times. 3 Vols. Post 8vo. 18s.

——— Early Christianity, from the Birth of Christ to the Abolition of Paganism in the Roman Empire. 3 Vols. Post 8vo. 18s.

——— Latin Christianity, including that of the Popes to the Pontificate of Nicholas V. 9 Vols. Post 8vo. 54s.

——— Annals of St. Paul's Cathedral, from the Romans to the funeral of Wellington. Portrait and Illustrations. 8vo. 18s.

——— Character and Conduct of the Apostles considered as an Evidence of Christianity. 8vo. 10s. 6d.

——— Quinti Horatii Flacci Opera. With 100 Woodcuts. Small 8vo. 7s. 6d.

——— Life of Quintus Horatius Flaccus. With Illustrations. 8vo. 9s.

——— Poetical Works. The Fall of Jerusalem—Martyr of Antioch—Balshazzar—Tamor—Anne Boleyn—Fazio, &c. With Portrait and Illustrations. 3 Vols. Fcap. 8vo. 18s.

——— Fall of Jerusalem. Fcap. 8vo. 1s.

——— (CAPT. E. A.) Wayside Cross. Post 8vo. 2s.

MIVART'S (ST. GEORGE) Lessons from Nature; as manifested in Mind and Matter. 8vo. 15s.

MODERN DOMESTIC COOKERY. Founded on Principles of Economy and Practical Knowledge. *New Edition.* Woodcuts. Fcap. 8vo. 5s.

MONGREDIEN (AUGUSTUS). Trees and Shrubs for English Plantation. A Selection and Description of the most Ornamental which will flourish in the open air in our climate. With Classified Lists. With 30 Illustrations. 8vo. 16s.

MOORE'S (THOMAS) Life and Letters of Lord Byron. *Cabinet Edition.* With Plates. 6 Vols. Fcap. 8vo. 18s.; *Popular Edition,* with Portraits. Royal 8vo. 7s. 6d.

MORESBY (CAPT.), R.N. Discoveries in New Guinea, Polynesia, Torres Straits, &c., during the cruise of H.M.S. Basilisk. Map and Illustrations. 8vo. 15s.

MOTLEY (J. L.). History of the United Netherlands: from the Death of William the Silent to the Twelve Years' Truce, 1609. *Library Edition.* Portraits. 4 Vols. 8vo. 60s. *Cabinet Edition.* 4 Vols. Post 8vo. 6s. each.

——— Life and Death of John of Barneveld, Advocate of Holland. With a View of the Primary Causes and Movements of the Thirty Years' War. *Library Edition.* Illustrations. 2 Vols. 8vo. 28s. *Cabinet Edition.* 2 vols. Post 8vo. 12s.

MOSSMAN (SAMUEL). New Japan; the Land of the Rising Sun; its Annals and Progress during the past Twenty Years, recording the remarkable Progress of the Japanese in Western Civilisation. With Map. 8vo. 15s.

PUBLISHED BY MR. MURRAY. 23

MOUHOT (HENRI). Siam, Cambojia, and Lao; a Narrative of
Travels and Discoveries. Illustrations. 2 Vols. 8vo.

MOZLEY'S (CANON) Treatise on Predestination. 8vo. 14s.
——— Primitive Doctrine of Baptismal Regeneration. 8vo. 7s.6d.

MUIRHEAD'S (JAS.) Vaux-de-Vire of Maistre Jean Le Houx,
Advocate of Vire. Translated and Edited. With Portrait and Illustrations. 8vo. 21s.

MUNRO'S (GENERAL) Life and Letters. By REV. G. R. GLEIG.
Post 8vo. 3s. 6d.

MURCHISON'S (SIR RODERICK) Siluria; or, a History of the
Oldest rocks containing Organic Remains. Map and Plates. 8vo. 18s.
——— Memoirs. With Notices of his Contemporaries,
and Rise and Progress of Palæozoic Geology. By ARCHIBALD GEIKIE.
Portraits. 2 Vols. 8vo. 30s.

MURRAY'S RAILWAY READING. Containing:—

WELLINGTON. By LORD ELLESMERE. 6d. | MAHON'S JOAN OF ARC. 1s.
NIMROD ON THE CHASE. 1s. | HEAD'S EMIGRANT. 2s. 6d.
MUSIC AND DRESS. 1s. | NIMROD ON THE ROAD. 1s.
MILMAN'S FALL OF JERUSALEM. 1s. | CROKER ON THE GUILLOTINE. 1s.
MAHON'S "FORTY-FIVE." 3s. | HOLLWAY'S NORWAY. 2s.
LIFE OF THEODORE HOOK. 1s. | MAXWELL'S WELLINGTON. 1s. 6d.
DEEDS OF NAVAL DARING. 3s. 6d. | CAMPBELL'S LIFE OF BACON. 2s. 6d.
THE HONEY BEE. 1s. | THE FLOWER GARDEN. 1s.
ÆSOP'S FABLES. 2s. 6d. | TAYLOR'S NOTES FROM LIFE. 2s.
NIMROD ON THE TURF. 1s. 6d. | REJECTED ADDRESSES. 1s.
ART OF DINING. 1s. 6d. | PENN'S HINTS ON ANGLING. 1s.

MUSTERS' (CAPT.) Patagonians; a Year's Wanderings over
Untrodden Ground from the Straits of Magellan to the Rio Negro.
Illustrations. Post 8vo. 7s. 6d.

NAPIER (SIR WM.). English Battles and Sieges of the Peninsular
War. Portrait. Post 8vo. 9s.

NAPOLEON AT FONTAINEBLEAU AND ELBA. A Journal of
Occurrences and Notes of Conversations. By SIR NEIL CAMPBELL,
C.B. With a Memoir. By REV. A. N. C. MACLACHLAN, M.A. Portrait.
8vo. 15s.

NARES (SIR GEORGE), R.N. Official Report to the Admiralty of
the recent Arctic Expedition. Map. 8vo. 2s. 6d.

NASMYTH AND CARPENTER. The Moon. Considered as a
Planet, a World, and a Satellite. With Illustrations from Drawings
made with the aid of Powerful Telescopes, Woodcuts, &c. 4to. 30s.

NAUTICAL ALMANAC (THE). (By Authority.) 2s. 6d.

NAVY LIST. (Monthly and Quarterly.) Post 8vo.

NEW TESTAMENT. With Short Explanatory Commentary.
By ARCHDEACON CHURTON, M.A., and ARCHDEACON BASIL JONES, M.A.
With 110 authentic Views, &c. 2 Vols. Crown 8vo 21s. bound.

NEWTH (SAMUEL). First Book of Natural Philosophy; an Introduction to the Study of Statics, Dynamics, Hydrostatics, Optics, and
Acoustics, with numerous Examples. Small 8vo. 3s. 6d.
——— Elements of Mechanics, including Hydrostatics,
with numerous Examples. Small 8vo. 8s. 6d.
——— Mathematical Examinations. A Graduated
Series of Elementary Examples in Arithmetic, Algebra, Logarithms,
Trigonometry, and Mechanics. Small 8vo. 8s. 6d.

NICHOLS' (J. G.) Pilgrimages to Walsingham and Canterbury.
By ERASMUS. Translated, with Notes. With Illustrations. Post 8vo. 6s.
——— (SIR GEORGE) History of the English Poor Laws.
2 Vols. 8vo.

NICOLAS' (SIR HARRIS) Historic Peerage of England. Exhibiting the Origin, Descent, and Present State of every Title of Peerage which has existed in this Country since the Conquest. By
WILLIAM COURTHOPE. 8vo. 30s.

NIMROD, On the Chace—Turf—and Road. With Portrait and Plates. Crown 8vo. 5s. Or with Coloured Plates, 7s. 6d.

NORDHOFF (Chas.). Communistic Societies of the United States; including Detailed Accounts of the Shakers, The Amana, Oneida, Bethell, Aurora, Icarian and other existing Societies; with Particulars of their Religious Creeds, Industries, and Present Condition. With 40 Illustrations. 8vo. 15s.

NORTHCOTE'S (Sir John) Notebook in the Long Parliament. Containing Proceedings during its First Session, 1640. From the Original MS. in the possession of the Right Hon. Sir Stafford Northcote, Bart., M.P. Transcribed and Edited, with a Memoir. By A. H. A. Hamilton. Crown 8vo. [In the Press.

OWEN (Lieut.-Col.). Principles and Practice of Modern Artillery, including Artillery Material, Gunnery, and Organisation and Use of Artillery in Warfare. With Illustrations. 8vo. 15s.

OXENHAM (Rev. W.). English Notes for Latin Elegiacs ; designed for early Proficients in the Art of Latin Versification, with Prefatory Rules of Composition in Elegiac Metre. 12mo. 3s. 6d.

PALGRAVE (R. H. I.). Local Taxation of Great Britain and Ireland. 8vo. 5s.

———— Notes on Banking in Great Britain and Ireland, Sweden, Denmark, and Hamburg, with some Remarks on the amount of Bills in circulation, both Inland and Foreign. 8vo. 6s.

PALLISER (Mrs.). Brittany and its Byeways, its Inhabitants, and Antiquities. With Illustrations. Post 8vo. 12s.

———— Mottoes for Monuments, or Epitaphs selected for General Use and Study. With Illustrations. Crown 8vo. 7s. 6d.

PARIS' (Dr.) Philosophy in Sport made Science in Earnest; or, the First Principles of Natural Philosophy inculcated by aid of the Toys and Sports of Youth. Woodcuts. Post 8vo. 7s. 6d.

PARKMAN (Francis). Discovery of the Great West; or, The Valleys of the Mississippi and the Lakes of North America. An Historical Narrative. Map. 8vo. 10s. 6d.

PARKYNS' (Mansfield) Three Years' Residence in Abyssinia: with Travels in that Country. With Illustrations. Post 8vo. 7s. 6d.

PEEK PRIZE ESSAYS. The Maintenance of the Church of England as an Established Church. By Rev. Charles Hole—Rev. R. Watson Dixon—and Rev. Julius Lloyd. 8vo. 10s. 6d.

PEEL'S (Sir Robert) Memoirs. 2 Vols. Post 8vo. 15s.

PENN (Richard). Maxims and Hints for an Angler and Chessplayer. Woodcuts. Fcap. 8vo. 1s.

PERCY (John, M.D.). Metallurgy. Vol. I., Part 1. Fuel, Wood, Peat, Coal, Charcoal, Coke, Refractory Materials, Fire-Clays, &c. With Illustrations. 8vo. 30s.

———— Vol. I., Part 2. Copper, Zinc, Brass. With Illustrations. 8vo. [In the Press.

———— Vol. II. Iron and Steel. With Illustrations. 8vo. [In Preparation.

———— Vol. III. Lead, including part of Silver. With Illustrations. 8vo. 30s.

———— Vols. IV. and V. Gold, Silver, and Mercury, Platinum, Tin, Nickel, Cobalt, Antimony, Bismuth, Arsenic, and other Metals. With Illustrations. 8vo. [In Preparation.

PHILLIPS' (John) Memoirs of William Smith. 8vo. 7s. 6d.

———— (John) Geology of Yorkshire, The Coast, and Limestone District. Plates. 2 Vols. 4to.

———— Rivers, Mountains, and Sea Coast of Yorkshire. With Essays on the Climate, Scenery, and Ancient Inhabitants. Plates. 8vo. 15s.

PHILLIPS' (SAMUEL) Literary Essays from "The Times." With
Portrait. 2 Vols. Fcap. 8vo. 7s.

POPE'S (ALEXANDER) Works. With Introductions and Notes,
by Rev. WHITWELL ELWIN. Vols. I., II., VI., VII., VIII. With Portraits. 8vo. 10s. 6d. each.

PORTER (REV. J. L.). Damascus, Palmyra, and Lebanon. With
Travels among the Giant Cities of Bashan and the Hauran. Map and Woodcuts. Post 8vo. 7s. 6d.

PRAYER-BOOK (ILLUSTRATED), with Borders, Initials, Vignettes, &c. Edited, with Notes, by REV. THOS. JAMES. Medium 8vo. 18s. cloth; 31s. 6d. calf; 36s. morocco.

PRINCESS CHARLOTTE OF WALES. A Brief Memoir.
With Selections from her Correspondence and other unpublished Papers. By LADY ROSE WEIGALL. With Portrait. 8vo. 8s. 6d.

PUSS IN BOOTS. With 12 Illustrations. By OTTO SPECKTER.
16mo. 1s. 6d. Or coloured, 2s. 6d.

PRIVY COUNCIL JUDGMENTS in Ecclesiastical Cases relating to Doctrine and Discipline. With Historical Introduction, by G. C. BRODRICK and W. H. FREMANTLE. 8vo. 10s. 6d.

QUARTERLY REVIEW (THE). 8vo. 6s.

RAE (EDWARD). Land of the North Wind; or Travels among
the Laplanders and Samoyedes, and along the Shores of the White Sea. With Map and Woodcuts. Post 8vo. 10s. 6d.

——— The Country of the Moors. A Journey from Tripoli in
Barbary to the City of Kairwan. Crown 8vo. [In the Press.

RAMBLES in the Syrian Deserts. Post 8vo. 10s. 6d.

RANKE (LEOPOLD). History of the Popes of Rome during the
16th and 17th Centuries. Translated from the German by SARAH AUSTIN. 3 Vols. 8vo. 30s.

RASSAM (HORMUZD). Narrative of the British Mission to Abyssinia. With Notices of the Countries Traversed from Massowah to Magdala. Illustrations. 2 Vols. 8vo. 28s.

RAWLINSON'S (CANON) Herodotus. A New English Version. Edited with Notes and Essays. Maps and Woodcut. 4 Vols 8vo. 45s.

——— Five Great Monarchies of Chaldæa, Assyria, Media,
Babylonia, and Persia. With Maps and Illustrations. 3 Vols. 8vo. 42s.

——— (SIR HENRY) England and Russia in the East; a
Series of Papers on the Political and Geographical Condition of Central Asia. Map. 8vo. 12s.

REED (E. J.). Shipbuilding in Iron and Steel; a Practical
Treatise, giving full details of Construction, Processes of Manufacture, and Building Arrangements. With 5 Plans and 250 Woodcuts. 8vo.

——— Iron-Clad Ships; their Qualities, Performances, and
Cost. With Chapters on Turret Ships, Iron-Clad Rams, &c. With Illustrations. 8vo. 12s.

——— Letters from Russia in 1875. 8vo. 5s.

REJECTED ADDRESSES (THE). By JAMES AND HORACE SMITH.
Woodcuts. Post 8vo. 3s. 6d.; or Popular Edition, Fcap. 8vo. 1s.

REYNOLDS' (SIR JOSHUA) Life and Times. By C. R. LESLIE,
R.A. and TOM TAYLOR. Portraits. 2 Vols. 8vo.

RICARDO'S (DAVID) Political Works. With a Notice of his
Life and Writings. By J. R. M'CULLOCH. 8vo. 16s.

RIPA (FATHER). Thirteen Years' Residence at the Court of Peking.
Post 8vo. 2s.

ROBERTSON (CANON). History of the Christian Church, from
the Apostolic Age to the Reformation, 1517. Library Edition. 4 Vols. 8vo. Cabinet Edition. 8 Vols. Post 8vo. 6s. each.

ROBINSON (Rev. Dr.). Biblical Researches in Palestine and the Adjacent Regions, 1838—52. Maps. 3 Vols. 8vo. 42s.
——— Physical Geography of the Holy Land. Post 8vo. 10s. 6d.
——— (Wm.) Alpine Flowers for English Gardens. With 70 Illustrations. Crown 8vo. 12s.
——— Wild Gardens; or, our Groves and Shrubberies made beautiful by the Naturalization of Hardy Exotic Plants. With Frontispiece. Small 8vo. 6s.
——— Sub-Tropical Gardens; or, Beauty of Form in the Flower Garden. With Illustrations. Small 8vo. 7s. 6d.
ROBSON (E. R.). School Architecture. Being Practical Remarks on the Planning, Designing, Building, and Furnishing of School-houses. With 300 Illustrations. Medium 8vo. 18s.
ROME (History of). See Liddell and Smith.
ROWLAND (David). Manual of the English Constitution. Its Rise, Growth, and Present State. Post 8vo. 10s. 6d.
——— Laws of Nature the Foundation of Morals. Post 8vo. 6s.
RUNDELL'S (Mrs.) Modern Domestic Cookery. Fcap. 8vo. 5s.
RUXTON (George F.). Travels in Mexico; with Adventures among the Wild Tribes and Animals of the Prairies and Rocky Mountains. Post 8vo. 3s. 6d.
SALE'S (Sir Robert) Brigade in Affghanistan. With an Account of the Defence of Jellalabad. By Rev. G. R. Gleig. Post 8vo. 2s.
SCEPTICISM IN GEOLOGY; and the Reasons for It. By Verifier. Crown 8vo. 6s.
SCHLIEMANN (Dr. Henry). Troy and Its Remains. A Narrative of Researches and Discoveries made on the Site of Ilium, and in the Trojan Plain. With Maps, Views, and 500 Illustrations. Medium 8vo. 42s.
——— Discoveries on the Site of Ancient Mycenæ. With numerous Illustrations, Plans, &c. Medium 8vo. [In Preparation.
SCOTT (Sir G. G.). Secular and Domestic Architecture, Present and Future. 8vo. 9s.
——— (Dean) University Sermons. Post 8vo. 8s. 6d.
SCROPE (G. P.). Geology and Extinct Volcanoes of Central France. Illustrations. Medium 8vo. 30s.
SHADOWS OF A SICK ROOM. With a Preface by Canon Liddon. 16mo. 2s. 6d.
SHAH OF PERSIA'S Diary during his Tour through Europe in 1873. Translated from the Original. By J. W. Redhouse. With Portrait and Coloured Title. Crown 8vo. 12s.
SMILES' (Samuel) British Engineers; from the Earliest Period to the death of the Stephensons. With Illustrations. 5 Vols. Crown 8vo. 7s. 6d. each.
——— George and Robert Stephenson. Illustrations. Medium 8vo. 21s.
——— Boulton and Watt. Illustrations. Medium 8vo. 21s.
——— Life of a Scotch Naturalist (Thomas Edward). With Portrait and Illustrations. Crown 8vo. 10s 6d.
——— Huguenots in England and Ireland. Crown 8vo. 7s. 6d.
——— Self-Help. With Illustrations of Conduct and Perseverance. Post 8vo. 6s. Or in French, 5s.
——— Character. A Sequel to "Self-Help." Post 8vo. 6s.
——— Thrift. A Book of Domestic Counsel. Post 8vo. 6s.
——— Industrial Biography; or, Iron Workers and Tool Makers. Post 8vo. 6s.

PUBLISHED BY MR. MURRAY. 27

SMILES' (SAMUEL) Boy's Voyage round the World. With Illustrations. Post 8vo. 6s.
SMITH'S (DR. WM.) Dictionary of the Bible; its Antiquities, Biography, Geography, and Natural History. Illustrations. 3 Vols. 8vo. 105s.
—— Concise Bible Dictionary. With 300 Illustrations. Medium 8vo. 21s.
—— Smaller Bible Dictionary. With Illustrations. Post 8vo. 7s. 6d.
—— Christian Antiquities. Comprising the History, Institutions, and Antiquities of the Christian Church. With Illustrations. Vol. I. 8vo. 31s 6d.
—— —— Biography, Literature, Sects, and Doctrines; from the Times of the Apostles to the Age of Charlemagne. Vol. I. 8vo. 31s. 6d.
—— Atlas of Ancient Geography—Biblical and Classical. Folio. 6l. 6s.
—— Greek and Roman Antiquities. With 500 Illustrations. Medium 8vo. 28s.
—— —————— Biography and Mythology. With 600 Illustrations. 3 Vols. Medium 8vo. 4l. 4s
—— —————— Geography. 2 Vols. With 500 Illustrations. Medium 8vo. 56s.
—— Classical Dictionary of Mythology, Biography, and Geography. 1 Vol. With 750 Woodcuts. 8vo. 18s.
—— Smaller Classical Dictionary. With 200 Woodcuts. Crown 8vo. 7s. 6d.
—— Smaller Greek and Roman Antiquities. With 200 Woodcuts. Crown 8vo. 7s. 6d.
—— Complete Latin-English Dictionary. With Tables of the Roman Calendar, Measures, Weights, and Money. 8vo. 21s.
—— Smaller Latin-English Dictionary. 12mo. 7s. 6d.
—— Copious and Critical English-Latin Dictionary. 8vo. 21s.
—— Smaller English-Latin Dictionary. 12mo. 7s. 6d.
—— School Manual of English Grammar, with Copious Exercises. Post 8vo. 3s. 6d.
—— —————— Modern Geography, Physical and Political. Post 8vo. 5s.
—— Primary English Grammar. 16mo. 1s.
—— —————— History of Britain. 12mo. 2s. 6d.
—— French Principia. Part I. A First Course, containing a Grammar, Delectus, Exercises, and Vocabularies. 12mo. 9s. 6d.
—— —————— Part II. A Reading Book, containing Fables, Stories, and Anecdotes, Natural History, and Scenes from the History of France. With Grammatical Questions, Notes and copious Etymological Dictionary. 12mo. 4s. 6d.
—— —————— Part III. Prose Composition, containing a Systematic Course of Exercises on the Syntax, with the Principal Rules of Syntax. 12mo. [In the Press.
—— Student's French Grammar. By C. HERON-WALL. With Introduction by M. Littré. Post 8vo. 7s. 6d.
—— Smaller Grammar of the French Language. Abridged from the above. 12mo. 3s. 6d.
—— German Principia, Part I. A First German Course, containing a Grammar, Delectus, Exercise Book, and Vocabularies. 12mo. 3s. 6d.

SMITH'S (Dr. Wm.) German Principia, Part II. A Reading Book; containing Fables, Stories, and Anecdotes, Natural History, and Scenes from the History of Germany. With Grammatical Questions, Notes, and Dictionary. 12mo. 3s. 6d.

——————— ——— Part III. An Introduction to German Prose Composition; containing a Systematic Course of Exercises on the Syntax, with the Principal Rules of Syntax. 12mo.
[*In the Press.*]

——————— Practical German Grammar. Post 8vo. 3s. 6d.

——————— Principia Latina—Part I. First Latin Course, containing a Grammar, Delectus, and Exercise Book, with Vocabularies. 12mo. 3s. 6d.
*** In this Edition the Cases of the Nouns, Adjectives, and Pronouns are arranged both as in the ORDINARY GRAMMARS and as in the PUBLIC SCHOOL PRIMER, together with the corresponding Exercises.

——————————————— Part II. A Reading-book of Mythology, Geography, Roman Antiquities, and History. With Notes and Dictionary. 12mo. 3s. 6d.

——————————————— Part III. A Poetry Book. Hexameters and Pentameters; Eclog. Ovidianæ; Latin Prosody. 12mo. 3s. 6d.

——————————————— Part IV. Prose Composition. Rules of Syntax with Examples, Explanations of Synonyms, and Exercises on the Syntax. 12mo. 3s. 6d.

——————— Principia Latina—Part V. Short Tales and Anecdotes for Translation into Latin. 12mo. 3s.

——————— Latin-English Vocabulary and First Latin-English Dictionary for Phædrus, Cornelius Nepos, and Cæsar. 12mo. 3s. 6d.

——————— Student's Latin Grammar. Post 8vo. 6s.

——————— Smaller Latin Grammar. 12mo. 3s. 6d.

——————— Tacitus, Germania, Agricola, &c. With English Notes. 12mo. 3s. 6d.

——————— Initia Græca, Part I. A First Greek Course, containing a Grammar, Delectus, and Exercise-book. With Vocabularies. 12mo. 3s. 6d.

——————————————— Part II. A Reading Book. Containing Short Tales, Anecdotes, Fables, Mythology, and Grecian History. 12mo. 3s. 6d.

——————————————— Part III. Prose Composition. Containing the Rules of Syntax, with copious Examples and Exercises. 12mo. 3s. 6d.

——————— Student's Greek Grammar. By CURTIUS. Post 8vo. 6s.

——————— Smaller Greek Grammar. 12mo. 3s. 6d.

——————— Greek Accidence. 12mo. 2s. 6d.

——————— Plato, Apology of Socrates, &c., with Notes. 12mo. 3s. 6d.

——————— Smaller Scripture History. Woodcuts. 16mo. 3s. 6d.

——————————— Ancient History. Woodcuts. 16mo. 3s. 6d.

——————————————— Geography. Woodcuts. 16mo. 3s. 6d.

——————————— Rome. Woodcuts. 16mo. 3s. 6d.

——————————— Greece. Woodcuts. 16mo. 3s. 6d.

——————————————— Classical Mythology. Woodcuts. 16mo. 3s. 6d.

——————————————— History of England. Woodcuts. 16mo. 3s. 6d.

——————————— English Literature. 16mo. 3s. 6d.

——————————————— Specimens of English Literature. 16mo. 3s. 6d.

SHAW (T. B.). Student's Manual of English Literature. Post 8vo. 7s. 6d.
——— Specimens of English Literature. Selected from the Chief Writers. Post 8vo. 7s. 6d.
——— (ROBERT). Visit to High Tartary, Yarkand, and Kashgar (formerly Chinese Tartary), and Return Journey over the Karakorum Pass. With Map and Illustrations. 8vo. 16s.
SHIRLEY (EVELYN P.). Deer and Deer Parks; or some Account of English Parks, with Notes on the Management of Deer. Illustrations. 4to. 21s.
SIERRA LEONE; Described in Letters to Friends at Home. By A LADY. Post 8vo. 3s. 6d.
SMITH (PHILIP). History of the Ancient World, from the Creation to the Fall of the Roman Empire, A.D. 476. Fourth Edition. 3 Vols. 8vo. 31s. 6d.
SIMMONS' (CAPT.) Constitution and Practice of Courts-Martial. Seventh Edition. 8vo. 15s.
SPALDING (CAPTAIN). Tale of Frithiof.' Translated from the Swedish of ESIAS TEGNER. Post 8vo. 7s. 6d.
STANLEY (DEAN). Sinai and Palestine, in connexion with their History. Map. 8vo. 14s.
——— Bible in the Holy Land; Extracted from the above Work. Woodcuts. Fcap. 8vo. 2s. 6d.
——— Eastern Church. Plans. 8vo. 12s.
——— Jewish Church. 1st & 2nd Series. From the Earliest Times to the Captivity. 2 Vols. 8vo. 24s.
——————— Third Series. From the Captivity to the Destruction of Jerusalem. 8vo. 14s.
——— Epistles of St. Paul to the Corinthians. 8vo. 18s.
——— Life of Dr. Arnold, of Rugby. With selections from his Correspondence. With portrait. 2 vols. Crown 8vo. 12s.
——— Church of Scotland. 8vo. 7s. 6d.
——— Memorials of Canterbury Cathedral. Woodcuts. Post 8vo. 7s. 6d.
——————— Westminster Abbey. With Illustrations. 8vo. 15s.
——— Sermons during a Tour in the East. 8vo. 9s.
——— ADDRESSES AND CHARGES OF THE LATE BISHOP STANLEY. With Memoir. 8vo. 10s. 6d.
STEPHEN (REV. W. R.). Life and Times of St. Chrysostom. With Portrait. 8vo. 15s.
ST. JAMES LECTURES. Companions for the Devout Life. 2 Vols. 8vo. 7s. 6d each.

First Series, 1875.
IMITATION OF CHRIST. CANON FARRAR.
PENSÉES OF BLAISE PASCAL. DEAN CHURCH.
S. FRANÇOIS DE SALES. DEAN GOULBURN.
BAXTER'S SAINTS' REST. ARCHBISHOP TRENCH.
S. AUGUSTINE'S CONFESSIONS. BISHOP ALEXANDER.
JEREMY TAYLOR'S HOLY LIVING AND DYING. REV. DR. HUMPHRY.

Second Series, 1876.
THEOLOGIA GERMANICA. CANON ASHWELL.
FÉNELON'S ŒUVRES SPIRITUELLES.
REV. T. T CARTER.
ANDREWES' DEVOTIONS. BISHOP OF ELY.
CHRISTIAN YEAR. CANON BARRY.
PARADISE LOST. REV. E. H. BICKERSTETH.
PILGRIM'S PROGRESS. DEAN HOWSON.
PRAYER BOOK. DEAN BURGON.

ST. JOHN (CHARLES). Wild Sports and Natural History of the Highlands. Post 8vo. 3s. 6d.
——————— (BAYLE) Adventures in the Libyan Desert. Post 8vo. 2s.

STUDENT'S OLD TESTAMENT HISTORY; from the Creation to the Return of the Jews from Captivity. Maps and Woodcuts. Post 8vo. 7s. 6d.
────────── NEW TESTAMENT HISTORY. With an Introduction connecting the History of the Old and New Testaments. Maps and Woodcuts. Post 8vo. 7s. 6d.
────────── ECCLESIASTICAL HISTORY. A History of the Christian Church from its Foundation to the Eve of the Protestant Reformation. Post 8vo. 7s. 6d.
────────── MANUAL OF ENGLISH CHURCH HISTORY, from the Reformation to the Present Time. By Rev. G. G. PERRY, Prebendary of Lincoln and Rector of Waddington. Post 8vo.
────────── ANCIENT HISTORY OF THE EAST; Egypt, Assyria, Babylonia, Media, Persia, Asia Minor, and Phoenicia. Woodcuts. Post 8vo. 7s. 6d.
────────── GEOGRAPHY. By REV. W. L. BEVAN. Woodcuts. Post 8vo. 7s. 6d.
────────── HISTORY OF GREECE; from the Earliest Times to the Roman Conquest. By WM. SMITH, D.C.L. Woodcuts. Crown 8vo. 7s. 6d.
⁎ Questions on the above Work, 12mo. 2s.
────────── HISTORY OF ROME; from the Earliest Times to the Establishment of the Empire. By DEAN LIDDELL. Woodcuts. Crown 8vo. 7s. 6d.
────────── GIBBON'S Decline and Fall of the Roman Empire. Woodcuts. Post 8vo. 7s. 6d.
────────── HALLAM'S HISTORY OF EUROPE during the Middle Ages. Post 8vo. 7s. 6d.
────────── HALLAM'S HISTORY OF ENGLAND; from the Accession of Henry VII. to the Death of George II. Post 8vo. 7s. 6d.
────────── HUME'S History of England from the Invasion of Julius Cæsar to the Revolution in 1688. Continued down to 1868. Woodcuts. Post 8vo. 7s. 6d.
⁎ Questions on the above Work, 12mo. 2s.
────────── HISTORY OF FRANCE; from the Earliest Times to the Establishment of the Second Empire, 1852. By REV. H. W. JERVIS. Woodcuts. Post 8vo. 7s. 6d.
────────── ENGLISH LANGUAGE. By GEO. P. MARSH. Post 8vo. 7s. 6d.
────────── LITERATURE. By T. B. SHAW, M.A. Post 8vo. 7s. 6d.
────────── SPECIMENS of English Literature from the Chief Writers. By T. B. SHAW. Post 8vo. 7s. 6d.
────────── MODERN GEOGRAPHY; Mathematical, Physical, and Descriptive. By REV. W. L. BEVAN. Woodcuts. Post 8vo. 7s. 6d.
────────── MORAL PHILOSOPHY. By WILLIAM FLEMING, D.D. Post 8vo. 7s. 6d.
────────── BLACKSTONE'S Commentaries on the Laws of England. By R. MALCOLM KERR, LL.D. Post 8vo. 7s. 6d.

SUMNER'S (BISHOP) Life and Episcopate during 40 Years. By Rev. G. H. SUMNER. Portrait. 8vo. 14s.

STREET (G. E.) Gothic Architecture in Spain. From Personal Observations made during several Journeys. With Illustrations. Royal 8vo. 30s.
────────── Italy, chiefly in Brick and Marble. With Notes of Tours in the North of Italy. With 60 Illustrations. Royal 8vo. 26s.

PUBLISHED BY MR. MURRAY. 31

STANHOPE (EARL) England from the Reign of Queen Anne to
the Peace of Versailles, 1701-83. *Library Edition.* 8 vols. 8vo.
Cabinet Edition, 9 vols. Post 8vo. 6s. each.
———————— British India, from its Origin to 1783. 8vo. 3s. 6d.
———————— History of "Forty-Five." Post 8vo. 3s.
———————— Historical and Critical Essays. Post 8vo. 3s. 6d.
———————— French Retreat from Moscow, and other Essays.
Post 8vo. 7s. 6d.
———————— Life of Belisarius. Post 8vo. 10s. 6d.
———————— Condé. Post 8vo. 3s. 6d.
———————— William Pitt. Portraits. 4 Vols. 8vo. 24s.
———————— Miscellanies. 2 Vols. Post 8vo. 13s.
———————— Story of Joan of Arc. Fcap. 8vo. 1s.
———————— Addresses on Various Occasions. 16mo. 1s.
STYFFE (KNUT). Strength of Iron and Steel. Plates. 8vo. 12s.
SOMERVILLE (MARY). Personal Recollections from Early Life
to Old Age. With her Correspondence. Portrait. Crown 8vo. 12s.
———————— Physical Geography. Portrait. Post 8vo. 9s.
———————— Connexion of the Physical Sciences. Portrait.
Post 8vo. 9s.
———————— Molecular and Microscopic Science. Illustrations. 2 Vols. Post 8vo. 21s.
SOUTHEY (ROBERT). Lives of Bunyan and Cromwell. Post
8vo. 2s.
SWAINSON (CANON). Nicene and Apostles' Creeds; Their
Literary History; together with some Account of "The Creed of St.
Athanasius." 8vo. 16s.
SYBEL (VON) History of Europe during the French Revolution,
1789—1795. 4 Vols. 8vo. 48s.
SYMONDS' (REV. W.) Records of the Rocks; or Notes on the
Geology, Natural History, and Antiquities of North and South Wales,
Siluria, Devon, and Cornwall. With Illustrations. Crown 8vo. 12s.
THIBAUT (ANTOINE) On Purity in Musical Art. Translated from
the German. With a prefatory Memoir by W. H. Gladstone, M.P.
Post 8vo. [*In preparation.*
THIELMANN (BARON) Journey through the Caucasus to
Tabreez, Kurdistan, down the Tigris and Euphrates to Nineveh and
Babylon, and across the Desert to Palmyra. Translated by CHAS.
HENEAGE. Illustrations. 2 Vols. Post 8vo. 18s.
THOMS' (W. J.) Longevity of Man; its Facts and its Fiction.
Including Observations on the more Remarkable Instances. Post 8vo.
10s. 6d.
THOMSON (ARCHBISHOP). Lincoln's Inn Sermons. 8vo. 10s. 6d.
———————— Life in the Light of God's Word. Post 8vo. 5s.
TITIAN. His Life and Times. With some account of his
Family, chiefly from new and unpublished Records. By J. A. CROWE
and G. B. CAVALCASELLE. With Portrait and Illustrations. 2 Vols.
8vo. 42s.
TOCQUEVILLE'S State of Society in France before the Revolution,
1789, and on the Causes which led to that Event. Translated by HENRY
REEVE. 8vo. 14s.
TOMLINSON (CHARLES); The Sonnet; Its Origin, Structure, and
Place in Poetry. With translations from Dante, Petrarch, &c. Post
8vo. 9s.

32 LIST OF WORKS PUBLISHED BY MR. MURRAY.

TOZER (Rev. H. F.) Highlands of Turkey, with Visits to Mounts Ida, Athos, Olympus, and Pelion. 2 Vols. Crown 8vo. 24s.
—————— Lectures on the Geography of Greece. Map. Post 8vo. 9s.
TRISTRAM (Canon) Great Sahara. Illustrations. Crown 8vo. 15s.
—————— Land of Moab; Travels and Discoveries on the East Side of the Dead Sea and the Jordan. Illustrations. Crown 8vo. 15s.
TWISLETON (Edward). The Tongue not Essential to Speech, with Illustrations of the Power of Speech in the case of the African Confessors. Post 8vo. 6s.
TWISS' (Horace) Life of Lord Eldon. 2 Vols. Post 8vo. 21s.
TYLOR (E. B.) Early History of Mankind, and Development of Civilization. 8vo. 12s.
—————— Primitive Culture; the Development of Mythology, Philosophy, Religion, Art, and Custom. 2 Vols. 8vo. 24s.
VAMBERY (Arminius) Travels from Teheran across the Turkoman Desert on the Eastern Shore of the Caspian. Illustrations. 8vo. 21s.
VAN LENNEP (Henry J.) Travels in Asia Minor. With Illustrations of Biblical Literature, and Archæology. With Woodcuts. 2 Vols. Post 8vo. 24s.
—————— Modern Customs and Manners of Bible Lands, in illustration of Scripture. With Maps and 300 Illustrations. 2 Vols. 8vo. 21s.
WELLINGTON'S Despatches during his Campaigns in India, Denmark, Portugal, Spain, the Low Countries, and France. Edited by Colonel Gurwood. 8 Vols. 8vo. 20s. each.
—————— Supplementary Despatches, relating to India, Ireland, Denmark, Spanish America, Spain, Portugal, France, Congress of Vienna, Waterloo and Paris. Edited by his Son. 14 Vols. 8vo. 20s. each. *_{*}* *An Index.* 8vo. 20s.
—————— Civil and Political Correspondence. Edited by his Son. Vols. I. to V. 8vo. 20s. each.
—————— Vol. VI., relating to the Eastern Question of 1829. Russian Intrigues, Turkish Affairs, Treaty of Adrianople, &c. 8vo.
—————— Speeches in Parliament. 2 Vols. 8vo. 42s.
WHEELER (G.). Choice of a Dwelling; a Practical Handbook of Useful Information on Building a House. Plans. Post 8vo. 7s. 6d.
WHITE (W. H.). Manual of Naval Architecture, for the use of Officers. Illustrations. 8vo. [*In the Press.*
WILBERFORCE'S (Bishop) Life of William Wilberforce. Portrait. Crown 8vo. 6s.
WILKINSON (Sir J. G.). Manners and Customs of the Ancient Egyptians, their Private Life, Government, Laws, Arts, Manufactures, Religion, &c. A new edition, with additions by the late Author. Edited by Samuel Birch, LL.D. Illustrations. 3 Vols. 8vo.
—————— Popular Account of the Ancient Egyptians. With 500 Woodcuts. 2 Vols. Post 8vo. 12s.
WOOD'S (Captain) Source of the Oxus. With the Geography of the Valley of the Oxus. By Col. Yule. Map. 8vo. 12s.
WORDS OF HUMAN WISDOM. Collected and Arranged by E. S. With a Preface by Canon Liddon. Fcap. 8vo. 3s. 6d
WORDSWORTH'S (Bishop) Athens and Attica. Plates. 8vo. 5s.
YULE'S (Colonel) Book of Marco Polo. Illustrated by the Light of Oriental Writers and Modern Travels. With Maps and 80 Plates. 2 Vols. Medium 8vo. 63s.

BRADBURY AGNEW & CO. PRINTERS, WHITEFRIARS.

www.ingramcontent.com/pod-product-compliance
Lightning Source LLC
Chambersburg PA
CBHW020319240426
43673CB00039B/864